*Sponsored by*
SRI International

*Funded by*
The Office of Planning, Budget and Evaluation
U.S. Department of Education
Under Contract Number LC 89089001

# Teaching Advanced Skills to At-Risk Students

Barbara Means,
Carol Chelemer, and
Michael S. Knapp,
Editors

# TEACHING ADVANCED SKILLS TO AT-RISK STUDENTS

*Views from Research and Practice*

Jossey-Bass Publishers

San Francisco • Oxford • 1991

TEACHING ADVANCED SKILLS TO AT-RISK STUDENTS
*Views from Research and Practice*
by Barbara Means, Carol Chelemer, and Michael S. Knapp, Editors

Copyright © 1991 by: Jossey-Bass Inc., Publishers
350 Sansome Street
San Francisco, California 94104
&
Jossey-Bass Limited
Headington Hill Hall
Oxford OX3 0BW

**Library of Congress Cataloging-in-Publication Data**

Teaching advanced skills to at-risk students: views from research and
    practice / Barbara Means, Carol Chelemer, Michael S. Knapp, editors
        p.    cm.—(The Jossey-Bass education series)
    Includes bibliographical references and index.
    ISBN 1-55542-393-0
    1. Socially handicapped children—Education—United States.
    2. Compensatory education—United States.   I. Means, Barbara, date.
    II. Chelemer, Carol, date.   III. Knapp, Michael S. (Michael
    Sturgis), date.   IV. Series.
    LC4091.T43    1991
    371.96'7—dc20                                          91-21683
                                                             CIP

Manufactured in the United States of America

The paper in this book meets the guidelines for
permanence and durability of the Committee on
Production Guidelines for Book Longevity of the
Council on Library Resources.

JACKET DESIGN BY VICTOR ICHIOKA
FIRST EDITION

*Code 9198*

The Jossey-Bass Education Series

# CONTENTS

Preface      xi

The Editors      xvii

The Contributors      xix

1. Introduction: Rethinking Teaching for Disadvantaged
   Students      1
   *Barbara Means and Michael S. Knapp*

2. Thinking in Arithmetic Class      27
   *Lauren B. Resnick, Victoria L. Bill,*
   *Sharon B. Lesgold, and Mary N. Leer*

   Commentary      54
   *Nancy J. Vye, Diana Miller Sharp, Kathy McCabe,*
   *and John D. Bransford*

3. Using Children's Mathematical Knowledge      68
   *Penelope L. Peterson, Elizabeth Fennema,*
   *and Thomas Carpenter*

   Commentary      102
   *Judith J. Richards*

4.   Dialogues Promoting Reading Comprehension    112
      *Annemarie Sullivan Palincsar and Laura J. Klenk*

      Commentary    131
      *Yolanda N. Padron*

5.   Teaching Writing to Students at Risk for
      Academic Failure    141
      *Mary Bryson and Marlene Scardamalia*

      Commentary    168
      *Harvey A. Daniels*

6.   What Schools Can Do to Improve Literacy Instruction    176
      *Robert Calfee*

      Commentary    204
      *Edys S. Quellmalz*

7.   A Cognitive Apprenticeship for Disadvantaged
      Students    216
      *Allan Collins, Jan Hawkins, and
      Sharon M. Carver*

      Commentary    244
      *Herb Rosenfeld*

8.   Conclusion: Implementing New Models for
      Teaching Advanced Skills    255
      *Michael S. Knapp, Barbara Means, and
      Carol Chelemer*

      Index    277

# PREFACE

Once again, we are in a period of widespread concern over the education of students regarded as least likely to achieve in school. Variously labeled "at risk," "disadvantaged," or "educationally deprived," these students come disproportionately from poor families and from ethnic and linguistic minority backgrounds.

## Background

In decades past, the diagnoses of school failure for this segment of the student population concentrated on what the students lacked— exposure to print outside of school, family support for education, and so on. Based on these diagnoses, the most widely accepted prescriptions for remedying the students' deficiencies emphasized teaching the "basics" through curricula organized around discrete skills taught in a linear sequence. Even today, compensatory education programs and other forms of remediation typically reflect these principles.

But education researchers and policymakers are now taking a hard look at compensatory education goals and practices. Scores from state and national testing programs suggest that the kind of discrete skill instruction stressed in most programs for disadvantaged students has had some positive (though not dramatic) effects on student scores on basic skills measures in the early years of elementary school, but there have not been comparable gains on measures of more advanced skills. In fact, despite years of compensatory education, the majority of educationally disadvantaged children appear to fall further and further behind their more advantaged peers as they progress in school and a greater emphasis is placed on advanced skills of comprehension, composition, and reasoning. Research shows that disadvantaged students are expected to do less in these areas and that they actually receive less instruction on these advanced skills than do more advantaged students.

In its 1988 reauthorization of Chapter 1, the largest federally funded compensatory education program, Congress stated the program's purpose was to improve achievement in more advanced as well as basic skills. These more advanced skills were defined to include reasoning, analysis, interpretation, problem solving, and decision making related to the subject areas taught by Chapter 1 programs. At the same time, leading education researchers have been calling for a new kind of instruction for at-risk students. This new thrust rejects the prevailing hierarchical concept of skills that places advanced skills at the end of a continuum and requires mastery of all basic skills first. It proposes, instead, an integration of basic and advanced skills, providing opportunities for students to apply skills to novel and complex tasks at all stages of their education.

Increasingly, those who educate at-risk students are being exhorted to integrate comprehension and mathematical reasoning with the teaching of basic skills, but educators have few models of how this can be done. This book fills the gap. It includes six chapters describing practical, theoretically sound approaches to teaching advanced skills to at-risk students. The chapters were written as part of an SRI International project (sponsored by the U.S. Department of Education's Office of Planning, Budget and Evaluation) by leading scholars and educators who have developed and studied the approaches. Together, the authors provide convincing evidence and arguments that powerful methods exist for teaching advanced skills to children who would be at risk of failing in more traditional classrooms. Commentaries by other scholars and practitioners offer further perspectives on the application of these ideas to the wide range of regular classroom and supplemental program settings in which disadvantaged children learn.

This book is intended for individuals who design, administer, or implement education programs in which disadvantaged students participate. The messages contained in these chapters are equally appropriate for educators who manage or implement the regular academic program and for those engaged in compensatory or supplemental programs of some kind. We hope that teachers will read the instructional model descriptions and ask themselves how these models can be applied to their own subject areas and classrooms. Administrators and program designers will want to read the chapters with a somewhat different perspective— examining the steps that they can take to facilitate the kind of teaching described here, particularly the kind of support required for in-service training and professional development.

By reconceiving what is taught to at-risk students, and how it is taught, schools stand a better chance of engaging students from poverty and minority backgrounds in an education that will be of use to those students in their lives. It is time that we recognized the fact that the sources of disadvantage and school failure lie as much with what schools do as with what children bring to the schoolhouse door. The challenge for the future is to reappraise what disadvantaged students need and how to serve them through compensatory and other programs.

## Overview of the Contents

Chapter One serves as an introduction, contrasting compensatory education as it is today with the kind of curriculum and instruction that would emerge based on the principles espoused in Chapters Two through Seven. Although those chapters focus on different ages, subject areas, and skills, common themes run through the six models. These involve a new attitude toward at-risk students, stressing their intellectual resources rather than deficits; reshaping the curriculum in terms of complex, meaningful problems; and applying new instructional strategies, in which teachers coach students through the application of powerful thinking strategies. The introduction concludes with a consideration of the steps that individual teachers, program planners, and school and district administrators can take to make reforms happen.

In Chapter Two, Lauren B. Resnick, Victoria L. Bill, Sharon B. Lesgold, and Mary N. Leer describe an experimental arithmetic curriculum that draws the child's informal knowledge about numbers and math concepts into the classroom and treats educationally disadvantaged children as mathematical reasoners. Commentary on this chapter is provided by Nancy J. Vye, Diana Miller Sharp, Kathy McCabe, and John D. Bransford, who have been working to provide students with meaningful contexts for exercising mathematics skills through the use of video-based presentation of complex problems embedded within adventure stories.

Penelope L. Peterson, Elizabeth Fennema, and Thomas Carpenter also focus on elementary school mathematics in Chapter Three. Their program, Cognitively Guided Instruction, has increased students' mathematics reasoning not by providing a new curriculum but rather by increasing teachers' understanding of the way children think about addition and subtraction. Judith J. Richards draws on her experience teaching mathematics in a K–8 age-integrated, ethnically diverse school in her commentary on this chapter. She emphasizes the importance of making the mathematics curriculum relevant to the daily lives and cultural traditions of all children.

In Chapter Four, Annemarie Sullivan Palincsar and Laura J. Klenk describe reciprocal teaching, an approach to fostering strategies of reading comprehension that has had dramatic success with disadvantaged children, whether or not they had fully mastered the basics of decoding. Yolanda N. Padron provides a commentary for this chapter, describing her experiences in applying reciprocal teaching methods with limited–English-proficient students.

The issue of how advanced skills of writing should be taught is taken up by Mary Bryson and Marlene Scardamalia in Chapter Five. They discuss a model for engaging at-risk students in "epistemic" writing, which is designed to inquire into a particular topic and to persuade readers of the fruits of the investigation. In his commentary on their chapter, Harvey A. Daniels compares their research-based model to the process writing approach.

In Chapter Six, Robert Calfee describes two programs aimed at instilling the comprehension and composition skills of critical literacy. He argues that real change requires not just a reorientation within individual classrooms but also a fundamental change in the school as a whole, with the interactions among teachers, administrators, school personnel, and parents reflecting the same principles that direct the instructional program. In her commentary, Edys S. Quellmalz reviews a wider set of schoolwide literacy programs as a context for reacting to the programs described by Calfee.

An influential concept within the current school reform movement is that of "cognitive apprenticeship," a return to apprenticeship as the prevailing metaphor for teaching, but with the important difference that the emphasis is on teaching internal, cognitive skills rather than concrete tasks such as tailoring and carpentry. In Chapter Seven, Allan Collins, Jan Hawkins, and Sharon M. Carver describe a cognitive apprenticeship for disadvantaged students, drawing on the experiences of two schools that have used technology to provide meaningful problem-solving experiences for disadvantaged middle and secondary school students. In his commentary, Herb Rosenfeld draws on his experiences as associate director of one of these, a Harlem secondary school, to describe how such an apprenticeship can take shape.

Issues surrounding the implementation of the instructional models described in Chapters Two through Seven are the focus of Chapter Eight. The discussion highlights the changes these models imply for the role of teachers, and the implications of these changes for teacher preparation and support.

### Acknowledgments

Preparation of the chapters for this book was supported by the Office of Planning, Budget and Evaluation (OPBE) of the U.S. Department of Education, but the ideas and opinions are those of the authors. The project was conceived by Carol Chelemer, who provided guidance and editorial review for preparation of the chapters. Additional guidance was provided by Joanne Wiggins, who served as the Department of Education project monitor during the concluding phase of the work, and by reviewers from the Office of Compensatory Education Programs, Office of Research, and Office of Bilingual Education and Minority Language Affairs within the Department of Education. We would also like to thank Marian S.

Stearns of SRI International for her review of the final chapter and
Klaus Krause for his editorial assistance throughout. Finally, we are
grateful to Katie Ann Kaattari, Marion Collins, Ann Ryan, and
Carolyn Estey, also of SRI, for overseeing all of the many operational and production details of bringing together a manuscript
written in so many different places.

*September 1991*                          Barbara Means
                                          *Menlo Park, California*

                                          Carol Chelemer
                                          *Washington, D.C.*

                                          Michael S. Knapp
                                          *Seattle, Washington*

# THE EDITORS

*Barbara Means* is director of the Education and Human Services Research Program at SRI International. Her research interests center on the application of cognitive psychology to education and instruction. A particular concern is the relationship between classroom instruction and performance in practical settings. She has written extensively on methods for analyzing the cognitive requirements of job tasks and coauthored (with Michael Cole) *Comparative Studies of How People Think*. Means holds an A.B. degree in psychology from Stanford University and a Ph.D. degree in intellectual development and education from the University of California, Berkeley.

*Carol Chelemer* is a supervisory education program specialist in the Office of Elementary and Secondary Education, U.S. Department of Education. She has coordinated evaluation and policy studies on compensatory education and school improvement initiatives. She currently serves as a branch chief in the Division of Drug Free Schools and Communities, administering six drug education and prevention programs.

*Michael S. Knapp* is an associate professor of education leadership and policy studies in the College of Education at the University of Washington. He specializes in studying issues regarding the education of special-needs populations, mathematics and science education, and staff development. He is the editor of *Schooling for Poor Children: Alternatives to Conventional Wisdom*. Knapp earned an M.Ed. degree at the Harvard Graduate School of Education and an M.A. degree in sociology and a Ph.D. degree in the sociology of education from Stanford University.

# THE CONTRIBUTORS

*Victoria L. Bill,* teacher of elementary mathematics at St. Agnes School (Pittsburgh) for eleven years, is the principal designer and lead teacher of the Reason Intu-it Mathematics Program. Her collaboration with the University of Pittsburgh includes a pilot program with seventeen elementary teachers from the Pittsburgh area. This effort will be extended to twenty-four additional teachers in 1991–1992. In addition to conducting workshops for the National Council of Teachers of Mathematics, the Pennsylvania Council of Teachers of Mathematics, and local agencies supporting teaching professionals and administrators, she instructs a mathematics teaching methods course for preservice teachers at Carlow College, Pittsburgh.

*John D. Bransford* is internationally known for his work on thinking and learning. Most recently, he and his colleagues have focused on the design of environments that make learning meaningful and that help students integrate knowledge from different subject areas, such as mathematics, science, history, and literature. The research of Bransford and his colleagues in this area highlights uses of technology that encourage generative learning rather than the mere passive reception of knowledge. The research involves applications of technology that are simple yet powerful, and it addresses issues of implementation into existing school curricula. After receiving his Ph.D. degree in cognitive psychology from the University of Minnesota, Bransford joined the faculty at the State University of New York, Stony Brook. In 1979, he became professor of psychology at Vanderbilt University; in 1983, he became professor of teaching and learning at Peabody College, Vanderbilt University. He currently is Centennial Professor of Psychology, codirector of the Learning Technology Center, and senior research scientist at the John F. Kennedy Center for Research on Education and Human Development. Bransford serves as consulting editor for several publications (*Cognition and Instruction, Human Learning, Discourse Processes, Technology and Learning,* among others). He has published extensively in the fields of psychology and education.

*Mary Bryson* is a faculty member of the Department of Educational Psychology and Special Education at the University of British Columbia (UBC), Vancouver, Canada, as well as an instructor in the UBC Women's Studies Program. Her current research focuses on feminist, postmodern reconstructions of cognitive approaches to theory and practice in the domain of literacy.

*Robert Calfee* is a cognitive psychologist with research interests in the effect of schooling on the intellectual potential of individuals and groups. He is a professor in the Committee on Language, Literacy, and Culture and the Committee on Psychological Studies within the School of Education of Stanford University. His interests have evolved over the past two decades from a focus on assessment of beginning literacy skills to a concern with the broader issue of the school as a literate environment. His theoretical efforts are directed toward the nature of human thought processes and the influence of language and literacy in the development of problem solving and communication.

*Thomas Carpenter* is professor of curriculum and instruction with an emphasis in mathematics education at the University of Wisconsin, Madison. He is editor of the *Journal of Research in Mathematics Education.* He has written extensively on young children's thinking about addition and subtraction. His ongoing work involves studying teachers' use of knowledge about children's thinking. He is codirector (with Elizabeth Fennema) of the Cognitively Guided Instruction Project.

*Sharon M. Carver* is assistant professor of education and psychology at the University of Rochester. She received her A.B. degree in psychology from Princeton University and her Ph.D. degree in cognitive development from Carnegie Mellon University. Carver's main research activities involve educational applications of cognitive theory, particularly in terms of the integration of technology across the middle school curriculum to facilitate the acquisition of problem-solving skills.

*Allan Collins* has been a leader in developing the field of cognitive science and has served as first chair of the Cognitive Science Society. He is principal scientist at Bolt Beranek and Newman Inc. and professor of education and social policy at Northwestern University. He is presently writing a book, with John Seely Brown, on "cognitive apprenticeship" methods of teaching and has been conducting experiments on the most effective uses of technology in schools.

*Harvey A. Daniels* is professor of reading, language, and interdisciplinary studies at National-Louis University in Evanston, Illinois. He received his B.A., M.A.T., and Ph.D. degrees from Northwestern University, where he also taught for two years before teaching at Rosary College in River Forest, Illinois. Daniels now codirects the Illinois Writing Project and the Walloon Institute, both of which offer teacher renewal programs on literacy instruction. He has been active in school reform efforts in the city of Chicago, helping to train a corps of teacher-consultants who now provide staff development programs on reading, writing, and whole language to colleagues throughout the city. Daniels has written or coauthored five books, including *A Community of Writers: Teaching Writing in the Junior and Senior High School* (1988) and *Language Diversity and Writing Instruction* (1988).

*Elizabeth Fennema* is professor of curriculum and instruction with an emphasis in mathematics education at the University of Wisconsin, Madison. Her research and writing have concentrated on two areas: gender issues in mathematics and teachers' use of knowledge about children's thinking. She is codirector (with Thomas Carpenter) of the Cognitively Guided Instruction Project.

*Jan Hawkins* is director of the Center for Children and Technology, acting director of the Center for Technology in Education, and acting dean of the research division at Bank Street College of Education, where she conducts research and development projects addressing central issues of technology and learning. She is directing a variety of projects for the National Center for Technology in Education on the redesign of classrooms, curricula, and materials for assessing student learning. She has directed work on gender issues in relation to expert and novice conceptualizations of different technologies and on the National Science Foundation-funded project *Inquire*, in which a set of software tools was designed to support inquiry-based science learning. Through her work on the multimedia "Voyage of the Mimi" materials, she has pioneered techniques of formative research for educational software development.

*Laura J. Klenk* is a doctoral student in educational studies at the University of Michigan. She earned a B. A. degree in elementary and special education from Augustina College (Sioux Falls, South Dakota) and an M.A. degree in curriculum and instruction from the University of Wyoming. Klenk's main research interests are in early literacy development, special education, and teacher preparation. She has been a recipient of the Marguerite Wilker Johnson fellowship for early childhood education (1990, 1991).

*Mary N. Leer* is a research specialist at the Learning Research and Development Center of the University of Pittsburgh. She served as a teacher-consultant for learning disabilities programs in Pennsylvania for thirteen years. The focus of her research is twofold: investigating the Reason Intu-it Mathematics (RIM) Program implemented by Victoria L. Bill in an inner-city setting and working on the RIM dissemination project.

*Sharon B. Lesgold* is project director for the Reason Intu-it Mathematics Program and a research specialist at the Learning Research and Development Center of the University of Pittsburgh. A former high school mathematics teacher, her research interests have included student understanding of basic mathematical properties, expert teachers' mathematical and pedagogical knowledge, and the mathematical content of classroom lessons.

*Kathy McCabe* is a kindergarten teacher in the public school system of Nashville, Tennessee. She received her B.S. degree in early childhood education from the George Peabody School for Teachers at Vanderbilt University and her M.Ed. degree in curriculum and instruction from Middle Tennessee State University. McCabe is an active member of the Metro Nashville Educational Association, the Tennessee Educational Association, and the National Association on Young Children. She has worked with at-risk children for five years.

*Yolanda N. Padron* is assistant professor at the University of Houston, Clear Lake, where she teaches courses in bilingual and multicultural education. She received her B.S. degree in elementary education and Spanish, her M.Ed. degree in curriculum and instruction/bilingual education, and her Ed.D. degree in curriculum and instruction/bilingual education from the University of Houston. Before receiving her Ed.D. degree, Padron had seven years of classroom teaching experience, during which time she taught limited–English-proficient students and English-monolingual students. Her research has focused primarily on bilingualism. Specifically, she has concentrated on students' bilingual cognitive strategies in the areas of reading and social studies, parent education, teacher-training programs, and bilingual/bicultural education. She has published in journals such as *TESOL Quarterly, Educational Horizons, Journal of Social Psychology, Journal of Educational Equity and Leadership,* and *The Reading Teacher.* In addition, she has been editor for the "Research and Field Practices" section of the *Journal of Educational Equity and Leadership* and has been on the editorial advisory board for the *National Reading Conference Yearbook.*

*Annemarie Sullivan Palincsar* is professor of educational studies at the University of Michigan. She has written extensively in the areas of literacy instruction, collaborative learning, and special education. She is coinvestigator (with Ann Brown) of the reciprocal teaching research program, a portion of which is summarized in a widely cited 1984 *Cognition and Instruction* article. Her research interests include investigating and improving the literacy instruction of disadvantaged children and the use of peer collaboration in problem-solving activity. Palincsar completed her M.S. and Ph.D. degrees at the University of Illinois.

*Penelope L. Peterson* is codirector of the Institute for Research on Teaching as well as the Center for the Learning and Teaching of Elementary Subjects at Michigan State University, where she is also a professor of educational psychology and teacher education. Previously, she was Sears-Bascom Professor of Education at the University of Wisconsin, Madison. Her current research focuses on children's mathematics knowledge, thinking, and learning and on teachers' knowledge, thinking, and beliefs. She is past vice president of the American Educational Research Association for Division C (Learning and Instruction) and the former editor of *Review of Educational Research*.

*Edys S. Quellmalz*, director of the Region F Technical Assistance Center, has been a classroom teacher, curriculum developer, evaluator, researcher, and technical service provider. She is a nationally recognized expert in the areas of writing assessment, performance assessment, and higher-order thinking skills. Quellmalz obtained her Ph.D. degree (1971) in instructional research and development from the University of California, Los Angeles. She has pursued her professional interests as director of curriculum and teacher-training programs at the Southwest Regional Laboratory for Educational Research and Development; as director of the Evaluation Testing, Test Design, and Writing Assessment projects at the Center for the Study of Evaluation at UCLA; and as a professor in the School of Education at Stanford University. She has provided technical assistance to districts and states throughout the country. Quellmalz's professional experience includes the development of composition skills and advanced reading programs and the design of K-12 programs to teach higher-order skills. She has developed systems to be used at the state, district, and classroom levels to assess writing and higher-order thinking skills. Quellmalz has published extensively in journals, edited a volume entitled *Studies in Test Design,* written a review for the *Buros Mental Measurement Yearbook,* and contributed chapters to several books on performance assessment and critical thinking.

*Lauren B. Resnick* is professor of psychology and education and director of the Learning Research and Development Center at the University of Pittsburgh. Resnick's primary interest is the cognitive psychology of learning and instruction. Her recent research has focused on the nature and development of thinking abilities and the relationship between school learning and everyday competence, with special attention to mathematics and literacy. She is founder and editor of *Cognition and Instruction* and author of the well-received monograph *Education and Learning to Think,* commissioned by the National Academy of Sciences. She is also coeditor of a new volume, *Socially Shared Cognition.*

*Judith J. Richards* is a teacher at the Saundra Graham and Rosa Parks Alternative Public School in Cambridge, Massachusetts. She has twenty years of teaching experience in urban public schools. She received her B.S. degree (1971) in early childhood education from Wheelock College. Richards's research interests focus on the classroom discourse of mathematics and science and on alternative forms of assessment. She has presented her discourse research at the annual meeting of the American Educational Research Association and coauthored, with Marlene Kliman, "Writing, Sharing and Discussing Arithmetic Stories," which appeared in *Arithmetic Teacher.* In 1987, she received a professional staff development grant from the Cambridge School Department for her work in disseminating Haitian culture and language activities. In 1990, she received an Arthur D. Little Fellowship to explore alternative assessment in mathematics. Richards teaches courses in mathematics education and multicultural learning and teaching at Wheelock College. She is also a curriculum development consultant at the Center for Learning Technology and a teacher-researcher at the Literacies Institute, both at the Education Development Center, Inc.

*Herb Rosenfeld* is a member of the staff at the Center for Children and Technology of the Bank Street College of Education and a consultant on mathematics education and school restructuring for the Coalition of Essential Schools and the Panasonic Foundation. He spent thirty years as a teacher, curriculum developer, school planner, and school administrator in the New York City public high schools. Rosenfeld received his B.A. degree in mathematics from Hunter College of the City University of New York and his M.S. degree in mathematics education at Yeshiva University. He helped plan the Manhattan Center, the only facility in New York City that houses a high school, a middle school, and an elementary school in the same building. He then established and chaired the mathematics department in the high school, which is known as the Manhattan Center for Science and Mathematics. He also cofounded the Central Park East Secondary School and was assistant director of the school until his recent retirement. At Central Park East, he led the development of a project-based math and science curriculum and the team approach to planning. Rosenfeld's current interests are a technology-supported, performance-based student assessment project at Bank Street and the development of a model secondary mathematics curriculum consistent with the thinking of the Coalition of Essential Schools. He is also planning a new public secondary school that will be based on the Central Park East model.

*Marlene Scardamalia* is currently head of the Center for Applied Cognitive Science at the Ontario Institute for Studies in Education. Prior to joining the Ontario Institute, she was a professor of developmental psychology at York University. She has coauthored two books with Carl Bereiter, *The Psychology of Written Composition* and *Process of Expertise,* and has written numerous articles on knowledge acquisition and Computer-Supported Intentional Learning Environments (CSILE). Scardamalia holds an M.A. degree from Bucknell University and a Ph.D. degree from the University of Toronto.

*Diana Miller Sharp* is a research associate in the Department of Psychology and Human Development at Vanderbilt University. She received her Ph.D. degree in cognitive psychology from Vanderbilt University, and she was the 1989–1990 recipient of the Barbara Strudler Wallston postdoctoral fellowship from the Southeastern Psychological Association. Her current research concentrates on issues in reading comprehension, with special focus on the construction of mental models for narratives.

*Nancy J. Vye* is assistant director of research at the Learning Technology Center of Vanderbilt University. She received her B.A. and M.Sc. degrees in psychology from Acadia University and her Ph.D. degree in cognitive psychology from Vanderbilt University. Vye's main research activities have been in cognition as it relates to classroom teaching and learning. Her recent work is concerned with the role of technology in creating effective contexts for problem solving and reasoning.

# Teaching
# Advanced Skills
# to At-Risk
# Students

# 1

# Introduction: Rethinking Teaching for Disadvantaged Students

## Barbara Means and Michael S. Knapp

A FUNDAMENTAL ASSUMPTION UNDERLYING MUCH OF THE CURRICU-
lum in America's schools is that certain skills are "basic" and must
be mastered before students receive instruction on more "advanced"
skills, such as reading comprehension, written composition, and
mathematical reasoning. One consequence of adherence to this assumption for many students, particularly those deemed most at risk
of school failure, is that instruction focuses on the so-called basics
(such as phonetic decoding and arithmetic operations) to the exclusion of reasoning activities and reading for meaning. Demonstrated
success on basic skills measures becomes a hurdle that must be
overcome before the student receives instruction in comprehension,
reading, or composition.

Research from cognitive science questions this assumption
and leads to a quite different view of children's learning and appropriate instruction. By discarding assumptions about skill hierarchies and attempting to understand children's competencies as
constructed and evolving both inside and outside of school, researchers are developing models of intervention that start with what
children know and provide access to explicit models of thinking in
areas that traditionally have been termed "advanced" or "higher
order." This volume offers descriptions of six instructional models
that have been highly successful in teaching advanced skills to stu-

dents who generally would be expected to fare poorly in the typical school program.

Together, these chapters comprise a critical mass of evidence that these children and youth, whom we will refer to collectively as educationally disadvantaged students, can profit from instruction in comprehension, composition, and mathematical reasoning from the very beginning of their education. In this summary, we highlight the issues that led to a search for alternative models, describe a set of overarching themes that set these models off from conventional approaches to compensatory education, and discuss the implementation problems that must be addressed if we are to see use of these models in the classrooms that serve the educationally "at risk."

### Compensatory Education as It Is Today

The prototypical compensatory education program is offered at the elementary school level. Children who score lower than their peers on standardized tests and teacher evaluations—many of these children are poor and are from culturally or linguistically different backgrounds—get special practice in reading, most often in a special pull-out room, sometimes in the regular classroom (Birman et al., 1987). While their classmates are working on reading new materials with comprehension, children in the compensatory program typically receive drill on phonics, vocabulary, and word decoding. Each of these is taught as a separate skill, with little or no integration. Often there is little or no coordination between the compensatory and regular classroom teachers and no congruence between the content of the two classes.

Compensatory programs in mathematics (second only to reading programs in number) tend to have a similar emphasis on teaching individual lower-level skills. Students practice basic arithmetic operations using workbooks or dittos. On the assumption that they cannot be expected to do even simple math-related problem solving until they have mastered the basics, students are drilled on the same numerical operations year after year.

Results from state and national testing programs suggest that this kind of instruction has had some positive (though not dramatic) effects on student scores on basic skills measures, especially in the early years of elementary school. What has been disheartening is the fact that comparable gains have not been seen on measures of more advanced skills. In fact, despite years of compensatory education, the majority of educationally disadvantaged children appear to fall farther and farther behind their more advantaged peers as they progress in school and a greater emphasis is placed on advanced skills of comprehension, problem solving, and reasoning.

For too long, there has been a tendency to blame this situation on the students. Tacitly or explicitly, it was assumed that they lacked the capability to perform complex academic tasks. Recently, however, there has been a reexamination of the premises underlying the instruction provided to educationally disadvantaged students in general and the most prevalent approaches to compensatory education in particular. Critics point out that we have decried educationally disadvantaged students' failure to demonstrate advanced skills while failing to provide them with instruction designed to instill those skills (Cole & Griffin, 1987). There is a growing understanding that the failures lie both in the compensatory program per se and in the regular classroom in which educationally disadvantaged students receive the rest of their instruction.

Classroom studies document the fact that disadvantaged students receive less instruction in higher-order skills than do more advantaged students (Allington & McGill-Franzen, 1989; Oakes, 1986). Their curriculum is less challenging and more repetitive. Teachers are more directive with educationally disadvantaged students, breaking each task down into smaller pieces, walking students through step-by-step, and leaving them with less opportunity to exercise higher-order thinking skills. As a consequence, disadvantaged students receive less exposure to problem-solving tasks in which there is more than one possible answer and they have to structure the problem for themselves (Anyon, 1980).

A recent summary of the critiques of this kind of instruction offered by a group of national experts in reading, writing, and mathematics education (Knapp & Turnbull, 1990) concluded that such approaches tend to

- Underestimate what disadvantaged students are capable of doing
- Postpone more challenging and interesting work for too long—in some cases, forever
- Deprive students of a meaningful or motivating context for learning or using the skills that are taught

### Why the Prevailing Emphasis on Lower-Level Skills?

The critique in the preceding section suggests that the dominant approaches to instructing educationally disadvantaged children are in fact holding them back—providing little or nothing to foster the growth of reasoning, problem solving, and independent thinking. Our goal in this volume is to offer some concrete alternatives to prevailing approaches. However, before turning to those alternatives, it is important to consider the reasons why educationally disadvantaged students are now taught the way they are. A thorough understanding of the theoretical tenets and organizational factors that support the current curriculum and instruction in compensatory education is needed if we are to design and implement alternative models.

A critical theoretical assumption underlying much of the curriculum and instruction provided to educationally disadvantaged students is that academic skills are hierarchical in nature. Some skills are "basics," and these must be mastered before more "advanced," "higher-order," or "complex" skills can be attained. This presumption is very deeply ingrained in the American curriculum. It is assumed that students must master the basics of vocabulary and phonics before they work on reading comprehension skills or critical literacy. In the area of writing, the mechanics of penmanship, grammar, and spelling are treated as prerequisites for learning to compose. The math curriculum presupposes that students must learn to execute basic numerical operations with accuracy and some speed before they tackle problems that require reasoning with mathematics. Once this assumption of a skills continuum from basic to advanced is adopted, compensatory education's focus on basic skills seems eminently reasonable.

This assumption about a skills hierarchy pervades the instructional and testing materials available to educators. Anyone attempting to implement an alternative instructional approach incorporating advanced skills throughout the curriculum must be prepared to face the barrier of a scarcity of compatible textbooks. (We are beginning to see indications of a change in this situation, as textbook publishers respond to the critiques of educational reformers such as the National Council of Teachers of Mathematics.) Today's reading texts are generally structured as a strict sequence of skills, beginning with phonetic decomposition and vocabulary. Math programs start with arithmetic operations performed on small numbers and proceed through a fairly standard hierarchy, with applications of math to real problems postponed until the necessary operations can be performed with consistent accuracy on abstract content—thus following the textbook results in treating discrete basic skills as a prerequisite for exposure to more complex, meaningful tasks.

The same thinking underlies the design of educational tests. Basic skills are emphasized in tests for students in the early elementary grades, with more advanced content added in later years. Even then, the minimum-competency movement and the difficulty in measuring meaningful higher-order tasks with economical paper-and-pencil measures have led to an emphasis on measuring discrete components of complex tasks rather than the tasks themselves (for example, grammar rather than composition). It is only natural that schools held accountable for student performance tend to orient their curricula around the content of those tests.

Mastery learning approaches bring curriculum content and classroom assessment together in a unified system that requires students to demonstrate achievement of lower-level skills before going on to receive instruction on advanced skills. Instructional packages based on this approach institutionalize mastery of basic skills as a prerequisite for getting instruction in skills considered more advanced.

One point made by the chapters in this volume is that we have been too accepting of the assumption that mastery of the skills traditionally designated as basic is an absolute prerequiste for learning those skills that we regard as advanced. Consider the case of reading comprehension. Cognitive research on comprehension processes has shown the importance of trying to relate what you read to what you already know, checking to see that your understanding of new information fits with what you have already read, setting up expectations for what is to follow and then seeing whether they are fulfilled. The research described by Palincsar and Klenk in Chapter Four demonstrates quite clearly that students can acquire these comprehension skills—which we have traditionally called advanced—well before they are good decoders of the printed word. Children can learn to reason about new information, relate information from different sources, ask questions, and summarize using orally presented text. We may or may not want to call these comprehension skills advanced, but it is clear that children—including educationally disadvantaged children—can acquire and exercise them before they master all of the so-called basics. Similarly, in Chapter Three, Peterson, Fennema, and Carpenter describe research showing that first-graders can solve a wide variety of math problems, using modeling and counting, before they have perfected the computational algorithms that are traditionally regarded as prerequisites. In Chapter Six, Calfee points out that children can perform sophisticated composition tasks before they have acquired the mechanics of writing.

In the early school years, children's achievement is typically measured in terms of their ability to perform basic skills in an academic context. Skills are formally assessed—children are asked to perform independently and to execute the skills for their own sake, not as part of any task they are trying to accomplish. Children from impoverished and linguistically different backgrounds often perform poorly on these assessments. Their performance leads educators to conclude that they are severely deficient academically, a conclusion predicated on the assumption that the skills being tested provide the necessary foundation for all later learning.

Ironically, the decontextualized measures of discrete skills that we have come to regard as basic offer less opportunity for connecting with anything children know from their past experiences than would more complex exercises emphasizing the skills we regard as advanced. As preparation for learning writing skills, children from different linguistic backgrounds are drilled on the conventions of written standard English. These will be harder for them than for other children because the conventions often conflict with the children's spoken language (Scott, 1988). In contrast, a task that focuses on higher-level issues of communication—for example, formulating a message that will be persuasive to other people—is perfectly consistent with many of the children's out-of-school experiences. At the level of language mechanics and communication formats, there are many inconsistencies between the backgrounds of many disadvantaged children and the conventions of the schoolhouse, but at the higher level of communication goals, there is much more common ground.

A similar argument can be made about reading instruction. Young readers deemed at risk of school failure are subjected to more drill and tighter standards regarding their pronunciation in oral reading (Allington, 1980; Brophy & Good, 1974). These children must struggle with a pronunciation system that is different from that of their spoken language or dialect at the same time that they are trying to master basic reading. When it comes to comprehension skills, in contrast, we have every indication that disadvantaged children can make use of their past experiences to help them understand a story. In Chapter Four, Palincsar and Klenk provide examples of young children regarded as academically "at risk" applying their background knowledge to make inferences about text. In one such example, a first-grade girl uses her prior knowledge about seasons to make inferences while listening to a story about a baby bear who played too roughly with his sister and fell off a tree into the water: "You know it kind of told you what time of year it was because it told you it went 'splash,' because if it was this time of year [February], I don't think he'd splash in the water; I think he'd crack." This inference making is exactly the kind of comprehension-enhancing strategy we regard as advanced. Real-life experiences and skills are relevant to these higher-level academic skills. Instruction in advanced skills offers opportunities for children to use what they already know in the process of developing and refining academic skills.

## Compensatory Education as It Could Be

This book contains six commissioned chapters describing alternative models for teaching advanced skills of mathematics reasoning, reading comprehension, problem solving, and composition to educationally disadvantaged students. These models represent a new attitude toward learners who have been labeled "disadvantaged" or "at risk," a fundamental rethinking of the content of the curriculum, and a set of instructional strategies that allow children to be active learners but do not require them to work in isolation. Although the chapters describe different academic content and different grade levels, we can extract the major themes emerging from the set. These themes are summarized in Exhibit 1.1 and are discussed below.

### Taking a New Attitude Toward Disadvantaged Learners

The instructional models described in this book reflect a new attitude toward the educationally disadvantaged learner. Rather than starting with a list of academic skills, administering formal assessments, and cataloging children's deficits, the researchers who contributed to this book start with the conviction that children from all kinds of backgrounds come to school with an impressive set of intellectual accomplishments. This conviction is bolstered by years

Exhibit 1.1. Principles of Cognitive Approaches to Teaching
Advanced Skills to Disadvantaged Students.

**Taking a New Attitude Toward Disadvantaged Learners**

- Appreciate intellectual accomplishments all young learners bring to school
- Emphasize building on strengths rather than just remediating deficits
- Learn about children's cultures to avoid mistaking differences for deficits

**Reshaping the Curriculum**

- Focus on complex, meaningful problems
- Embed instruction on basic skills in context of more global tasks
- Make connections with students' out-of-school experience and culture

**Applying New Instructional Strategies**

- Model powerful thinking strategies
- Encourage multiple approaches
- Provide scaffolding to enable students to accomplish complex tasks
- Make dialogue central medium for teaching and learning

of research in cognitive psychology and linguistics. When we start to do a detailed analysis of what it means to understand numbers, what it takes to master a language's grammar, what is required to be able to categorize and recategorize objects, we come to appreciate the magnitude of young children's intellectual accomplishments. When we look closely at how these kinds of understanding are achieved, we begin to understand that concepts are not something given to the child by the environment but rather are constructed by the child who interacts with that environment.

Children from poor and affluent backgrounds alike come to school with important skills and knowledge. They have mastered the receptive and expressive skills of their native language. The particular language or dialect they have acquired may or may not match that of the classroom, but the intellectual feat is equivalent in any case. They have learned basic facts about quantity (for example, the fact that rearranging objects does not change their number). They have learned much about social expectations, such as the need to take turns talking when participating in a conversation. Moreover, they have a host of knowledge about the world: for example, that grocery stores are places where you pay money for food, new flowers bloom in the spring, and nighttime is for sleeping.

Instead of taking a deficit view of the educationally disadvantaged learner, the researchers developing the alternative models described here focus on the knowledge, skills, and abilities that the child brings. Early accomplishments, attained before coming to school, demonstrate that disadvantaged children can do serious intellectual work. What we need to do is design curricula and instructional methods that will build on that prior learning and complement rather than contradict the child's experiences outside of school.

*Reshaping the Curriculum*

The instructional approaches described in this volume eschew the assumption that students cannot meaningfully engage in activities involving advanced skills of comprehension, composition, and reasoning unless they have mastered the so-called basic skills. Once the conventional assumption about a necessary skills hierarchy has been abandoned, a new set of curricular principles follows.

*Focus on Complex, Meaningful Problems.* The dominant curricular approach over the last two decades has broken academic content down into small skills, with the idea that each piece would be easy to acquire. An unfortunate side effect is that by the time we break something down into its smallest parts, the whole is often totally obscured. Children drill themselves on the spellings and definitions of long lists of words, often without really understanding the words' meanings or having any motivation for using them. High school students practice computations involving logarithms but leave school with no idea what the purpose of logarithms is or how they might aid in solving practical problems (Sherwood, Kinzer, Hasselbring, & Bransford, 1987).

The alternative is to keep tasks at a global enough level that the purpose of the tasks is apparent and makes sense to students. Thus, children might write to their city council in support of a public playground. In the course of the exercise, they might need to acquire new vocabulary (*alderman, welfare,* and *community*), but each word would be acquired in a context that gave it meaning. At the same time, children would be attending to higher-level skills. What are the arguments for a good playground? Which of these arguments would be most persuasive to a politician? What counterarguments can be expected? How can these be refuted?

The programs described in this volume abound with examples of providing students with more global, complex tasks. In Chapter Seven, Collins, Hawkins, and Carver describe a math and science curriculum organized around the problem of understanding motion. Students engage in extended investigations of topics such as the physical principles of motion underlying an amusement park ride of their own design or a foul shot in basketball. In Chapter Two, Vye, Sharp, McCabe, and Bransford describe a program using interactive video to present students with complex problem situations, such as moving a wounded eagle to a distant veterinarian by the safest and fastest route. A whole series of rate, fuel consumption, and distance problems must be recognized and solved in the process of devising a plan.

Certainly these tasks are more complex than simple computations or phonics exercises, but there are instructional techniques (described below as part of our discussion of new instructional strategies) that lessen the burden on any one student. Moreover, as we argued earlier, these more complex tasks build on things that students already know.

*Embed Instruction on Basic Skills in the Context of More Global Tasks.* Teaching advanced skills from the beginning of a child's education does not mean failing to teach those skills generally called basic. Rather, what alternative approaches advocate is using a complex, meaningful task as the context for instruction on both advanced and basic skills. Instead of constant drill on basic addition and subtraction facts, these skills are practiced in the context of trying to solve real problems. In Chapter Three, Peterson, Fennema, and Carpenter describe the pedagogical use of problems stemming from daily classroom activities—for example, figuring out how many children will be having hot lunches and cold lunches at school that day. Children can practice addition, subtraction, fractions, and record keeping in the course of this authentic classroom activity.

There are multiple advantages to this approach. First, the more global task provides a motivation for acquiring all the knowledge and skills entailed in its accomplishment. It is worth learning the conventions of writing if that will enable you to communicate with a distant friend. Word decoding is much more palatable if the word is part of a message you care about. Second, embedding basic skills in more complex task contexts means that students receive practice in executing the skill in conjunction with other skills. Cognitive research on learning has shown that it is possible to be able to perform all the subskills of a task without being able to put the pieces together into any type of coherent performance. Cognitive psychologists call this the problem of orchestration. The ability to orchestrate discrete skills into performance of a complex task is critical. After all, the desired outcome of schooling is not students who can perform arithmetic calculations on an arithmetic test but students who can use these skills in performing real-world tasks. The latter will require that the calculations be performed in conjunction with the higher-level skills of problem recognition and formulation.

Finally, teaching basic skills in the context of more global, meaningful tasks will increase the probability that those skills will transfer to real-world situations. The decontextualized academic exercises within which many basic skills have been taught are so different from what any of us encounter in the everyday world that it is little wonder students question the relevance of most of what they learn in school. Some students come to accept the idea of performing academic exercises for their own sake. Others reject the whole enterprise. Neither group could be expected to use what they learned in school when they encounter problems in their everyday lives. Thus, we have students like those described above who perform calculations with logarithms in class but have no idea why the topic is taught or how logarithms might ever be used in problem solving. Much classroom instruction focuses on how to execute a skill without adequate attention as to when to execute it. Students learn how to make three different kinds of graphs but receive no instruction or practice in deciding what kind of graph is most useful for what purpose. This issue of how to decide which skill to apply does not come up when skills are taught in isolation; it is unavoidable when skills are taught in a complex, meaningful task context.

***Make Connections with Students' Out-of-School Experience and Culture.*** Implicit in the argument above is the notion that in-school instruction will be more effective if it both builds on what children have already learned out of school and is done in such a way that connections to situations outside of school are obvious. In Chapter Two, Resnick, Bill, Lesgold, and Leer describe a program in which young children not only are given realistic problems to solve with arithmetic in class but also are encouraged to bring in their own real-life problems for their classmates to solve.

It is important to recognize that there is great cultural diversity in the United States and that many children in compensatory education come from homes with language, practices, and beliefs that are at variance with some of those assumed in "mainstream" classrooms. Moll (1990) argues that the strengths of a child's culture should be recognized and that instruction should capitalize on them. He describes an intricate network for sharing practical knowledge and supporting acquisition of English skills among a Hispanic community. This cultural practice of knowledge sharing can become an effective model for cooperative learning and problem solving in classrooms. In Chapter Five, Bryson and Scardamalia argue that students can learn to use writing as a medium for thinking while working on literary forms compatible with their particular cultural background. An example is provided by Griffin and Cole (1987), who had black students compose rap lyrics in collaborative sessions using computers. Although rap is not a form of literature found in many standard textbooks, it is no different from the sonnet in terms of having a structure and a set of conventions. When working with this form, which was both relevant to their culture and motivating, black students from low-socioeconomic-status homes demonstrated a high degree of sophistication in their composition and revision skills.

*Applying New Instructional Strategies*

The rethinking of the curriculum described above must be matched by a change in the methods used to impart that curriculum. The programs described in this book stress teaching methods that are quite different from the structured drill and practice that typify most compensatory education.

*Model Powerful Thinking Strategies.* With its focus on teaching cognitive (as opposed to physical) skills, research in cognitive psychology has long been concerned with making the thinking of expert performers manifest. A key goal has been to understand the processes that expert performers use in addressing complex tasks and solving novel problems and to explicitly model these processes for novice learners. Great strides have been made in understanding the strategies that accomplished readers use to monitor and enhance their understanding of what they read, that mathematicians use when faced with novel problems, and that skilled writers employ. The research described in this book demonstrates the instructional value of making these strategies explicit for learners.

All of the authors recommend that teachers explicitly and repeatedly model the higher-order intellectual processes they are trying to instill in their students. This means thinking out loud while reading a text and trying to understand how the information in it fits with previously known facts, externalizing the thought process in trying to solve a mathematical puzzle, demonstrating the planning and revision processes involved in composition. For too long we have shown students the product they are supposed to achieve (the right answer to a math problem or a polished essay) without demonstrating the critical processes required to achieve it.

*Encourage Multiple Approaches.* The alternative programs differ from the instruction conventionally provided in most classrooms in their encouragement of multiple solution strategies. Rather than trying to teach the one right way to solve a problem, these programs want to foster students' ability themselves to invent strategies for solving problems. In some cases, this kind of thinking is elicited by providing students with open-ended problems to which there is no single right answer. Given the assignment to develop a description of one's city that would attract other people to live there, for example, students are free to follow very different paths and to produce different kinds of solutions. In other cases, such as elementary mathematics, problems do have one correct solution. Still, there is often more than one way to reach that solution, and one of the clearest demonstrations of real understanding of mathematics concepts is the ability to use those concepts to invent solution strategies on one's own.

To support the development of this essential component of problem solving, the programs described here invite students to think of their own ways to address a problem. In a classroom described in Chapter Three by Peterson et al., for example, small groups of students are given mathematics problems that each child solves individually. As each child finds an answer, the teacher asks him or her to describe how the problem was solved. When all students have finished, their different paths to the answer are compared and discussed so that students can see alternative approaches modeled and come to realize that there is no single right way to find the answer.

*Provide Scaffolding to Enable Students to Accomplish Complex Tasks.* A natural reaction to our recommendation that disadvantaged students be presented with authentic, complex tasks from the outset of their education would be concern about how these students will handle all the requirements for such tasks. We need to be sensitive to the fact that many of the components of the task will be difficult and require mental resources. How is the student, particularly the young student, to handle all of this?

A key instructional concept is that of scaffolding—enabling the learner to handle a complex task by taking on parts of the task. One example of scaffolding is the instructor's performing all the computations required when first introducing students to algebra problems. Another, described by Bryson and Scardamalia in Chapter Five, is scaffolding of the writing process by supplying novice authors with cue cards reminding them to do things such as consider alternative arguments. The reciprocal teaching program described by Palincsar and Klenk in Chapter Four uses many kinds of scaffolding. In the early stages of teaching, the teacher cues the students to employ the various comprehension-enhancing strategies, leaving students free to concentrate on executing those strategies. A more extensive form of scaffolding is provided for students who have yet to master decoding skills: the teacher reads the text orally, allowing students to practice comprehension strategies before they have fully mastered word decoding.

Like the physical scaffolding that permits a worker to reach higher places than would otherwise be accessible, instructional scaffolding makes it possible for students to accomplish complex tasks with assistance from the teacher, special materials, or other students. The ultimate goal, of course, is for the student to be able to accomplish the task without assistance. This requires the judicious removal of the teacher's support as the student gains more skill.

*Make Dialogue the Central Medium for Teaching and Learning.* In conventional modes of instruction, the key form of communication is transmission—the teacher has the knowledge and transmits it to the students. Just as the television viewer cannot change the content of a program transmitted to his home, the student is viewed as the passive recipient of the message the teacher chooses to deliver. The student can pay attention or not, but the message will be the same regardless. A dialogue is a very different form of communication. It connotes an interchange in which two parties are full-fledged participants, both with significant influence on the nature of the exchange. This concept of dialogue is central to the programs described here.

Reciprocal teaching occurs through dialogue—initially between the teacher and a small group of students, later among the students themselves. The specifics of the instructional content emerge in the back-and-forth interchange between teacher and students. In Chapter Three, Peterson et al. describe how student-teacher dialogue provides the basis for teachers to diagnose each student's level of understanding and design appropriate mathematics problems. In Chapter Seven, Collins et al. provide an example of the value of student-student dialogue: Students who had developed hypermedia information displays found that students from another school were bored by the work they had regarded as exemplary. This experience led the student developers to look at their work from an audience's perspective and to undertake design changes to make their product better.

## How Do Such Reforms Happen?

The chapters in this book provide a concrete picture of alternative models for teaching advanced skills to disadvantaged students. We are fully aware, however, that there are many steps and roadblocks between enthusiasm for a new approach and effective implementation. Here, we consider what individual teachers, staff developers, compensatory program managers, and school or district administrators can do to make such reforms happen. All these individuals have an important role to play. Furthermore, implementing new approaches to teaching advanced skills to a particular segment of the student population—the educationally disadvantaged—implies adjustments in the academic program for all students.

*What Individual Teachers Can Do in Their Classrooms: Experiment with New Approaches.* Whether they work in a regular classroom or a separate compensatory education setting, individual teachers can do much to bring about the changes discussed in this book. Using knowledge about children's understanding and the processes and strategies that support performance of advanced skills, they can select or develop more challenging problems for their students. They can seek "authentic" problems as a context for teaching and practicing skills, often combining reading comprehension with mathematics, writing with science, and so on. They can consciously provide their own thinking processes as models and probe students to get at their thinking. They can become knowledgeable about their students' culture and seek to develop problems and activities that will draw on the strengths of that culture. They can develop classroom assessment techniques that get at higher-order skills and the ability to apply them to novel content rather than the dutiful repetition of designated phrases or stereotypical procedures. Finally, they can work with other teachers to share interesting problems and techniques and to make connections across the different subject areas and classrooms to which students are exposed.

For most teachers, these ways of approaching students, instruction, and assessment are unfamiliar. To realize them in the classroom implies considerable experimentation, once teachers have a clear concept of the approach in mind. The most adventurous of teachers will pick up the ideas on their own, but the large majority will need help and support. Staff developers have a particularly important role to play in this regard.

*What Staff Developers Can Do: Provide Teachers with Appropriate Learning Experiences.* Staff development opportunities are one of the most direct—and potentially powerful—ways for teachers to become attuned to new ways of teaching. Here, we consider the kinds of experiences teachers need to prepare them for new approaches to teaching advanced skills.

The same principles underlie learning new approaches to teaching as underlie student learning in the classroom. In the view of cognitive psychologists, human learning is not a matter of passive absorption of whatever information an instructor happens to provide. Rather, it involves an active role on the part of the learner, who tries to make sense of new information in terms of what she or he already knows. The way in which the new information is understood, the extent to which it is remembered, and the degree to which it will have an impact on future behavior depend on the learner's prior knowledge and the connections that are made between new information and old. Thus, the learner is actively engaged both in assimilating the new knowledge and, if there are inconsistencies with old knowledge, in restructuring or refining prior understandings to incorporate the new concept.

This is just as true of teachers as of their pupils. The way teachers will understand and apply innovative teaching approaches depends on the way those approaches fit in with their prior knowledge and beliefs. If the alternative approaches require a fundamental reshaping of those beliefs, teachers will have to be provided with a great deal of evidence and some experience applying the new approaches before real change in their views and behaviors is possible.

The alternative models described here differ from conventional compensatory education in their underlying assumptions about the capability of educationally disadvantaged students to exercise higher-level comprehension, composition, and math reasoning skills. Whether because they believe that some children's backgrounds leave them inherently limited or because they believe that advanced skills cannot be acquired until all the basics are mastered, many teachers have lower expectations for educationally disadvantaged children. An important part of preparing teachers for alternative models is changing this belief. This is not effectively accomplished by telling teachers to change. Rather, teachers need the experiences that will lead them to new conclusions about children's capabilities. Videotapes of children engaging in sophisticated comprehension strategies or reasoning about novel mathematics problems have proved very useful in this regard.

In addition to an alteration in conceptions about the capabilities of educationally disadvantaged students, a change in well-learned methods of teaching is required. Many of the instructional techniques described in this book are quite different from those with which most teachers themselves were taught in school or those stressed in teacher training. The techniques of modeling, coaching, and providing for reflection on performance are just as relevant when teaching these instructional techniques to teachers as they are when trying to teach children. Those responsible for in-service training need to model skills such as interviewing children to get at their level of understanding. Teachers then need to practice this kind of interaction with real students. Teachers who are expert in these techniques can act as coaches, providing support during the interview and offering detailed critiques of transcripts or videotaped interviews. At the same time that teachers are gaining skill in this kind of interaction, they also gain more information about what students do and do not understand. This experience can help teachers appreciate the importance of concepts children bring to school and at the same time perceive the cases where school-taught procedures fail to connect with children's intuitive knowledge.

Similarly, these techniques of modeling and coaching can be applied to helping teachers learn how to model their own thinking and provide scaffolding to students as they work in specific task areas. Teachers need the opportunity to try out these instructional techniques and to receive feedback on the strengths and weaknesses of their efforts.

The literatures on professional development, school change, and cognitive learning all suggest that teachers will both understand and embrace a system more thoroughly if they have had a role in shaping it. Rather than providing an instructional package that teachers are expected to adopt in its entirety, we recommend that staff developers work with teachers and administrators to adapt the instructional principles discussed here in ways that fit their particular teaching situations and then develop or adapt curricula and techniques that embody those principles. We have provided descriptions of models for instruction, but any of them would have to be thought through and refined to fit the goals and circumstances of a particular classroom and school.

*What Program Planners and Managers Can Do: Incorporate New Approaches into the Design of Compensatory Programs.* Compensatory education teachers rarely operate with a free rein to fashion a curriculum as they see fit. More often, they teach their students as part of a program designed at the school district level, in response to state and federal program requirements and guidelines. The program is often fine-tuned in the school building, however, and, depending on the relationship between compensatory teachers and those in the regular classrooms, may be adapted to suit the needs of particular teachers and classes.

The design of a compensatory education program has much to do with the prospects that the ideas presented in this volume will take root. Program planners and staff will need to consider, for example:

- *The emphasis placed on discrete basic skills in compensatory program objectives and materials.* Despite rhetorical support for advanced skills teaching, the materials and even the specific objectives of the program may still emphasize isolated skill teaching. Careful attention must be paid to the details of the compensatory education curriculum if it is significantly to increase students' exposure to advanced skills.
- *The use of tests or other assessment devices that tap only the students' grasp of basic skills.* Compensatory education programs may subvert their own attempts at teaching advanced skills by using and judging their effectiveness on measures that tap primarily basic skills. Alternative measures tapping advanced skills as described in this book are not always available, but wherever possible, emphasis should be given to those available measures that aim most closely toward advanced skills (for example, reading comprehension subscores as opposed to measures of language mechanics or decoding, math concepts and applications subscores rather than math computation).
- *The use of staff (for example, aides) who lack the training to teach advanced skills.* Choices of compensatory education staffing need to be made with attention to the capabilities of staff— current and potential—for teaching advanced skills and to the resources required to train staff in appropriate techniques. This is a major issue in many compensatory programs, especially those favoring the use of in-class paraprofessional aides.
- *Limitations on the range of curriculum in the purview of the*

*compensatory program.* Often the content domain stipulated
for compensatory education is too restricted to encompass some
of the interdisciplinary approaches we have advocated for teaching advanced skills. A prime example of such limitations is the
failure to include writing in most compensatory language arts
programs, effectively depriving students of an important class of
higher-order thinking experience that can not only impart skills
in written expression but also facilitate learning to read.

• *Connections with the regular academic program.* Compensatory
programs are linked to varying degrees with a regular academic
program, which may or may not feature or encourage the kind
of advanced skills teaching described in this volume. Doing a
good job of teaching advanced skills implies closer coordination
of regular and compensatory instruction than currently happens
in many settings, assuming the regular academic program is
designed to foster the learning of advanced skills.

These considerations are generally within the control of local
program planners and coordinators, in collaboration with staff responsible for the regular academic program. The challenge is to
explore the implications of the models presented in this book for
all aspects of compensatory education program design and implementation.

*What School and District Administrators Can Do: Develop
a Supportive Framework in the Regular Academic Program.* The
kinds of approaches described in this volume imply other forms of
school and district support besides appropriate staff development
and compensatory program design. As noted earlier, compensatory
programs are usually intended to supplement the regular academic
program. The skills learned by educationally disadvantaged children are the joint result of their experience in the regular classroom
and supplemental program settings. Therefore, the school and district policies that govern curriculum, scheduling, assessment, and
other features of the regular academic program are intimately connected to the prospects for better teaching of advanced skills to the
disadvantaged and other children as well.

At a minimum, school and district policies need to foster the professional interchange and provide the requisite learning time for both regular and compensatory teachers. Developing a network of teachers who can model new approaches and help train their colleagues is vital. Administrators need to develop mechanisms for providing release time so that teachers can attend training and develop new instructional materials for their classes. Strategies that have been used include providing for team teaching, hiring of substitutes, and use of administrators to teach some classes while teachers are participating in training and development activities. Similarly, arrangements that enable teachers to visit each other's classrooms (for example, videotaping classes, hiring substitutes) promote coherence across the educational program and make it possible for teachers to learn from each other.

A more extensive review of policies governing the regular academic program is also called for to ensure that the structure, philosophy, and support systems built into the regular academic program reinforce the teaching of advanced skills. Thus, a set of considerations must be addressed in the regular program as in the compensatory program:

- *Organization of the school day.* School structures that divide the curriculum into discrete pieces with only twenty to fifty minutes for a given subject limit the teaching of advanced skills. The kinds of complex, authentic tasks we are advocating often take much more extended time to address and involve more than one academic domain.
- *Curricula.* State or local curricula and instructional materials that enforce a rigid sequence of discrete basic skills make it difficult to engage in extended instruction of the sort described here. Requirements to use a basal reader or to use different materials for regular and compensatory education can hinder implementation of these models.
- *Testing and assessment.* Testing programs that emphasize basic skills and do not assess higher-order thinking or extended samples of intellectual performance (such as writing) convey a message that advanced skills are unimportant.
- *How teachers are viewed.* Administrators' views that many teachers are not capable of offering more challenging, dynamic

instruction foreclose the possibility that teachers will be pushed or encouraged to grow.

- *Resources to support changes in practice.* Lack of release time for developing new curricula and instructional materials or for sharpening instructional skills limits teachers' exposure to the kind of models discussed in this book and makes it highly unlikely that any real change in teaching content or strategies will take place.

The innovations we are advocating need to permeate educationally disadvantaged students' regular classrooms as well as their compensatory programs. In this regard, it is important to note that our recommendations for teaching advanced skills to educationally disadvantaged students apply equally well to other students. The disadvantaged students' current program offers the starkest contrast to the kind of teaching advocated in this volume; we would argue, however, as have many others, that all students experience too little coherent instruction dealing with real problems and calling for meaningful application of ideas and skills. Thus, the kinds of innovations recommended for educationally disadvantaged students would be advantageous for other students as well.

*A Whole-School Perspective on Teaching the Educationally Disadvantaged.* When one considers what teachers, staff developers, program managers, and school administrators can do to implement the kinds of approaches described in this book, it soon becomes clear that whole-school solutions are especially powerful. In Chapter Six, Calfee argues that effective implementation of these kinds of instructional models requires change not just on the classroom level but also in the school as a whole. He urges that the kind of dialogue that becomes the medium of exchange in the classroom be adopted among teachers and between teachers and administrators as well. In addition to raising its expectations for educationally disadvantaged students, the school must provide a coherent program that places sustained intellectual effort above categorical distinctions among subject areas or between regular and compensatory programs.

Compensatory education programs are evolving in ways that encourage whole-school solutions, and administrators should give increased attention to schoolwide programs as a mechanism for innovation. Regulations for Chapter 1, the major program providing federal funds to school districts serving children from economically disadvantaged homes, permit such schoolwide efforts, by way of supporting instructional innovations that will help all students, including those who otherwise would have received separate Chapter 1 services. School, district, and state reform efforts and Chapter 2 programs (which provide a small amount of federal money but give local education agencies broad discretion in how to use the funds) are providing additional sources of support for new approaches to education.

Any schoolwide approach must confront questions about the role of assessment in promoting advanced skills. A requirement for schoolwide Chapter 1 programs is that they be able to demonstrate that those children eligible for Chapter 1 services do as well as or better than they would have done given separate services. This generally requires use of nationally normed tests and raises the issue of the congruence between what the program is trying to teach and what the tests are measuring. Although many of the standardized tests given now tend to emphasize discrete basic skills, there are several reasons to believe that schools instituting alternative programs aimed at teaching advanced skills will be able to make their case.

First, although the programs described here have inculcation of advanced skills as their primary focus, the more discrete basic skills that tend to be measured by most standardized tests are dealt with in the context of more complex tasks. The available evidence suggests that on tests of basic skills students involved in the type of program described here often do as well as or better than students participating in more traditional programs of drill and practice on basic skills. Second, test developers are moving toward including meaningful measures of advanced skills (such as extended reading passages, writing samples) on their instruments, and such tests can be expected to become more available and more widely used in the next five years. Finally, the movement toward "authentic" or "performance" testing both signals increasing state and federal interest in measuring advanced skills and provides support for schools' use of supplementary evidence, such as portfolios or locally developed tests, to support the claim that students have made progress in the advanced skills that are the focus of alternative programs.

## Conclusion

The chapters in this book attest that much more can be done in teaching comprehension, composition, and math reasoning to educationally disadvantaged students than most compensatory education programs have done in the past. It is time to rethink our assumptions about the relationship between basic and advanced skills and to examine critically the content and teaching methods we bring to the classroom. The models described in these chapters were inspired by research in cognitive psychology and focus on teaching the kind of content generally regarded as "conceptual," "higher order," or "advanced." The curricular emphasis and some of the instructional elements of these models have long been accepted as appropriate for teaching gifted children, older students, or students from educationally advantaged backgrounds. What has not been adequately appreciated is the relevance of these models for all learners—advantaged and disadvantaged, young and old alike. We hope that these chapters will serve as a resource and an inspiration for educators undertaking the hard work involved in providing students with a new, more challenging educational experience.

## References

Allington, R. L. (1980). Teacher interruption behavior during primary-grade oral reading. *Journal of Educational Psychology, 72,* 371–377.

Allington, R. L., & McGill-Franzen, A. (1989). School response to reading failure: Chapter 1 and special education students in grades 2, 4, and 8. *Elementary School Journal, 89,* 529–542.

Anyon, J. (1980). Social class and the hidden curriculum of work. *Journal of Education, 162* (1), 67–92.

Birman, B. F., Orland, M. E., Jung, R. K., Anson, R. J., Garcia, G. N., Moore, M. T., Funkhouser, J. T., Morrison, D. R., Turnbull, B. J., & Reisner, E. R. (1987). *The current operation of the Chap-*

*ter 1 program: Final report from the National Assessment of Chapter 1*. Washington, DC: U.S. Government Printing Office.

Brophy, J. E., & Good, T. (1974). *Teacher-student relationships: Causes and consequences*. New York: Holt, Rinehart, & Winston.

Cole, M., & Griffin, P. (Eds.). (1987). *Improving science and math education for minorities and women*. Madison, WI: Center for Educational Research.

Griffin, P., & Cole, M. (1987). New technologies, basic skills, and the underside of education: What's to be done? In J. A. Langer (Ed.), *Language, literacy, and culture: Issues of society and schooling*. Norwood, NJ: Ablex.

Knapp, M. S., & Turnbull, B. J. (1990). *Better schooling for the children of poverty: Alternatives to conventional wisdom: Vol. 1. Summary*. Washington, DC: U.S. Department of Education, Office of Planning, Budget and Evaluation.

Moll, L. (1990). Social and instructional issues in educating "disadvantaged" students. In M. S. Knapp & P. M. Shields (Eds.), *Better schooling for the children of poverty: Alternatives to conventional wisdom: Vol. 2. Commissioned papers and literature review*. Washington, DC: U.S. Department of Education, Office of Planning, Budget and Evaluation.

Oakes, J. (1986). Tracking, inequality, and the rhetoric of school reform: Why schools don't change. *Journal of Education, 168*, 61–80.

Scott, J. C. (1988). Nonmainstream groups: Questions and research directions. In J. L. Davidson (Ed.), *Counterpoint and beyond*. Urbana, IL: National Council of Teachers of English.

Sherwood, R. D., Kinzer, C., Hasselbring, T., & Bransford, J. (1987). Macro-contexts for learning: Initial findings and issues. *Journal of Applied Cognition, 1*, 93–108.

# 2

# Thinking in Arithmetic Class

*Lauren B. Resnick, Victoria L. Bill,*
*Sharon B. Lesgold, and Mary N. Leer*

FOR MANY YEARS NOW, MOST EFFORTS TO IMPROVE EDUCATIONAL OUT-
comes for disadvantaged students have been based on the premise
that what such children need is higher expectations for learning
coupled with intensified and careful application of traditional
classroom methods. Thus, what is typically prescribed is more careful explanations, more practice, and more frequent testing to monitor progress. Such methods seem to work—up to a point. That is,
they produce gains on basic skills tests. But they are not designed
to teach children to reason and solve problems. Today, such abilities are fundamental for participation in the economy and society
in general.

The nearly exclusive focus on the kinds of "basic skills" that
can be taught by repetitive drill does not necessarily derive from a
lack of ambition for disadvantaged students or from a belief that the
children are inherently incapable of thinking and problem solving.
Rather, it is rooted in an assumption that most educators share
about all learning by nearly all children (some would except the
"gifted"): that successful learning means working step by step
through a hierarchical sequence of skills and concepts. The common view is that skills and concepts are ordered in rather strict
hierarchies and that asking children to perform complex skills before they master the prerequisite simpler ones is to doom them to

failure, or at least to frustration, in the course of learning. This hierarchical mastery learning approach dictates that children who have trouble learning some of the simpler skills practice them longer. But in practice this turns out to deny disadvantaged children the opportunity to learn higher-order abilities. Because many disadvantaged are among those who learn slowly at the outset, they are doomed to more and more supervised practice on the "basics." They never get to graduate to the more demanding and interesting problems that constitute the "higher-order" part of the curriculum.

The work we describe in this chapter is premised on a radically different set of assumptions. We argue that disadvantaged children, like all children, can begin their educational life by engaging in active thinking and problem solving. We argue further that when thinking-oriented instruction is carefully organized for this purpose, children can acquire the traditional basic skills in the process of reasoning and solving problems. As a result, they can acquire not only the fundamentals of a discipline but also the ability to apply those fundamentals, and—critically—a belief in their own capacities as learners and thinkers.

Reviewing research and practical efforts to teach higher-order thinking skills a few years ago, Resnick (1987) concluded that shaping a disposition to critical thought is as important in developing higher-order cognitive abilities in students as is teaching particular skills of reasoning and thinking. Acquiring such dispositions, she proposed, requires regular participation in activities that exercise reasoning skills within social environments that value thinking and judgment and that communicate to children a sense of their own competence in reasoning and thinking. This, in turn, calls for educational programs suffused with thinking and reasoning, programs in which basic subject matter instruction serves as the daily occasion for exercising and extending cognitive abilities. Explicit attention to thinking and reasoning seems particularly important for children who are not experiencing daily practice in such reasoning in their homes or who do not trust their own out-of-school experience as being relevant to school success. Such children often fail to learn the "hidden curriculum" of thinking and reasoning that more favored children acquire without much explicit help from teachers.

We report here on the early results of an effort to apply these ideas to early mathematics teaching for disadvantaged children. To embed basic mathematics learning in a thinking curriculum, we had to design a new set of practices for the mathematics classroom. We wanted to create an environment in which children would practice mathematics as a field in which there are open questions and arguments, in which interpretation, reasoning, and debate—all key components of critical thought—play a legitimate and expected role. To do this, we needed to revise mathematics teaching in the direction of treating mathematics as if it were an ill-structured discipline. That is, we needed to take seriously, with and for young learners, the propositions that mathematical statements can have more than one interpretation, that interpretation is the responsibility of every individual using mathematical expressions, and that argument and debate about interpretations and their implications are a normal part of mathematical activity. Participating in such an environment, we thought, would develop capabilities and dispositions for finding relationships among mathematical ideas and between mathematical statements and problem situations. It would develop skill not only in applying mathematics but also in thinking mathematically. In short, it would socialize children into a developmentally appropriate form of the practice of mathematics as a mode of thought, reasoning, and problem solving.

This goal, however, seemed at first to pose an insurmountable problem for school beginners—especially, perhaps, those we label *disadvantaged*. To engage in the kind of mathematical discussions we were aiming for, children would have to know *some* mathematics at the outset. They would need something to think *about* if the exercise was not to be an empty one. A first question, then, was whether children entering school knew enough about numbers and quantities to permit a reasoning- and discussion-oriented program from the outset. Fortunately, a large body of research accumulated over the past decade suggests that almost all children come to school with a substantial body of knowledge about quantity relations and that children are capable of using this knowledge as a foundation for understanding numbers and arithmetic (see Resnick, 1989, and Resnick & Greeno, 1990, for interpretive reviews). This knowledge, we thought, could provide the initial foundations for children's participation in a reasoning-based mathematics program.

## The Intuitive Basis for Early Mathematical Reasoning

Children come to school with two kinds of intuitively developed knowledge relevant to mathematics learning. First, they know a good deal about amounts of physical material and the relations among these amounts, even though they cannot yet use numbers to describe these relations. Second, most children know the rules for counting sets of objects. This gives them the beginning tool for using numbers to manipulate and describe quantity relations.

### Protoquantitative Schemas

During the preschool years, children develop a large store of knowledge about how quantities of physical material behave in the world. This knowledge, acquired from manipulating and talking about physical material, allows children to compare amounts and sizes and to reason about changes in amounts and quantities. Because this early reasoning about amount of material is done without measurement or exact numerical quantification, we refer to it as *protoquantitative* reasoning. We can document development during the preschool years of three sets of protoquantitative schemas: *compare, increase/decrease,* and *part-whole* (see Figure 2.1).

The *protoquantitative compare* schema makes greater-smaller comparative judgments of amounts of material. Before they are two years old, children express quantity judgments in the form of absolute size labels such as *big, small, lots,* and *little.* Only a little later, they begin to put linguistic labels on the comparisons of sizes they made as infants. Thus, they can look at two circles and declare one bigger than the other, see two trees and declare one taller than the other, examine two glasses of milk and declare that one contains more than the other. These comparisons initially are based on direct perceptual judgments without any measurement process. However, they form a basis for eventual numerical comparisons of quantity.

The *protoquantitative increase/decrease* schema interprets changes as increases or decreases in quantities. This schema allows

## Figure 2.1. The Protoquantitative Schemas.

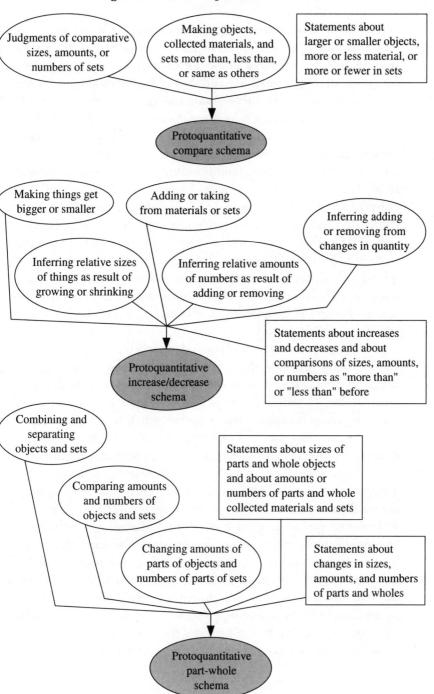

*Source:* Adapted from Resnick & Greeno (1990).

children as young as three or four years of age to reason about the effects of adding an amount to or taking an amount away from a starting amount. Children know, for example, that if they have a certain amount of something and they get another amount of the same thing (perhaps Mother adds another cookie to the two already on the child's plate), they have more than before. Or, if some of the original quantity is taken away, they have less than before. Equally important, children know that if nothing has been added or taken away, they have the same amount as before. For example, children show surprise and label as "magic" any change in the number of objects on a plate that occurs out of their sight (Gelman, 1972). This shows that children have the underpinnings of number conservation well before they can pass the standard Piagetian tests. They can be fooled by perceptual cues or language that distracts them from quantity, but they possess a basic understanding of addition, subtraction, and conservation. The protoquantitative increase/decrease schema is also the foundation for eventual understanding of unary addition and subtraction.

The *protoquantitative part-whole* schema is really a set of schemas that organize children's knowledge about the ways in which material around them comes apart and goes together. The schemas specify that material is *additive*. That is, one can cut a quantity into pieces that, taken together, equal the original quantity. One can also put two quantities together to make a bigger quantity and then join that bigger quantity with yet another in a form of hierarchical additivity. Implicitly, children know about this additive property of quantities. This protoquantitative knowledge allows them to make judgments about the relations between parts and wholes, including class inclusion (Markman & Siebert, 1976) and the effects of changes in the size of parts on the size of the whole. The protoquantitative part-whole schema is the foundation for later understanding of binary addition and subtraction and for several fundamental mathematical principles, such as the commutativity and associativity of addition and the complementarity of addition and subtraction. It also provides the framework for a concept of additive composition of number that underlies the place value system.

*Counting*

Counting is the first step in making quantitative judgments exact. It is a measurement system for sets. Gelman and her colleagues have shown that children as young as three or four years of age implicitly know the key principles that allow counting to serve as a vehicle of quantification (Gelman & Gallistel, 1978). These principles include the knowledge that number names must be matched one for one with the objects in a set and that the order of the number names matters but that the order in which the objects are touched does not. Knowledge of these principles is inferred from the ways in which children solve novel counting problems. For example, if asked to make the second object in a row "number 1," children do not neglect the first object entirely but, rather, assign it one of the higher number names in the sequence.

Other research has challenged Gelman's assessment of the ages at which children can be said to have acquired all of the counting principles. Some of the challenges are really arguments about the criteria for applying certain terms. For example, Gelman has attributed knowledge of *cardinality*, a key mathematical principle, to children as soon as they know that the last number in a counting sequence names the quantity in the whole set; others would reserve the term for a more advanced stage in which children reliably conserve quantity under perceptual transformations. A challenge that goes beyond matters of terminology comes from research showing that, although children may know all the principles of counting and be able to use counting to quantify given sets of objects or to create sets of specified sizes, they may not, at a certain point, have fully integrated their counting knowledge with their protoquantitative knowledge. Several investigators (for example, Sophian, 1987) have shown that many children who know how to count sets do not spontaneously count in order to compare sets. This means that counting and the protoquantitative schemas exist initially as separate knowledge systems, isolated from each other.

*Integrating Counting with the Protoquantitative Schemas.* Such findings make it clear that, even after knowledge of counting principles is established, there is substantially more growth in number concepts still to be attained. A first major step in this growth is integration of the number-name sequence with the proto-quantitative comparison schema. This seems to happen as young as about four years of age. At this point, children behave as if the counting word sequence constitutes a kind of "mental number line" (Resnick, 1983). They can quickly identify which of a pair of numbers is more by mentally consulting this number line, without actually stepping through the sequence to determine which number comes later.

In the child's subsequent development, counting as a means of quantifying sets is integrated with the protoquantitative part-whole and increase/decrease schemas. This integration seems to develop as a result of participating in situations in which changes and combinations of quantity are called for and there is a cultural mandate for exact quantification. Out of school, this can occur in various play or household activities—particularly when age segregation is not strict so that young children engage freely with older children and adults. School settings can mimic the conditions of everyday life to some extent. However, a principal resource for promoting quantification of the schemas in school is the story problem. Several researchers (for example, De Corte & Verschaffel, 1987; Riley & Greeno, 1988) have shown that children entering school can solve many simple story problems by applying their counting skills to sets they create as they build physical models of the story situations. Because the stories involve the same basic relationships among quantities as the protoquantitative schemas, extensive practice in solving problems via counting should help children quantify their original schemas. Such practice should not only develop children's ability to solve problems using exact numerical measures but also lead them to interpret numbers themselves in terms of the relations specified by the protoquantitative schemas. Eventually, children should be able to construct an enriched meaning for numbers—treating numbers (rather than measured quantities of material) as the entities that are mentally compared, increased and decreased, or organized into parts and wholes.

### Principles for a Reasoning-Based Arithmetic Program

With this research base as a grounding for our efforts, we set out to develop a primary arithmetic program (for grades 1 through 3) that would engage children from the outset in invention, reasoning, and verbal justification of mathematical ideas. The school in which we worked served mainly minority (94 percent were African-Americans), low-income (69 percent were eligible for free or reduced-price lunches) children. Our goal was to use as little traditional school drill material as possible in order to provide for children a consistent environment in which they would be socialized to think of themselves as mathematical reasoners and to behave accordingly. This meant that we needed a program in which children would successfully learn the traditional basics of arithmetic calculation as well as more complex forms of reasoning and argumentation. The program evolved gradually over a period of months. We describe it here in somewhat schematized form as the instantiation of a set of six principles that guided our thinking and experimentation.

*1. Develop Children's Trust in Their Own Knowledge.* Traditional instruction, by focusing on specific procedures and on special mathematical notations and vocabulary, tends to teach children that what they already know is not legitimately mathematics. To develop children's trust in their own knowledge as mathematics, our program stresses the possibility of multiple procedures for solving any problem, invites children's invention of these multiple procedures, and asks that children explain and justify their procedures using everyday language. In addition, the use of manipulatives and finger counting ensures that children have a way of establishing for themselves the truth or falsity of their proposed solutions. Exhibit 2.1 provides examples of multiple procedures used by second-grade children to solve the same addition problem, 158 + 74. The examples are copied from six different children's homework papers. Child A used a procedure of adding the value of the leftmost digits, first 100 + 70, then 50 + 4. This unusual decomposition left the 8 of 158 still to be added, which the child added to the already accumulated 54. To add the resulting 62 to 170, the child decomposed it to 60 and 2. He added to 60 first, yielding 230, and then the 2, to yield the final answer. Child F used a more conventional place value decomposition, first adding up the hundreds (note that she indicates that there are 0 hundreds in 74), then the tens, then the units, and finally combining the three partial

**Exhibit 2.1. Several Second-Graders' Solutions
to a Computational Problem.**

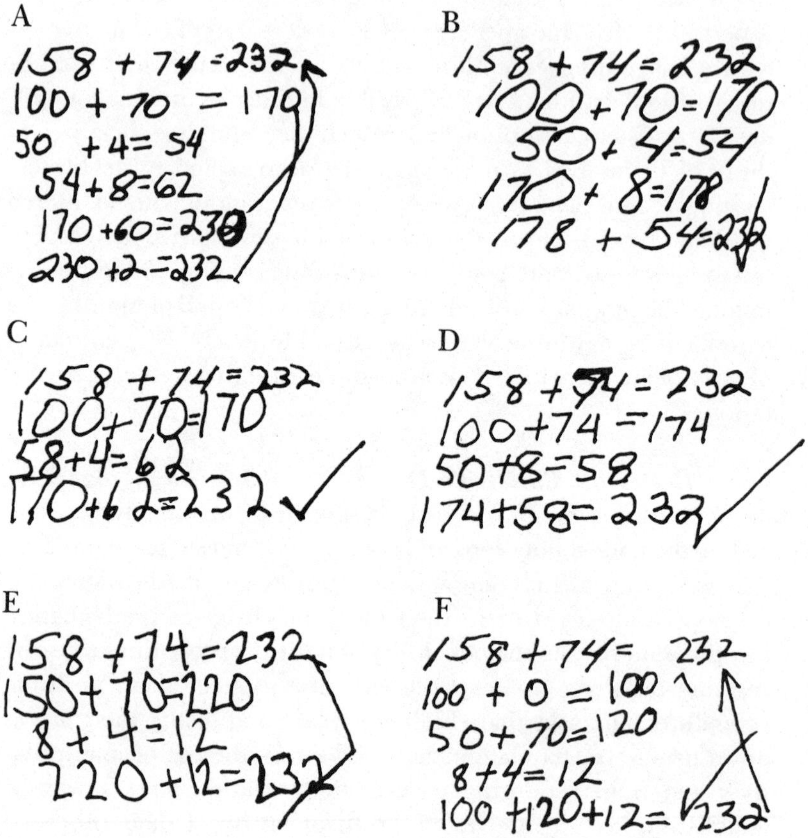

A

$$158 + 74 = 232$$
$$100 + 70 = 170$$
$$50 + 4 = 54$$
$$54 + 8 = 62$$
$$170 + 60 = 230$$
$$230 + 2 = 232$$

B

$$158 + 74 = 232$$
$$100 + 70 = 170$$
$$50 + 4 = 54$$
$$170 + 8 = 178$$
$$178 + 54 = 232$$

C

$$158 + 74 = 232$$
$$100 + 70 = 170$$
$$58 + 4 = 62$$
$$170 + 62 = 232$$ ✓

D

$$158 + 74 = 232$$
$$100 + 74 = 174$$
$$50 + 8 = 58$$
$$174 + 58 = 232$$

E

$$158 + 74 = 232$$
$$150 + 70 = 220$$
$$8 + 4 = 12$$
$$220 + 12 = 232$$

F

$$158 + 74 = 232$$
$$100 + 0 = 100$$
$$50 + 70 = 120$$
$$8 + 4 = 12$$
$$100 + 120 + 12 = 232$$

sums. Child E also used a place value decomposition but worked initially on the hundreds and tens combined (150 + 70). These and the other solutions in the exhibit illustrate the ways in which written notation and mental arithmetic are combined in the children's procedures.

*2. Draw Children's Informal Knowledge, Developed Outside School, into the Classroom.* An important early goal of the program is to stimulate the use of counting in the context of the compare, increase/decrease, and part-whole schemas to promote children's construction of the quantified versions of those schemas.

This is done through extensive problem-solving practice, using both story problems and acted-out situations. Counting (including counting on one's fingers) is actively encouraged. Exhibit 2.2 gives an example of a typical class problem, showing how it can generate several solutions; the notations shown are copied from the notebook in which a child recorded the solutions proposed by several teams who had worked on the problem.

*3. Use Formal Notations (Identify Sentences and Equations) as a Public Record of Discussions and Conclusions.* Children's intuitive knowledge must be linked to the formal language of mathematics. By using a standard mathematical notation to record conversations carried out in ordinary language and rooted in well-understood problem situations, the formalisms take on a meaning directly linked to children's mathematical intuitions. First used by the teacher as a way of displaying for the class what a child had proposed, equations quickly became common currency in the classroom. Most of the children began to write equations themselves only a few weeks into the school year. Figure 2.2 shows part of a typical teacher-led sequence in which children propose a solution to a story problem. The teacher carefully linked elements of the proposed solution to the actual physical material involved in the story (the tray of cupcakes) and an overhead schematic of the material. Only after the referential meaning of each number had been carefully established was the number written into the equation. The total sequence shown took about 1 minute, 20 seconds.

*4. Introduce Key Mathematical Structures as Quickly as Possible.* Children's protoquantitative schemas already allow them to think reasonably powerfully about how amounts of material compare, increase and decrease, and come apart and go together. In other words, they already know, in nonnumerically quantified form, something about properties such as commutativity, associativity, and additive inverse. A major goal of the first year or two of school mathematics is to "mathematize" this knowledge—that is, quantify it and link it to formal expressions and operations. It was our conjecture that this could best be done by laying out the additive structures (for example, for first grade: addition and subtraction problem situations, the composition of large numbers, and re-

**Exhibit 2.2. A Second-Grade Problem and Several Solutions.**

---

*Mary told her friend Tonya that she would give her ninety-five barrettes. Mary had four bags of barrettes, and each bag had nine barrettes. Does Mary have enough barrettes?*

The class first developed an estimated answer. Then they were asked, "How many more does she need?" The solutions below were generated by different class groups.

Group 1 first solved for the number of barrettes by repeated addition. Then they decomposed 4 × 9 into 2 × 9 plus 2 × 9. Then they set up a missing addend problem, 36 + 59, which they solved by a combination of estimation and correction.

Group 2 set up a subtraction equation and then developed a solution that used a negative partial result.

Group 4 began with total number of barrettes needed and subtracted out the successive bags of 9.

Est. 4×10=40 NO

1-24-90

#1 9+9+9+9=36

4×9=36
2×9=18
2×9=18
18+18=36

60

36 + 59 = 95
36 + 60 = 96
96 − 1 = 95
60 − 1 = 59

#2 95 − 36 = 59
90 − 30 = 60
5 − 6 = −1
60 − 1 = 59

#4 95 − 9 = 86
86 − 9 = 77
77 − 9 = 68
68 − 9 = 59

---

grouping as a special application of the part-whole schemas) as quickly as possible and then allowing full mastery (speed, flexibility of procedures, articulate explanations) of elements of the system to develop over an extended time. Guided by this principle, we found it possible to introduce addition and subtraction with regrouping in February of first grade. However, no specific procedures were taught; rather, children were encouraged to invent (and explain) ways of solving multidigit addition and subtraction problems, using appropriate manipulatives and/or expanded notation formats that they developed.

It is important to note that a program built around this principle constitutes a major challenge to an idea that has been widely accepted in the past twenty to thirty years of educational research and practice. This is the notion of learning hierarchies—specifically, that it is necessary for learners to master simpler components before they try to learn complex skills. According to theories of hierarchical and mastery learning, children should thoroughly master single-digit addition and subtraction, for example, before attempting multidigit procedures, and they should be able to smoothly perform multidigit arithmetic without regrouping before they tackle the complexities of regrouping. We propose instead a *distributed* curriculum in which multiple topics are developed all year long, with increasing levels of sophistication and demand, rather than a strictly sequential curriculum.

To convey the flavor of the process, Table 2.1 shows the range of topics planned for a single month of the second-grade program. All topics shown are treated at changing levels of sophistication and demand throughout the school year. This distributed curriculum discourages decontextualized teaching of components of arithmetic skill. It encourages children to draw on their existing knowledge framework (the protoquantitative schemas) to interpret advanced material, while gradually building computational fluency.

*5. Encourage Everyday Problem Finding.* In stating this principle, we deliberately use the term *everyday* in two senses. First, it means literally doing arithmetic every day, not only in school but also at home and in other informal settings. Children need massive practice in applying arithmetic ideas, far more than the classroom

## Figure 2.2. Part of a Whole-Class Discussion of a Story Problem.

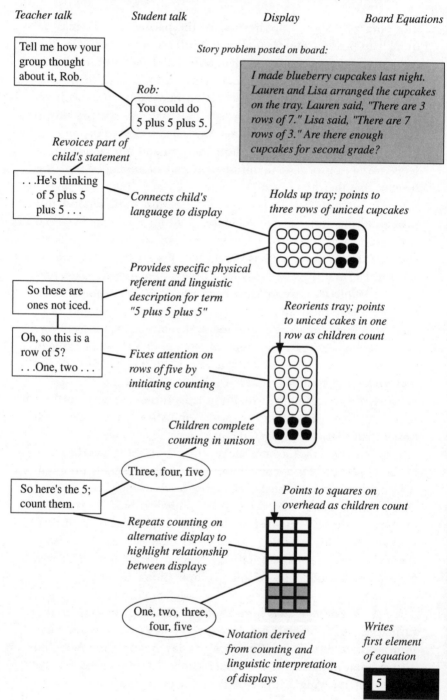

Teacher talk     Student talk     Display     Board Equations

Tell me how your group thought about it, Rob.

Rob:
You could do 5 plus 5 plus 5.

*Story problem posted on board:*

*I made blueberry cupcakes last night. Lauren and Lisa arranged the cupcakes on the tray. Lauren said, "There are 3 rows of 7." Lisa said, "There are 7 rows of 3." Are there enough cupcakes for second grade?*

*Revoices part of child's statement*

...He's thinking of 5 plus 5 plus 5 ...

*Connects child's language to display*

*Holds up tray; points to three rows of uniced cupcakes*

*Provides specific physical referent and linguistic description for term "5 plus 5 plus 5"*

So these are ones not iced.

*Reorients tray; points to uniced cakes in one row as children count*

Oh, so this is a row of 5? ...One, two ...

*Fixes attention on rows of five by initiating counting*

*Children complete counting in unison*

Three, four, five

So here's the 5; count them.

*Points to squares on overhead as children count*

*Repeats counting on alternative display to highlight relationship between displays*

One, two, three, four, five

*Notation derived from counting and linguistic interpretation of displays*

*Writes first element of equation*

5

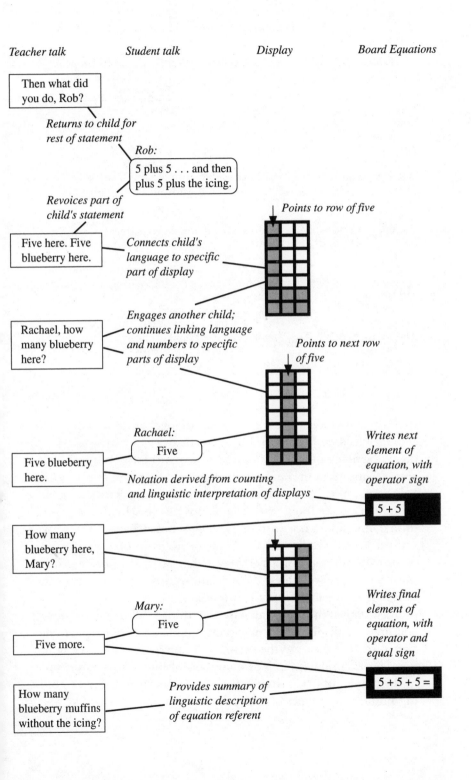

| Teacher talk | Student talk | Display | Board Equations |
|---|---|---|---|

Then what did you do, Rob?

*Returns to child for rest of statement*

Rob:
5 plus 5 . . . and then plus 5 plus the icing.

*Revoices part of child's statement*

*Points to row of five*

Five here. Five blueberry here.

*Connects child's language to specific part of display*

*Engages another child; continues linking language and numbers to specific parts of display*

Rachael, how many blueberry here?

*Points to next row of five*

Rachael:
Five

Five blueberry here.

*Notation derived from counting and linguistic interpretation of displays*

*Writes next element of equation, with operator sign*

5 + 5

How many blueberry here, Mary?

Mary:
Five

*Writes final element of equation, with operator and equal sign*

Five more.

5 + 5 + 5 =

How many blueberry muffins without the icing?

*Provides summary of linguistic description of equation referent*

Table 2.1. Topic Coverage Planned for a Single Month in Grade 2.

| Domain | Specific Content |
|---|---|
| Reading/writing numerals | 0–9,999 |
| Set counting | 0–9,999 |
| Addition | 2- and 3-digit regrouping, basic facts 20 |
| Subtraction | 2-digit renaming, basic facts 20 |
| Word problems | Addition, subtraction, multiplication |
| Problem solving | Work backward, solve an easier problem, patterns |
| Estimation | Quantities, strategies, length |
| Ratio/proportion | Scaling up, scaling down |
| Statistics/probability | Scaling up, scaling down, spinner (1/4), dice (1/16), 3 graphs |
| Multiplication | Array (2, 4 tables), allocation, equal groupings |
| Division | Oral problems involving sharing sets equally |
| Measurement | Arbitrary units |
| Decimals | Money |
| Fractions | Parts of whole, parts of set, equivalent pieces |
| Telling time | To hour, to half hour |
| Geometry | Rectangle, square (properties) |
| Negative integers | Ones, tens |

itself can provide. For this reason, we thought it important to encourage children to find problems for themselves that would keep them practicing number facts and mathematical reasoning. Second, *everyday* means nonformal, situated in the activities of everyday life. It is important that children come to view mathematics as something that can be found everywhere, not just in school, not just in formal notations, not just in problems posed by a teacher. We wanted to get children in the habit of noticing quantitative and other pattern relationships wherever they are and of posing questions for themselves about those relationships. Two aspects of the program represent efforts to instantiate this principle. First, the problems posed in class are drawn from things children know about and are actually involved in. Second, homework projects are designed so that they use the events and objects of children's home lives: for example, finding as many sets of four things as possible in the home; counting fingers and toes of family members; recording numbers and types of things removed from a grocery bag after a shopping trip. From child and parent reports, there is good, although informal, evidence that this strategy works. Children in the program are noticing numbers and relationships and setting problems for themselves in the course of their everyday activities. Exhibit 2.3 shows part of a letter from a parent to the teacher, sharing a story of a child's everyday math engagement.

   *6. Talk About Mathematics; Don't Just Do Arithmetic.* Discussion and argument are essential to creating a culture of critical thought. To encourage this talk, our program uses a combination of teacher-led whole-class discussion and structured small-group activity by the children. In a typical daily lesson, a single relatively complex problem is presented on the chalkboard. The first phase is a class discussion of what the problem means—what kind of information is given, what is to be discovered, what possible methods of solution there are, and the like. In the second phase, teams of children work together on solving the problem, using drawings, manipulatives, and role playing to support their discussions and solutions. The teams are responsible not only for developing a solution to the problem but also for being able to explain why their solution is mathematically and practically appropriate.

   The following transcript of a four-minute segment of a third-grade team's conversation as they work independently on a problem

**Exhibit 2.3. Excerpt of a Letter from a Parent.**

Dear Mrs. Bill,

   As a parent, I must share this with you.
   On Saturday, Raymond, Jamella and I were having lunch at Monroeville Mall. Raymond and Jamella love to spend their own money, so I told both of them that I would pay for half of their lunch. I asked Ray if he remembered what he had paid for his hot dog, fries and drink. He said "Yes, $4.33." My reply was, "O.K., tell me what I owe you. What is half of $4.33?"
   He leaned back in his chair and you could just look into his eyes and see him concentrating. On the other hand, Jamella was doing the calculations on a make-believe piece of paper on the table. (This is what I usually do). Not Raymond, Mrs. Bill, he was feeling and thinking the math problem. His answer was, "$2.15, Mommy." Well, I almost fell over into my Chinese food. When I told him that he was correct, he just beamed.

shows how linguistic interpretation and development of manipulative displays interact in the children's work.

Mick, Joe, Anna, and Ms. B. were working on the following story problem:

> Mr. Bill bought three boxes of Ninja Turtle cookies for $3.79. One box costs $1.50 at other stores. Which is the better buy?

> How much are the $3.79 Ninja Turtles per box?

*Ms. B.:*   I want to discuss it with your groups. I want you to show how you figured it out. And when you have it, raise your hand. I'll let you put it on. If you need manipulatives, you may just get them.

Ms. B. circulates around the room while children work at solving the problem in their respective discussion teams.

*Joe:*   Four dollars and that's automatically over.

*Anna:*   So here's the three boxes. [Anna puts three pieces of colored paper on the desk.]

*Joe:*   Now it's time to . . . now it's time to . . . Wait, wait a minute.

*Mick:*   What . . .

*Anna:*   What kind of problem could we do?

*Mick:*   We could say, we could say three dollars and seventy-nine cents. Okay, three dollars and seventy-nine cents divided by the three boxes, because we're taking the three seventy-nine and trying to see how much each box would cost if it wasn't in a bulk. [Ms. B. appears at group table carrying the three-box unit of Ninja Turtle cookies.]

*Joe:*   All right.

*Anna:*   I agree, I agree because we have three seventy-nine in three boxes. . . . Ms. B. brought it for second grade. Third grade will divide it up . . . in into and divided it up for second-grade and third-grade class.

*Joe:*   All right, now.

*Anna:*   So I agree.

*Joe:*   All right, now [inaudible]. What's over three dollars [writing in notebook]?

*Mick:*   I agree.

*Anna:*   I agree.

*Joe:*   I agree with myself [all three students writing in notebooks]. We have to show [three dollars divided by three]. We have to put the date.

*Anna:*   I agree. I agree . . . three dollars divided by three.

*Joe:*   We have to show this. [Joe stands and reaches into the manipulatives bin, which contains bundles of ten and one hundred popsickle sticks, as well as single popsickle sticks.]

*Anna:*   How can we show this, Joe?

*Mick:*   You could say . . .

*Joe:*   Three dollars. These are our three dollars [puts down three bundles of hundred and writes something in his notebook].

*Mick:*   So what is this, Anna, three dollars or three pennies?

*Anna:*   Three pennies.

*Mick:*   Okay, so three, so what do we do with this three dollars?

*Anna:*   We divide it . . . three hundred. [Anna picks up a bundle of one hundred and begins to take off the rubber band.]

*Mick:*   Wait a minute . . .

*Joe:*   We have the other two hundred.

*Mick:*   Yeah, so . . . but are we taking off the rubber band [addressing Anna]?

*Anna:*   Yeah, we have to.

*Joe:*   No, we don't. Here are two more. One, two, three [picks up and puts down the three bundles].

*Anna:*   One goes here, one goes here, and one goes there [puts bundles of one hundred, one at a time, on top of the pieces of colored paper].

In the third phase of the lesson, teams successively present their solutions and justifications to the whole class, and the teacher records these on the chalkboard. The teacher presses for explanations and challenges those that are incomplete or incorrect; other children join in the challenges or attempt to help by expanding the presented argument. By the end of the class period, multiple solutions to the problem, along with their justifications (as in Exhibits 2.1 and 2.2) have been considered, and there is frequently discussion of why several different solutions could all work, or why certain ones are better than others. In all these discussions, children are permitted to express themselves in ordinary language. Mathematical language and precision are deliberately not demanded in the oral discussion. However, the equation representations that the teacher and children write to summarize oral arguments provide a mathematically precise public record, thus linking everyday language to mathematical language (as in Figure 2.2).

### Results of the Program

We are describing here a program that has been under development for a little over two years. The project began not as a research project but as an effort to help an ambitious teacher apply research findings to improve her teaching. During the developmental period, we did not want to impose testing programs beyond those that the school regularly administered. We are thus limited, in this period of the project's life, to data from the school's standardized testing program and from clinical interviews that we conducted with some of the children, along with some impressionistic reports of child and parent reactions to the overall program.

Formal evaluation data consist of scores from the California Achievement Test (CAT), which is administered in the school each

September. First-graders were tested at the beginning of second grade, second-graders at the beginning of third grade. Scores on the Metropolitan Reading Readiness Test, administered by the school in March of the kindergarten year, provide data on children's general academic level before entering first grade. We have data on two cohorts of children who participated in the program, one beginning in first grade, one beginning in second grade. Figure 2.3a shows three years of reading and math data for cohort A, who began the program in first grade. The children were low performers (about the 25th percentile) in both math and reading in kindergarten and remained quite low in reading in grades 1 and 2. However, their math scores rose dramatically, to a mean of the 80th percentile and stayed high (mean of 70th percentile) during the second year of the program. Figure 2.3b shows four years of data for cohort B, who began the program during second grade. Like cohort A, they were low scorers before the program. When the program was introduced in second grade, their math scores jumped to nearly the 70th percentile on average and stayed in that range through third grade. For this cohort, reading scores also rose somewhat. Reading was taught by a different teacher in the school. We are now investigating what might have been responsible for this gain. For comparison, Figure 2.3c shows three years of data for a cohort of children taught by the intervention program teacher before she adopted the new program. Throughout the period, mean scores remained at a low 40th to 45th percentile. An important point, one that cannot be seen in the means of the graphs, is that the math gains were not limited to only a few of the children. In cohort A, for example, the *lowest*-scoring child at the end of the first grade was at the 66th percentile. Thus, the program appeared effective for children of all ability levels.

These global data tell only part of the story, of course. We would like to know much more for which systematic data are not yet available. Nevertheless, we can point to some indicators based on our interviews, class observations, and reports from the school. We interviewed all first-graders three times during the year, focusing on their knowledge of counting and addition and subtraction facts, along with their methods for calculating and their understanding of the principles of commutativity, conservation, and the complementarity of addition and subtraction. At the outset, these

**Figure 2.3. California Achievement Test Scores.**

### 3a. Intervention cohort A

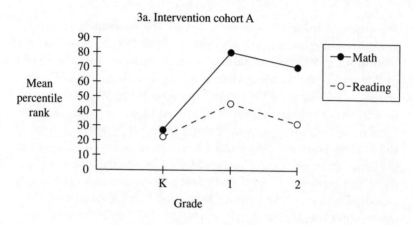

### 3b. Intervention cohort B

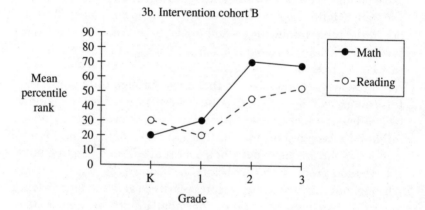

### 3c. Control cohort

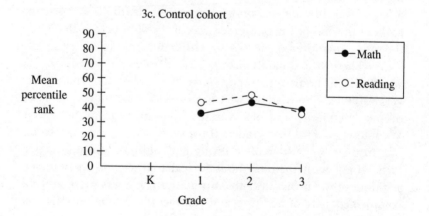

children, as might be expected given their socioeconomic status and their parents' generally low educational background, were not highly proficient. Only one-third of them could count orally to one hundred or beyond, and most were unable to count reliably across decade boundaries (for example, from twenty-nine to thirty or fifty-nine to sixty). The size of the sets that they could quantify by counting ranged from six to twenty. About one-third of these children could not solve small-number addition problems, even with manipulatives or finger counting and plenty of encouraging support from the interviewer. Only about six appeared able to perform simple subtractions using counting procedures. Thus, these children seemed very weak in entering arithmetic knowledge, especially compared with data presented by a number of investigators for middle-class and educationally favored populations. By December the picture was sharply different. All but a handful of children were performing both addition and subtraction problems successfully, and all of these demonstrated knowledge of the commutativity of addition. At least half also were using invented procedures, such as counting on from the larger of two addends, or using procedures that showed that they understood principles of complementarity of addition and subtraction. By the end of the school year, all children were performing in this way, and many were successfully solving and explaining multidigit problems.

The following additional evidence indicates that the program was having many of the desired effects. The children displayed various examples of confidence in doing mathematical work. Many sang to themselves as they took the standardized test. When visitors came to the classroom, they would offer to show off by solving math problems. They frequently asked for harder problems. These displays came from children of almost all ability levels. They had not been typical of any except the most able children the preceding year. Homework was more regularly turned in than in preceding years, without nagging or pressure from the teacher. Children often asked for extra math periods. Many parents reported that their children loved math and wanted to do math all the time. Parents also sent to school examples of problems that children had solved on their own in some everyday family situation. Knowing that the teacher frequently used such problems in class, parents asked that their child's problems be used. It is notable that this kind of parent engagement occurred in a population of parents that is traditionally aliented from the school and tends not to interact with teachers or school officials.

## Conclusion

We believe we have made a promising start at reaching our goals. We have shown that an interpretation- and discussion-oriented mathematics program can begin at the outset of school by building on the intuitive mathematical knowledge that children have as they enter school. Our standardized test score data show that this kind of thinking-based program also succeeds in teaching the basic number facts and arithmetic procedures that are the core of the traditional primary mathematics program. It is not necessary to teach facts and skills first and only then go on to thinking and reasoning. The two can be developed simultaneously. Assuming that we can maintain and replicate our results, this means that an interpretation- and discussion-oriented program can serve as the basic program in arithmetic, not just as an adjunct to a more traditional knowledge and skills curriculum.

Moreover, our results show that an interpretation-oriented mathematics program can be suitable even for children who are not socially favored, or initially, educationally able. The children with whom we have worked come disproportionately from among the least favored of American families. Many are considered to be educationally at risk; their educational prognosis, without special interventions or changed educational programs, is poor. Yet these children learned effectively in a type of program that, if present in schools at all, has been reserved for children judged able and talented—most often those from favored social groups.

What is at issue here, as we suggested at the outset, is not only an apparently successful program but also some fundamental challenges to dominant assumptions about learning and schooling. As we worked to develop this program, we realized that a new theoretical direction was increasingly dominating our thinking about the nature of development, learning, and schooling. This is the view, shared by a growing minority of thinkers in the various disciplines that comprise cognitive science, that human mental functioning must be understood as fundamentally situation specific and context dependent rather than as a collection of context-free abilities and knowledge. This apparently simple shift in perspective in fact entails reconsideration of a number of long-held assumptions in both psychology and education.

Until recently, educators and scholars have defined the educational task as one of teaching specific knowledge and skills. As concern has shifted from routine to higher-order or thinking abilities, we have developed more complex definitions of the skills to be acquired and even introduced various concepts of *meta*skill in the search for teachable general abilities. But we have continued to think of our major concern as one of identifying and analyzing particular skills of reasoning and thinking and then finding ways to teach them, on the assumption that successful students then will be able to apply these skills in a wide range of situations.

As we developed our program, we found ourselves less and less asking what constitutes mathematics competence or ability for young schoolchildren and more and more analyzing the features of the mathematics classroom that provide activities that exercise reasoning skills. This meant choosing story problems on the basis of the mathematical principles they might illustrate and developing forms of classroom conversation designed to evoke public reasoning about these principles. Our focus on mathematics as a form of cultural practice did not deny that children engaging in mathematical activity must be knowledgeable and skillful in many ways. However, our emerging perspective led us to focus far less on the design of "lessons" than on the development of a sequence of problem-solving situations in which children could successfully participate. Another way of saying this is that we were trying to create an *apprenticeship* environment for mathematical thinking in which children could participate daily. We expected them to acquire thereby not only the skills and knowledge that expert mathematical reasoners possess but also social identities as persons able and expected to engage in such reasoning (see Lave, in press).

Our program constitutes a version of the *cognitive apprenticeship* called for by Collins, Brown, and Newman (1989) in a recent influential paper. Its very success, however, calls into question some aspects of the apprenticeship metaphor as applied to early learning in a school environment. Among these is the nature of the master-apprentice relationship. In traditional apprenticeship, apprentices seek to become like their masters, and masters continually display all elements of skilled productive activity in their field of expertise. Teaching is only a secondary function of the traditional master. This simple—indeed, perhaps oversimplified— relationship does not seem applicable to the school setting, where the teacher's predominant function is not to *do* mathematics but to *teach* it. We will need to work out the particular role of the teacher in designing an environment *specifically for learning purposes*. A second issue surrounding cognitive apprenticeship in school is how to ensure that necessary particular skills will be acquired, even though the daily focus of activity is on problem solving and reasoning. Our first-year standardized test results suggest that we have not done badly on this criterion, but we need to understand better than we do now just *what* it is in our program that has succeeded and what the limits of our methods might be. In short, we offer this chapter as only a very preliminary report on what we expect to be a long-term effort to revise instructional practice in ways that will bring educators closer to being able to meet the goal of shaping dispositions and skills for thinking through a form of socialization into cultural environments that value and practice thinking.

## References

Collins, A., Brown, J. S., & Newman, S. E. (1989). Cognitive apprenticeship: Teaching the crafts of reading, writing, and mathematics. In L. B. Resnick (Ed.), *Knowing, learning, and instruction: Essays in honor of Robert Glaser* (pp. 453-494). Hillsdale, NJ: Erlbaum.

De Corte, E., & Verschaffel, L. (1987). The effect of semantic structure on first graders' strategies for solving addition and subtraction word problems. *Journal for Research in Mathematics Education, 18,* 363-381.

Gelman, R. (1972). Logical capacity of very young children: Number invariance rules. *Child Development, 43,* 75-90.

Gelman, R., & Gallistel, C. R. (1978). *The child's understanding of number*. Cambridge, MA: Harvard University Press.

Lave, J. (in press). Situated learning in communities of practice. In L. B. Resnick, J. Levine, & S. D. Behrend (Eds.), *Perspectives on socially shared cognition*. Washington, DC: American Psychological Association.

Markman, E. M., & Siebert, J. (1976). Classes and collections: Internal organization and resulting holistic properties. *Cognitive Psychology, 8,* 516–577.

Resnick, L. B. (1983). A developmental theory of number understanding. In H. P. Ginsburg (Ed.), *The development of mathematical thinking* (pp. 109–151). New York: Academic Press.

Resnick, L. B. (1987). *Education and learning to think.* Washington, DC: National Academy Press.

Resnick, L. B. (1989). Developing mathematical knowledge. *American Psychologist, 44,* 162–169.

Resnick, L. B., & Greeno, J. G. (1990). *Conceptual growth of number and quantity.* Unpublished manuscript.

Riley, M. S., & Greeno, J. G. (1988). Developmental analysis of understanding language about quantities and of solving problems. *Cognition and Instruction, 5,* 49–101.

Sophian, C. (1987). Early developments in children's use of counting to solve quantitative problems. *Cognition and Instruction, 4,* 61–90.

# COMMENTARY

## Nancy J. Vye, Diana Miller Sharp, Kathy McCabe, and John D. Bransford

In their chapter for this book, Resnick, Bill, Lesgold, and Leer describe a mathematics program for young children that they believe is especially good for those who are at risk of school failure. We have been asked to provide comments on their chapter. As co-authors, we bring to bear on the task several different perspectives and types of expertise. We bring the expertise of a classroom teacher with many years of experience teaching mathematics to young disadvantaged children. We also bring the expertise of several cognitive psychologists specializing in ways to enhance learning and instruction, especially through the use of technology.

We want to begin by briefly underscoring two basic features of the program of Resnick and her colleagues that make it especially timely. First, the program was developed and tested in classrooms made up of children from disadvantaged backgrounds with records of poor performance in traditional academic settings. There is a current, critical need for instruction that will be effective for children such as these who are at risk of school failure. Recent estimates warn that at least 30 percent of elementary and secondary students in the United States are educationally at risk and that this proportion may rise rapidly in the future. Second, the program represents a shift away from the format of traditional remedial programs. Resnick and her colleagues do not emphasize drill and practice in "the basics," nor do they attempt to simplify the content that is taught. Instead, their program is designed to help children recognize the

Preparation of this commentary was supported in part by grants from the James S. McDonnell Foundation (Grant No. 10026), the National Institute of Child Health and Development (Grant No. HD15051-11), and the National Science Foundation (Grant No. MDR9050191).

power of their own mathematical intuitions and to introduce them to sophisticated ideas about mathematical concepts and procedures. The value of teaching skills and knowledge in the context of meaningful, practical activities, rather than as decontextualized exercises, has only recently received much attention by educational researchers (for example, Brown, Collins, & Duguid, 1989; The Cognition and Technology Group at Vanderbilt, 1990; Resnick & Klopfer, 1989). To our knowledge, this is one of the first systematic efforts to teach mathematics to children of this age and skill level using a reasoning-based approach, and we applaud the efforts of Resnick and her colleagues in their endeavor.

In the remainder of our paper we will address three major issues:

- The program's theoretical framework and its relevance to areas other than mathematics
- The program from the perspective of what teachers would need to know in order to try it in their classrooms
- Factors that may underlie the effectiveness of the program and ways that the program might be made even stronger through the introduction of videodisc-based problem-solving environments such as those being developed at our technology center at Vanderbilt

### Theory-Based Curriculum Development

The program of Resnick et al. is based on two major lines of research. One emphasizes the importance of developing argumentation and reasoning skills; the other focuses on important mathematics concepts and skills. One of the strengths of the program—a strength that sets it apart from many other curricula—is that the program is theory based. In developing their instructional content and approach, the authors were guided by theory and research on the development of children's early mathematical thinking and on the importance of creating apprenticeshiplike situations for learning mathematics.

*Children's Early Number Skills.* The authors' approach draws heavily on research on young children's knowledge of mathe-

matics (Gelman & Gallistel, 1978; Resnick, 1989). Research indicates that by the time most children come to school, they have
already acquired the rudimentary quantitative skills or "protoquantitative schemas" that form the basis of formal mathematical knowledge. For example, one type of protoquantitative schema is the
"increase/decrease" schema. Research suggests that, before any formal schooling, children are able to correctly interpret changes in
quantities as increases or decreases. Children know that if they have
a certain amount of something—say, cookies—and someone takes
some of them away, they have fewer than before (children would
also be able to interpret correctly the addition of cookies). It is
assumed that children have a basic understanding of subtraction
and addition, even though they do not engage in counting to make
their judgments.

Resnick et al. used the research base on protoquantitative
schemas to derive instructional principles for their curriculum. A
major principle is to draw on children's informal mathematical
knowledge as they learn formal mathematics. This is done in several
ways. One way is to introduce formal mathematics concepts and
principles in the context of problem situations that students might
encounter in their everyday lives and that in the past students might
have solved using their "less precise" protoquantitative schemas. In
other words, an attempt is made to connect situations in which one
does school math to problem-solving situations outside of school.
Another way in which the authors' program attempts to draw on
children's informal mathematical knowledge is by encouraging
children to use their informal mathematical knowledge as a basis
for solving problems in mathematics class. Many times the message
that we give children, unintentionally or not, is that mathematics
consists of only the formal concepts and algorithms explicitly
taught in mathematics class. We unintentionally teach children to
devalue their intuitive knowledge or, worse yet, to believe that formal and informal mathematical knowledge bear no relation to one
another. The program of Resnick et al. encourages children to trust
their mathematical intuitions by encouraging them to solve problems in any way they are able, not merely by means of standard
algorithms. The program fits the guidelines recommended by the
National Council of Teachers of Mathematics (1989).

Another major instructional principle is to introduce children to formal mathematical content as early as possible. Guided by this principle, Resnick et al. introduce some content much earlier and in a different sequence than is done traditionally (for example, addition and subtraction with regrouping in first grade). Their goal is to equip students with more powerful ways to think mathematically, that is, to quantify information and link it with formal expressions and operations. The assumption is that children are ready for this content if they are helped to map it onto their protoquantitative schemas and if they are provided with appropriate manipulatives and opportunities for extended practice. As Resnick et al. note, their nontraditional approach discourages the teaching of isolated skills and enables children to draw more fully on their existing knowledge.

From our perspective, the strategy of Resnick et al. of selecting curricular content based on what is known about children's knowledge at different ages is extremely valuable. Ample evidence suggests that tailoring instruction to students' current knowledge, formal or informal, is a critical factor in determining whether and how much students learn (Anderson & Smith, 1984; Bransford & Vye, 1989; Carey, 1986; Feltovich, Spiro, & Coulson, 1988).

The authors' commitment to creating a curriculum sensitive to children's mathematical development leads us to question whether similar concern is given to other areas of children's cognitive and social-emotional development. For example, to what extent does the curriculum presuppose a particular level of language and social development? We raise the issue of children's language skills in part because an important part of the curriculum involves having children engage in dialogue related to mathematics concepts and problems and in part because at-risk students are very often language delayed. We have a similar question regarding the level of social development presupposed by the program. Once again, we raise the issue because the program incorporates group discussion where students need to be able to reflect on and respond to other students' comments in ways that promote learning.

***Cognitive Apprenticeships in Mathematics.*** Another theoretical influence that can be discerned in the program of Resnick et al.

is work on "situated learning" (Brown, Collins, & Duguid, 1989; The Cognition and Technology Group at Vanderbilt, 1990; Rogoff & Lave, 1984). According to this approach, one of the major "failings" of schools is that the kinds of activities and tasks comprising various school subjects (history, mathematics, and so forth) tend to be arbitrary and unrelated to the activities engaged in by experts and professionals who work in these domains. For example, students of mathematics are likely to spend their time computing answers to already formulated problems, whereas the kind of mathematical thinking that an expert mathematician might engage in would more likely involve inventing mathematical procedures, exploring mathematical relations, and so forth (see Schoenfeld, 1989, for more detailed illustrations of authentic mathematics tasks). Proponents of this approach also argue that schools tend to emphasize abstract concepts and knowledge and often do not help students understand how and when to apply this knowledge. As a result, this knowledge is not used to help solve problems in contexts other than the particular school context in which it was originally learned.

The curriculum of Resnick et al. is consistent with a cognitive apprenticeship approach, and aspects of the curriculum are reminiscent of other curricula for older children based on the same approach (for example, Lampert, 1986; Schoenfeld, 1989). The curricular activities described in their chapter are very different from the activities of traditional mathematics classes and are very like the kinds of cognitive activities in which expert mathematicians take part. There is an emphasis on problem solving and on inventing mathematical procedures. Students are also encouraged to think about mathematics as something that is found outside of school; they are encouraged to notice quantitative and other pattern relationships in everyday situations and to notice everyday situations where mathematics is used to solve problems.

We believe that helping students construct the meanings of mathematics from their own perspectives will make the curricula more effective than traditional curricula. Indeed, initial evaluation data of Resnick et al. suggest that students better understand basic mathematical concepts and procedures. We also suspect that students will be better able to apply what they have learned to other situations, both in and out of the classroom, partly because students are given ample opportunity to reflect on quantitative concepts and procedures and partly because they practice this knowledge in authentic problem situations.

### The Curriculum from the Perspective of Classroom Teachers

From the perspective of the classroom teacher, the program of Resnick et al. presents some exciting possibilities. It illustrates ways teachers can help disadvantaged children learn to reason better and at the same time acquire a deep understanding of quantitative concepts and operations. A key to the program's success is its emphasis on mapping new knowledge onto the skills and experiences of children. A major difficulty that teachers of disadvantaged children face is that their children's range of experience and familiarity with school-like tasks and skills are often limited. The program provides some excellent examples of how to create meaningful problem solving by carefully selecting familiar problem situations, by helping children notice mathematical situations in their everyday lives, and by motivating parents to teach their children. Teachers will be especially interested in learning more about how the program stimulated parental involvement, since many disadvantaged children come from dysfunctional families or families where the parents have little education, and where there is often limited contact with school personnel.

Although the program presents exciting possibilities, it is likely to present some additional challenges as well. The teacher's role in the program of Resnick et al. differs in major ways from the teacher's role in the typical arithmetic classroom; as a result, teachers will have questions—and in some cases reservations—about the program. For instance, the program involves extensive use of small-group and teacher-led discussion. Many teachers will have questions about whether the program will work in their classrooms because of their children's limited language skills. In thinking about disseminating their program, it will be important for Resnick and colleagues to address the question of whether some minimum language competency is required and what strategies can help teachers circumvent problems that may arise in class because of language deficiencies. Another challenge of the program is that many classroom teachers rarely if ever use small-group activities with young disadvantaged children. Because of the belief that disadvantaged children tend to exhibit behavior problems, some teachers may be afraid to try small groups for fear of losing control of the class. These teachers will need special reassurances. In general, teachers will be interested in learning how to facilitate social interactions when children work in groups.

In addition to concerns about whether their children possess the requisite competencies and about the teaching strategies to use to obviate problems that these deficiencies create, we suspect that many teachers will feel that they need specialized skills training before they would be able to implement the program in their classrooms. First, we think that teachers will want to learn techniques for conducting small groups. We assume that when children first work in small groups, they will need a great deal of support from teachers, and that teachers will have to model the kinds of interactions that they want children to engage in. Second, teachers will also need training in techniques that help children create procedures for solving problems. Teachers are more likely to be used to teaching one "right" procedure for solving a class of problems; therefore, they may have difficulty knowing how to help children invent their own procedures for solving problems. Finally, as surprising as it may seem, many teachers may also need special training in how to teach mathematics in a way that helps children understand the number system. Sadly, mathematics instruction frequently emphasizes drill and practice on procedures, with little attention to comprehending the underlying basis for these procedures, and many teachers do not use manipulatives as a comprehension tool. These teachers will need special guidance in transforming their instruction, particularly as it relates to helping children understand how mathematical operations such as addition, subtraction, multiplication, and division relate to the base 10 system. We think that teaching teachers how to use a comprehension-based approach to instruction, particularly as this relates to the use of manipulatives, is especially important for reasons that we describe in greater detail below.

## A Curriculum for Building Mental Models

*What Is a Mental Model, and Why Is It Useful?* We now turn our attention to discussions of particular cognitive aspects of problem solving and how the program that Resnick and her colleagues describe may be especially successful in enabling children to gain a deeper understanding of mathematics. We think that two of the more effective components of the program, especially for children who are at risk for school failure, are the extensive use of manipulatives and the use of familiar contexts for problem solving. Our view arises from recent theories that conceive of comprehension and problem solving as tasks that require students to construct "mental models." Mental models are similar to physical models or pictures of specific situations. In fact, for the purposes of this discussion, mental models can be thought of as mental pictures.

Why is it important that a child be able to construct a mental model or a mental picture of a problem? Because to construct a mental model, a child has to be clear on what the objects in the situation are like, how they are arranged, and what relationships they have to each other. Unless the child has a mental model of what the situation is, he or she will not know how to manipulate the elements of the situation to come up with a solution. For example, in the barrette problem that Resnick et al. describe, students need to form a mental model that specifies that (1) there are four main elements (the bags), (2) inside each of those four bags are nine items (the barrettes), and (3) the total number of all the barrettes in all the bags need to be combined and compared with the number 95. By having a mental model of the situation, the child can understand why it makes more sense to combine four groups of 9 together than to add the numbers 4 and 9. The correct operation is the one that makes sense in that situation. In short, the notion of using a mental model to understand and solve a problem is very different from the notion of using a set of "rules," such as "*and* means to add" and "*more than* means to subtract" (Littlefield & Rieser, 1991).

*How the Program Supports Mental Model Construction.* Just as the creation of a picture or a physical model takes physical effort, so does the creation of a mental model or image. For example, an image of four bags of barrettes is very different from how the words of the story problem sound or look on a page, so students need to mentally translate the words in the problem into correctly arranged elements in a mental model. This translation process may require considerable mental effort for the young child, and the amount of mental resources required may exceed the limits of the child's pool of memory resources.

This analysis suggests how physical aids like manipulatives, pictures, and "acting out situations" can help problem solving. Instead of having to perform all the translations from words to mental models "in the head," the child can use these physical aids to help keep track of what the elements in the problem are and how they are arranged. Moreover, the use of familiar objects and contexts is helpful because the child can more easily image familiar objects and can draw on memories of past familiar scenes for information on how the mental model should look.

As children become practiced in translating word problems to mental models, the translation process should require less and less effort, so that eventually children are able to construct the mental model from the text and numbers in the problem alone. Whether a reliance on physical aids is something that will automatically diminish, or whether children need to be systematically taught to construct mental models under less supportive conditions in which physical aids are not available, is a question likely to be answered in further research using the approach of Resnick et al.

*The Generality and Transfer of Mental Model Skills.* The construction of mental models from text is something that is necessary not just for understanding story problems; recent research suggests that good readers construct mental models for all types of text, and the construction of mental models leads to improved comprehension and memory of text information (Glenberg, Meyer, & Lindem, 1987; Johnson-Laird, 1983; Sharp, 1991; Sharp & McNamara, 1991). Therefore, if children learn in a math program how to translate text information into a mental model, we hope they will use this skill for understanding other kinds of reading material. We note that the reading scores of one of the groups in the program of Resnick et al. improved, whereas the reading scores of the other group did not. The authors mention that they are investigating why the reading scores improved for one group, but we suggest that they turn the question around and investigate why the reading scores of the other group did *not* improve. Research has shown that students often fail to transfer skills that they learn in one content domain to other content domains, so if the skills that students learn in the math program are in fact applicable to reading, then students may need to be explicitly taught to transfer these skills from the math class to the reading class.

*Videodisc Environments for Building Mental Models.* In this section, we describe how videodisc environments may be used to achieve some of the same instructional goals that Resnick and colleagues describe, and also why we think that videodiscs may provide a means for expanding these goals. Like Resnick and her colleagues, we think that children should learn math in the context of real-world problems and should learn how to reason about and discuss mathematical solutions. In the previous sections, we described our belief that the key to enabling children to reason about math is to provide them with the tools for building rich mental models of problem situations. We now will discuss why we think that videodiscs can be extremely effective in providing those tools.

For example, one of our projects at the Cognition and Technology Group is a videodisc mathematics problem-solving series called *The Adventures of Jasper Woodbury* (The Cognition and Technology Group at Vanderbilt, 1990). Although the series is designed for students who are several years older than those of Resnick et al.—the series is for fifth- and sixth-graders—we are also developing materials for younger students. Each disc in the Jasper series is an adventure story. At the end of the story, the main character is faced with a complex problem whose solution involves mathematics. For example, in one video the main character, Emily, is faced with the problem of rescuing a wounded eagle. The eagle is stranded in a remote area where the nearest road is several miles away. To rescue the eagle, Emily must decide which of several different routes to take and what means of transportation to use (ultralight, foot, truck, or some combination of means). Each route must be evaluated in turn with respect to the distance to be traveled, speed and range of the selected vehicle, and, or course, estimated trip time. All the mathematical information needed to solve Emily's problem is in the story. To reach a solution, students must formulate various plans for rescuing the eagle, decide how to evaluate each plan mathematically, search the video for the relevant mathematical information, and perform computations using this information.

Our research using the *Jasper* series, as well as other videodisc-based materials, has shown that students learn more from the video instruction than from traditional instruction on the same content. For example, *Jasper*-taught students are more adept at the higher-order reasoning skills involved in complex mathematical problem solving than students who receive traditional instruction and practice on story problems. They are better able to generate and logically evaluate plans for solving complex problems, and they are also more successful at solving problems.

We believe that the videos directly provide students with rich mental models of problem situations and in this way help students bypass problems they may experience in constructing mental models based on verbal or written scenarios of problems (for example, written story problems). The videos also provide extensive background knowledge, without which many students, particularly at-risk students, would not be able to form mental representations of problems they are given. Mental models created from video thus provide the scaffold for lower-level skills that enables children to practice higher-level problem-solving skills.

Video problem solving seems to have important effects on motivation as well. Teachers consistently observe a high degree of enthusiasm and on-task behavior among students when using *Jasper*. Furthermore, they see this in Chapter 1 and high-achieving classes alike. Chapter 1 students are positive about this program despite the fact that in general they tend to have relatively negative attitudes toward mathematics. At this point we can only speculate on what accounts for the increased motivation that we have observed. Novelty may play a role, and the use of video—a very comfortable medium for children—may also be a factor. But we also think that a very important factor is that students come to understand that mathematics has a function outside the classroom in helping solve problems from everyday life. In this way, the videos help forge what Resnick et al. suggest is an important link between everyday experience and formal mathematics.

We think that children in the program of Resnick et al. might benefit from problem-solving instruction where some of the problems are depicted in video format. Of course, one could argue that the best way to practice problem solving is in the context of everyday problems that students themselves identify. In fact, one principle of the program of Resnick et al. is to encourage finding everyday problems. Although we agree that everyday problems are the ultimate "authentic" context and that it is important to encourage children in this way, we also argue that everyday problems have instructional limitations. For example, problems that are part of one child's experience are not necessarily part of other children's experiences, making them less effective for instruction. This is where video has an important advantage. Because video can be taken into the classroom, all children can share the experience. We also argue that everyday problems that children identify are likely to be less useful than video because they are apt to be problems that are already within children's competence levels. In this way, finding everyday problems may be most effective as a vehicle for having children *practice* mathematical skills. Video problem-solving environments, on the other hand, can also be used to extend children's mathematical competence into new skill areas.

Another way in which the program of Resnick et al. might benefit from the introduction of videodisc problem solving is in the quality of the classroom discussion among students and between teacher and students. We have found that students initiate more questions and that there is more sustained discussion among students when they are working on video-based tasks. This is very different from typical classroom talk, which consists of a repetitive cycle where the teacher asks a question and a student responds. In part we think this higher-quality discussion occurs because all students share a rich understanding, or what we have been calling a mental model, of the problem situation, which enables more students to take an active part in classroom activities. Video problem-solving contexts may prove especially effective in reasoning-based programs such as that of Resnick et al., where dialogue among students is an essential vehicle for learning. Furthermore, the videos may make it easier for teachers to implement the kinds of instruction that Resnick and others recommend (National Council of Teachers of Mathematics, 1989).

## Summary of Comments

The curriculum described by Resnick et al. meets two important educational needs: the need for more early elementary programs that help disadvantaged children and the need for more programs that help these children develop thinking skills. We think the authors have developed a program that will have an important impact on young children's mathematical thinking. Our goal has been to acknowledge the curriculum's strong theory base and to discuss specific cognitive mechanisms that may mediate students' learning. At the same time, we raised questions concerning the language and social skills presupposed by the program and about the new roles required of teachers. We have suggested possible ways to enhance instruction in everyday problem solving by incorporating videodisc problem-solving context. We believe that video can provide the scaffold for lower-level skills that enables children to practice higher-level problem solving in authentic contexts. Video environments may also make it easier for teachers to implement new instructional ideas.

## References

Anderson, C. W., & Smith, E. L. (1984). Children's preconceptions and content-area textbooks. In G. Duffy, L. Roehler, & J. Mason (Eds.), *Comprehension instruction: Perspectives and suggestions*. New York: Longman.

Bransford, J. D., & Vye, N. J. (1989). A perspective on cognitive research and its implications for instruction. In L. Resnick & L. Klopfer (Eds.), *Toward the thinking curriculum* (pp. 173–205). Alexandria, VA: Association for Supervision and Curriculum Development.

Brown, J. S., Collins, A., & Duguid, P. (1989). Situated cognition and the culture of learning. *Educational Researcher, 18* (1), 32–42.

Carey, S. (1986). Cognitive science and science education. *American Psychologist, 41,* 1123–1130.

The Cognition and Technology Group at Vanderbilt. (1990). Anchored instruction and its relationship to situated cognition. *Educational Researcher, 19* (5), 2–10.

Feltovich, P. J., Spiro, R. J., & Coulson, R. L. (1988). The nature of conceptual understanding in biomedicine: The deep structure of complex ideas and the development of misconceptions. In D. Evans & V. Patel (Eds.), *The cognitive sciences in medicine.* Cambridge, MA: MIT Press.

Gelman, R., & Gallistel, C. R. (1978). *The child's understanding of number.* Cambridge, MA: Harvard University Press.

Glenberg, A. M., Meyer, M., & Lindem, K. (1987). Mental models contribute to foregrounding during text comprehension. *Journal of Memory and Language, 26,* 69–83.

Johnson-Laird, P. N. (1983). *Mental models.* Cambridge, MA: Harvard University Press.

Lampert, M. (1986). Knowing, doing, and teaching mathematics. *Cognition and Instruction, 3* (4), 305–342.

Littlefield, J., & Rieser, J. (1991). Semantic features of similarity in children's identification of relevant information in mathematical story problems. Accepted for publication in *Cognition & Instruction.*

National Council of Teachers of Mathematics. (1989). *Curriculum and evaluation standards for school mathematics.* Reston, VA: National Council of Teachers of Mathematics.

Resnick, L. (1989). Developing mathematical knowledge. *American Psychologist, 44,* 162–169.

Resnick, L., & Klopfer, L. (1989). *Toward the thinking curriculum: Current cognitive research.* Alexandria, VA: Association for Supervision and Curriculum Development.

Rogoff, B., & Lave, J. (1984). *Everyday cognition: Its development in social context.* Cambridge, MA: Harvard University Press.

Schoenfeld, A. (1989). Teaching mathematical thinking and problem solving. In L. Resnick & L. Klopfer (Eds.), *Toward the thinking curriculum: Current cognitive research.* Alexandria, VA: Association for Supervision and Curriculum Development.

Sharp, D.L.M. (1991). *Individual differences in mental models for ambiguous text.* Unpublished manuscript, Vanderbilt University, Nashville, TN.

Sharp, D.L.M., & McNamara, T. P. (1991). *Spatial mental models in narrative comprehension: Now you see them, now you don't.* Unpublished manuscript, Vanderbilt University, Nashville, TN.

# 3

# Using Children's Mathematical Knowledge

*Penelope L. Peterson, Elizabeth Fennema,*
*and Thomas Carpenter*

> Maria has four peanuts. Her mother gave her some
> more. Now she has eleven peanuts. How many pea-
> nuts did her mother give her?

MOST FIRST- AND SECOND-GRADE TEACHERS, AND PROBABLY MOST
adults, see the above problem as a subtraction problem that will be
difficult for young children to solve. However, consider what Elissa
(a four-year-old) did when asked to solve this problem. First, Elissa
counted out four counters. Then she added more counters until she
had eleven. With her hand she separated out the original four counters, then she pointed to the group she had left and said to the
interviewer, "This many." The interviewer asked her, "How many
is that?" Elissa counted, "One, two, three, four, five, six, seven."
Turning to the interviewer, Elissa announced firmly, "Seven
peanuts!"

Elissa did what most young children do. She invented a way
to solve the problem that was based on how she thought about the

The research reported in this chapter was funded in part by a grant to
Elizabeth Fennema, Thomas Carpenter, and Penelope Peterson from the
National Science Foundation (Grant No. MDR-8550263). The opinions
expressed do not necessarily reflect the position, policy, or endorsement of
the National Science Foundation.

problem, not on any procedure that had been taught to her. She recognized that the problem involves joining some things together, and she did that. Elissa is not unusual. In fact, we have learned from research that all children come to school knowing a great deal about mathematics. If adults take children's mathematical knowledge seriously, they can help children use their knowledge to solve problems and learn more mathematics.

Adults have not always taken children's knowledge seriously. Typically, parents and teachers have assumed that children begin school with little or no knowledge of mathematics. This assumption was not unreasonable when the primary goal of the elementary mathematics curriculum was to develop skill in computation (for example, to learn the basic facts and the algorithms of addition and subtraction). Children did not come to school with much knowledge of formal algorithms, so it made sense to assume that children did not have much mathematical knowledge. Although most educators knew that computational skills were not sufficient, they presumed that before children could understand the algorithms and use them to solve problems, children needed to have mastered computational skills. Thus, primary school instruction has focused on students' practice of these skills to attain mastery. This emphasis is even more pronounced in the instruction of children in less advantaged socioeconomic areas, who spend more time in computational tasks than do children in schools with more resources (Zucker, 1990). The tacit assumption is that once children have learned to compute with a reasonable level of facility, they can be taught to understand why the various procedures work and to apply the procedures to solve problems.

Findings from the National Assessment of Educational Progress and other research programs have documented, however, that this heavy emphasis on computation has been misplaced (Dossey, Mullis, Lindquist, & Chambers, 1988). Although children in the United States can demonstrate computational skills at a reasonable level of proficiency, most children do not appear to understand the mathematics in the skills, and they cannot apply the skills to even simple problem situations. This situation has led the National Council of Teachers of Mathematics (1989) and the Mathematical Sciences Educational Board of the National Research Council

(1989) to propose that problem solving and the development of mathematical understanding should be the focuses of the mathematics curriculum *for all students* and that problem solving should be integrated throughout the mathematics curriculum rather than tacked on after computational skills are mastered.

### Reconsidering Children's Mathematical Knowledge

A new approach to teaching and curriculum, which holds promise for achieving the expanded goals of mathematics instruction, takes seriously the knowledge that children have when they enter school. In this approach, teachers use the knowledge of each child to make instructional decisions so that the child learns mathematics with understanding, learns how to solve problems, and learns the computational skills. This approach uses knowledge that has been accumulating from research on children's thinking in mathematics.

*The Research Base on Children's Thinking.* A growing body of research documents that children develop understanding, problem-solving abilities, and skills concurrently as they engage in active problem solving (Fennema, Carpenter, & Peterson, 1989a). This research also shows that children invent ways of solving problems that are not tied to traditional arithmetic solutions (Carpenter, 1985; Ginsburg, 1983; Lave, 1988). In fact, children's problem-solving experiences actually form the basis for their development of basic arithmetic concepts and skills.

Over the last ten years, an extensive body of research has also accumulated on the development of basic addition and subtraction concepts and skills in primary schoolchildren (Carpenter, 1985; Fuson, 1988). This research shows that young children are adept at solving simple word problems, and their solutions often involve relatively sophisticated problem-solving processes. Even before children receive any formal instruction in addition and subtraction, they consistently solve simple addition and subtraction word problems by modeling and counting.

Consider, for example, the problem that Elissa solved at the beginning of the chapter. Maria had four peanuts. Her mother gave her some more. Now she has eleven peanuts. How many peanuts did her mother give her? Most adults solve this problem by subtracting four from eleven, but it is not easy to explain why to subtract. Subtraction is usually taught as representing a separation action like the situation in the following problem: Angelica had fourteen dollars. She spent six dollars on a kitten. How many dollars does she have left? The problem about the peanuts, however, might be perceived as asking how much needs to be added to the four to get eleven peanuts. Accordingly, young children do not think of this as a subtraction or take-away problem. They solve the problem by modeling the additive action. If children have counters, they make a set of four counters and then add counters to this initial set until there are a total of eleven counters. By counting the counters that have been added on, children find the number of peanuts that Maria's mother gave her.

The above example illustrates two features that are important for understanding children's thinking and how elementary mathematics instruction might be designed to build on it. First, different problem situations exist that represent different conceptions of addition and subtraction, not just the simple joining and separating situations that are used to define addition and subtraction in most standard elementary mathematics textbooks. Second, children do not interpret all addition and subtraction problems in terms of pluses and minuses; they attempt to model the action and the relationships described in the problem.

Current research on children's thinking about addition and subtraction problems is based on a detailed analysis of the problem space (Carpenter, 1985). Addition and subtraction word problems are partitioned into several basic classes that distinguish among different types of actions and relationships. Distinctions are made among problems involving joining action, separating action, part-part-whole relationships, and comparison situations. Examples of each of these basic problem types are presented in Table 3.1. (For a complete description of this problem space and the related solution strategies, see Carpenter, 1985, or Fennema & Carpenter, 1989.) Within each class, three distinct problem types can be generated by systematically varying the unknown in the problem. For example, Elissa's problem is a joining problem with the change unknown, while the joining problem in Table 3.1 is one with the result un-

Table 3.1. Basic Classes of Addition and Subtraction Problems.

| Problem Type | Example Problem |
| --- | --- |
| Joining | There were seven birds on a wire. Five more birds joined them. How many birds were on the wire then? |
| Separating | Twelve frogs were in the pond. Five frogs hopped out. How many frogs were left? |
|  | There were some frogs in the pond. Five hopped out. Then there were seven frogs left. How many were there to start with? |
| Comparing | Charles picked seven flowers. Penelope picked twelve flowers. How many more flowers did Penelope pick than Charles? |
| Part-part-whole | There are seven boys and five girls on the playground. How many children are on the playground? |

known. The first separating problem in Table 3.1 is a result-unknown problem, while the second one is a start-unknown problem. This classification scheme provides a highly principled analysis of problem types such that knowledge of a few general rules is sufficient to generate a complete range of problems.

The power of this analysis is that it is consistent with the way children think about and solve problems. When young children initially solve word problems, they directly model the action or relationships in the problem using counters, fingers, or counting patterns. For example, a young child would solve the first separating problem in Table 3.1 by making a collection of twelve counters and removing five of them. A young child would solve the comparing problem most readily by making two sets and matching them to find out how many are left over. Elissa's solution to the problem at the beginning of this paper illustrates how one type of joining problem is solved.

Children at this level generally have difficulty with problems that cannot be easily modeled. For example, the second separating problem in Table 3.1 is difficult to model because the initial quantity is the unknown, so children have no place to start in attempting to model the action in the problem.

Over time, children invent more efficient strategies for solving these problems. They base these strategies on their growing understanding of number concepts. For example, a child might solve the problem about the peanuts by counting up from four and saying, "Five, six, seven, eight, nine, ten, eleven. The answer is seven." In this case, the child does not exactly model any of the quantities described in the problem but simply keeps track of the number of steps in the counting sequence using fingers or some other device. Similarly, a child might solve the first separating problem in Table 3.1 by counting back from twelve.

Even when first- and second-grade children appear to be using recall of number facts to solve problems, they are often actually using these modeling and counting strategies. Gradually, they begin to learn the number facts first by using a core of facts they know in order to derive or generate unknown facts. For example, to solve the first joining problem, six-year-old Juan might respond, "Well, I know that five and five is ten, so since seven is two more than five, the answer is twelve because twelve is two more than ten."

Although for many teachers and adults this kind of thinking seems abstract, for Juan it makes perfect sense because he is building on and using what he knows in order to solve a mathematics problem. Derived facts are not used by only a handful of very bright students. Even without specific instruction, many children use derived facts before they have mastered all their number facts at a recall level. In a three-year longitudinal study in Madison, Wisconsin, over 80 percent of the children used derived facts at least occasionally at some time in grades 1 to 3, and 40 percent of the children used derived facts as their primary strategy at some time during the three years.

Indeed, all these kinds of thinking by children in the primary grades are typical. Almost all children spontaneously use the kinds of solution strategies that we have discussed. By the middle of the first grade, most children can solve many different types of addition and subtraction problems, and they are beginning to use more efficient counting strategies as well as direct modeling.

Children's solutions demonstrate in two ways the kind of mathematical thinking that we want to encourage. First, children can solve a variety of problems by attending carefully to the information given in the problem, not by looking for key words or using other tricks to bypass understanding. Second, the procedures they invent to find the answer demonstrate creative problem solving based on an understanding of fundamental number concepts. In the early elementary school years, children are capable of much more sophisticated thinking than adults have assumed. Children do not start school as blank slates but bring with them a rich store of mathematical knowledge that they have already acquired.

The research on children's solving of addition and subtraction problems demonstrates that children enter school with a rich store of informal knowledge that can serve as a basis for developing meaning for the formal symbolic procedures they learn in school. But the research does more than demonstrate that children know more and are capable of learning more than they have been given credit for. It also provides a principled framework for selecting problems and analyzing students' thinking that allows teachers to understand better their own students' thinking so that they can select appropriate instruction to build on the mathematical knowledge that their students have already acquired. Disadvantaged as well as advantaged children have interacted with numbers in a variety of ways. They have counted many things, have some knowledge of money, and have had many natural interactions with numbers.

The analysis of the addition/subtraction problem space and the related research on children's solution strategies comprise a systematic body of knowledge useful in developing an approach to mathematics teaching and curriculum for all children in the primary grades. We consider now the Cognitively Guided Instruction (CGI) Project, in which we have been studying the use of this knowledge by teachers and children.

### The CGI Approach

The CGI approach is based on two key assumptions: first, that knowledge of children's thinking about addition and subtraction problems can be useful to teachers; second, that just as children interpret and make sense of new knowledge in light of their existing knowledge and beliefs, so do teachers.

***Sharing Research Knowledge with Teachers.*** Rather than attempt to use this research to specify a program of instruction, we decided to share the research-based knowledge about children's mathematical knowledge and thinking directly with teachers and to let teachers interpret for themselves what it meant to their instructional programs. Our approach is similar to how we believe children learn and is also compatible with site-based approaches to school improvement. Each child has to make sense of the world for herself or himself. Understanding comes only when a child is able to assimilate new knowledge in a way that is not in conflict with what she or he already knows and believes. Why should teachers be any different? In fact, research suggests strongly that teachers' understandings and beliefs profoundly influence their instruction (Clark & Peterson, 1986) and that teachers gain understanding in much the same way that children do (Duckworth, 1987; Lampert, 1984). Teachers in their classrooms are the ones who make the decisions that influence learning, and they make decisions congruent with what they understand and believe (Fennema, Carpenter, & Peterson, 1989b).

At the beginning of our National Science Foundation–supported CGI project, forty experienced first-grade teachers from the Madison, Wisconsin, area agreed to work with us. We assigned teachers randomly to one of two groups. The first group (CGI) participated in the training workshop during the summer of 1986. These teachers spent twenty hours per week for four weeks with us learning about children's thinking in addition and subtraction. The second group served as a comparison or control group during the first year and participated in a similar workshop in the summer of 1987.

During the workshop, we shared with the teachers the framework of problem types shown in Table 3.1 and the related children's solution strategies. The teachers viewed videotapes of children solving addition/subtraction word problems until the teachers could identify both problem types and strategies with relative ease. The teachers also interviewed five- and six-year-old children to ascertain whether children actually used the solution strategies that had been discussed.

We did not tell the teachers what to do with the knowledge they had gained. We discussed the importance of a teacher's knowledge of how each child solves problems, the place of drill on number facts, and the necessity for children to think and talk about their own problem solutions with each other and with the teacher. We talked about adapting the problems (by type of problem or size of number in the problem) given to a child, depending on what the child understands and can do. We discussed writing problems around themes related to children's lives and classroom activities. (For a complete description of activities and readings used in the workshop, see Fennema & Carpenter, 1989.)

We gave the teachers time to plan how they would use their new knowledge in their classrooms during the following year. Teachers talked extensively with us and with other teachers about possible implications of the knowledge about addition and subtraction. Most teachers wrote examples of all the problem types to use in their classrooms and tentatively planned one unit that they would teach sometime during the schoolyear.

***What Research Says About the Use and Effectiveness of CGI.*** We pre- and posttested children in the CGI and control teachers' classes, and we observed these teachers' mathematics teaching regularly during the 1986–87 school year. We also assessed the teachers' knowledge and beliefs about teaching mathematics both before the workshop and at the end of the school year (Carpenter, Fennema, Peterson, & Carey, 1988; Peterson, Carpenter, & Fennema, 1989; Peterson, Fennema, Carpenter, & Loef, 1989). We compared the instructional practices, beliefs, and knowledge of the CGI teachers and the learning of CGI students with those of the control group of teachers and their students.

When compared with control teachers, the CGI teachers spent significantly more time on word problem solving in addition and subtraction and significantly less time drilling on addition and subtraction number facts. CGI teachers also encouraged their students to solve problems in many more different ways, listened more to their students' verbalizations of ways they solved problems, and knew more about their individual students' problem-solving strategies. CGI students outperformed control students on written and interview measures of problem solving and number fact knowledge, including a measure of complex word problem solving on the Iowa Test of Basic Skills, and they reported greater understanding and confidence in their problem-solving abilities. Although CGI teachers spent only half as much time as control teachers did in teaching number fact skills explicitly, CGI students demonstrated greater recall of number facts than did control students.

Those teachers who believed more in the ideas of CGI and had more knowledge about their children listened more to their children's verbalizations of their thinking, and they implemented CGI more than did those teachers who had lesser knowledge and weaker beliefs. In sum, at the end of only one year, the research evidence demonstrated that teachers' use of the knowledge of children's mathematical thinking that they had gained from the workshop and developed in their classroom practice made a significant difference in their children's confidence and abilities to solve mathematics problems. (For complete descriptions of these results, see Carpenter, Fennema, Peterson, Chiang, & Loef, 1989; Peterson, Carpenter, & Fennema, 1989; Peterson, Fennema, & Carpenter, 1988/ 1989.)

But would a CGI approach be effective with disadvantaged children in inner-city schools? Indeed, some would argue that disadvantaged children still need drill on computation skills and number facts. However, we have recent evidence that a CGI approach can be quite successful in an inner-city setting.

Significant effects of CGI on students' problem solving were reported recently by Villasenor (1990), who worked with first-grade teachers in inner-city public and private schools in Milwaukee, Wisconsin. Villasenor participated in a CGI workshop taught in Madison, Wisconsin, by two members of our original project staff. He then used the Cognitively Guided Instruction Program implementation guide, readings, and materials developed by Fennema and Carpenter (1989) to conduct a one-week, four-hour-per-day workshop (for a total of twenty hours) for twelve inner-city Milwaukee first-grade teachers in the summer of 1989. These teachers volunteered to participate, and they became the CGI "treatment" group. Villasenor also recruited another group of twelve first-grade teachers from schools in inner-city Milwaukee who formed the "nontreatment" control group. During the workshop, teachers in the CGI group focused on understanding the different types of word problems in addition and subtraction and on understanding students' strategies for solving these word problems. Teachers explored ways to assess students' mathematical knowledge as well as ways to use this knowledge to design instruction, and they planned their instruction using CGI for the upcoming schoolyear. During the schoolyear, these CGI teachers met once a month on Saturday mornings to share their ideas about CGI and talk about their implementation of CGI ideas in their first-grade classrooms. Teachers in the control group participated in two one-and-a-half hour workshops on problem solving in October and January.

To assess students' problem-solving achievement at the end of the year, Villasenor used the written test of problem solving that we developed (Carpenter et al, 1989). Students in CGI teachers' classes achieved significantly higher scores than did students in control teachers' classes, achieving an average of 9.67 out of 14 items correct, a mean score that was nearly 4 standard deviations higher than the average score of 2.92 for students in the control group. CGI students also showed significantly greater knowledge of number facts, achieving an average of 4.75 out of 5 items correct, or about 5 standard deviations above the mean of 2.29 for the control group students. These significant results are shown in Figure 3.1.

One possible limitation of the study involves the comparability of the control group to the CGI group of teachers and students. The groups were similar in at least one respect. In both groups, teachers taught in schools with an enrollment that averaged 76 percent minority students, drawn from predominantly Hispanic and black populations. However, the groups were dissimilar in that teachers in the CGI group had students who performed one standard deviation higher on the problem-solving pretest than did students in the control group (although in both groups students' averages on the pretest were only one or two problems correct out of fourteen). Nonetheless, CGI students' average increase in problem-solving achievement was still significantly greater than that of control students, even when initial pretest scores were taken into account. In sum, Villasenor's results are important because they provide concrete evidence for the effectiveness of the CGI approach with a disadvantaged population of students—the same kinds of students who often participate in compensatory education programs.

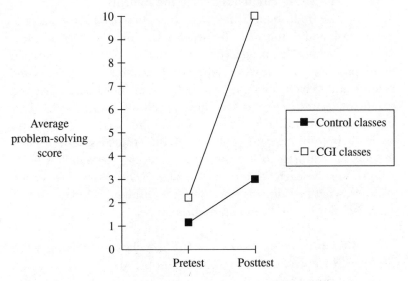

Figure 3.1. Average Pretest and Posttest Problem-Solving Scores of Students in CGI Classes and Control Classes in Villasenor's (1990) Study.

## A Look at CGI Classrooms

After the original year of studying CGI and its impact, we have continued to study CGI teachers. As a result, we know that CGI classrooms are different from traditional classrooms. Consider, for example, the following descriptions of a traditional second-grade classroom and a first-grade CGI classroom.

*Traditional Classroom.* The lesson begins with a three-minute timed test in which each student tries to beat a personal best in writing answers to number facts with speed and accuracy. Then Mr. K. reads aloud two word problems involving addition or subtraction of multidigit numbers. Students work on these problems at their tables. Mr. K. calls on a few students to explain their strategies. The students respond by stating the algorithms they used. Finally, the teacher passes out worksheets containing more word problems that are result-unknown problems. The students are to solve these with traditional multidigit algorithms. The teacher asks the students to complete three of these problems before the end of the lesson. All students work the problems with the traditional algorithms while Mr. K. circulates to help the students.

In the traditional primary mathematics classroom, children are on task and doing what the teacher has told them to do. Most activities focus on learning a computational procedure to solve each word problem. The teacher expects all children to do the same routine and to have the same knowledge in mathematics. The word problems seem to serve as a context for children to practice their algorithms rather than as a context for children to make visible and share their thinking and problem-solving strategies. The teacher expects all children to use the same strategy—the standard algorithm—to solve each word problem. The teacher bases all his decisions on what he thinks is important for children to learn—in this case, the addition and subtraction procedures.

*CGI Classroom.* While most of the class are solving word problems independently or in small groups, Ms. J. is sitting at a table with three students, Raja, Erik, and Ernestine. Each child has plastic cubes that can be connected together, a pencil, and a big sheet of paper on which are written the same word problems. As the students peruse the problems, they notice their names:

*Raja:*    My name is already there!

*Ms. J.:*    Your name is there? Yes!

*Ernestine:*    My name is on! Her name is on!

*Ms. J.:*    Yeah, and so is your name, eventually. Okay. Who wants to read the first one?

*All:*    Me!

*Ms. J.:*    Well, let's read them together.

*All:*    [Reading] Raja made eighteen clay dinosaurs. Ernestine has nine clay dinosaurs. How many more clay dinosaurs does Raja have than Ernestine [a compare problem]?

*Ms. J.:*    Okay [reads problem again as students listen].

The students work on the problem in different ways. Raja puts together eighteen cubes. She removes nine of them and counts the rest. She gets eleven. She writes the answer down, then looks up at the teacher for confirmation. Ms. J. looks at the answer, looks back at the problem, and then says, "You're real close." As Raja recounts the cubes, Ms. J. watches her closely. This time Raja counts nine.

Ernestine exclaims, "I've got it!" Ms. J. looks at Ernestine's answer and says, "No. You're real close."

Erik connects nine cubes, and in a separate group he connects eighteen. He places them next to each other and matches them up, counting across each row to make sure there are nine matches. Then Erik breaks off the unmatched cubes and counts them. "I've got it!" he announces. Erik writes down his answer. He says to Ms. J., "Got it. Want me to tell you?" Ms. J. nods "Yes." Erik goes to Ms. J. and whispers his answer in her ear. Ms. J. nods "Yes" in reply. Turning to the group, she queries, "Okay, now, how did you get your answers? Remember, that's what's always the important thing: How did you get it? Let's see if we can come up with different ways this time. [Erik has his hand raised.] Erik, what did you do?"

*Erik:* I had nine cubes and then I had and then I put eighteen cubes and then I put them together. And the eighteen cubes, I took away some of the eighteen cubes.

*Ms. J.:* Okay, let's see if we can understand what Erik did. Okay, you got—show me eighteen cubes.

*Erik:* Okay. [He puts together two of the three sets of nine he has lined up in front of him.]

*Ms. J.:* Okay, so you have eighteen cubes. Then you had nine.

*Erik:* [He takes nine cubes in his other hand and puts them side by side.] Yeah.

*Ms. J.:* Then you compared.

*Erik:* [Simultaneously with Ms. J.] Then I put them together.

*Ms. J.:* Then you put them together.

*Erik:*   Then I took . . .

*Ms. J.:*   Nine away.

*Erik:*   Nine away, and I counted them [the ones left], and there were nine.

*Ms. J.:*   Okay. So that's one way that you did it. Nice job, Erik. Which way did you do it, Raja?

*Raja:*   [She has a set of eighteen cubes connected in front of her.] Well, I counted eighteen cubes.

*Ms. J.:*   Erik, let's listen to her way.

*Raja:*   Then I counted nine. [She counts nine of the eighteen.]

*Ms. J.:*   You counted nine. [Another student comes up to the table and puts a paper in front of Ms. J. Ms. J. puts her arm around this student while she continues listening to Raja.]

*Raja:*   Then I [she breaks the nine cubes away from the eighteen], then I got nine.

*Ms. J.:*   Okay, great! [To Ernestine] What did you do? [To Raja as she pats her on the hand] Nice job.

*Ernestine:*   I knew nine plus nine was, nine plus nine is eighteen. I took away one nine, and it was nine.

*Ms. J.:*   Okay. Say that again. I'm sorry, I missed your problem.

*Ernestine:*   I said I knew nine plus nine was eighteen.

*Ms. J.:*   You knew that nine plus nine was eighteen. Okay.

*Ernestine:*   I took away one nine and it was nine.

*Ms. J.:*   Okay. Good. So we had—how many different ways did we do that problem? Erik, you did it one way, right? Raja, was your way different from Erik's? [Raja nods "Yes."] Was your way different from Ernestine's [Raja nods "Yes."] So that was two ways. Ernestine, was your way different from Raja's?

*Ernestine:*   Yes.

*Ms. J.:*   Was your way different from Erik's?

*Ernestine:*   Yes.

*Ms. J.:*   So we did the problem in three different ways. Let's read the next problem.

The three children in Ms. J.'s class worked on one problem for about five minutes. These children, who could be characterized as disadvantaged, were solving a relatively difficult comparison problem. Ms. J. had written the problem just for these children and had even put two of the children's names in the problem. In deciding on the type of problem and the size of the numbers in the problem, Ms. J. drew on her knowledge of these children's mathematical knowledge and thinking. Each child figured out a way to solve the problem and described clearly what he or she had done. Ms. J. is experienced at listening to her children talking about their thinking. She is adept at understanding what they are trying to say and at gently probing when she does not understand how they are thinking. When the above dialogue occurred, Ms. J. had been working with these children for a number of months, so she knew the kinds of thinking they might do. She also had a well-organized body of knowledge that included how young children typically solve comparison problems. She recognized each strategy as one that many children use to solve comparison problems.

In the CGI classroom, the teacher poses problems that each child can solve at her or his level of mathematics knowledge and understanding. The teacher encourages each child to solve mathematical problems using ways that make sense to the child. Ms. J. encourages each child to tell her how he or she solved the problems and uses what the child tells her to make instructional decisions. Children are aware that their thinking is as important as the answer and are not only comfortable but also determined that Ms. J. understand how they have solved each problem.

In other CGI classrooms, teachers work with the whole class and take into account individual differences in students in two ways. First, teachers pose problems that can be solved in a variety of ways so that each child can solve the problem according to her or his level of mathematical knowledge. Second, teachers substitute smaller or larger numbers in the same word problem, depending on their judgments of the size of numbers that different children can work with and use. After posing a problem to the whole class, teachers typically call on several children, one at a time, to say and show how they solved the problem. Often the teacher expects the next child to provide a different solution strategy from the ones given previously.

## Key Elements of CGI Classrooms

Because teachers were not given prescriptions, they have adapted CGI ideas according to their own teaching styles and according to what is comfortable and right for them. Thus, each CGI classroom is, in some sense, unique. However, we have observed three key elements that all CGI classrooms have in common. As we have discussed already, one important element is that *multiple solution strategies to problems are recognized, encouraged, and explored.* These solution strategies are brought out as the thinking of children becomes visible within the context of solving problems. This points to a second key element of CGI classrooms: *a focus on problem solving.* A third key element of CGI classrooms is that *teachers have an expansive view of children's mathematical knowledge and thinking.* CGI teachers believe that all children know something about mathematics and that teachers need to figure out continually what children know about mathematics and then use this knowledge to plan and adapt their mathematics instruction. We consider these last two elements further in the sections that follow.

### Focus on Problem Solving

Problem solving is the focus of all CGI classrooms. Teachers pose many problems for children. They carefully write or select these problems to be appropriate for their children. Generally, teachers construct problems relevant to the children's real lives in school and out, such as a forthcoming class trip to the school forest or the real need to figure out at the beginning of each school day how many children will eat hot and cold lunches. Problems emerge during social studies lessons, or from a book the teacher happens to be reading to the class, or from a fantasy world constructed by the class, such as the Friendly Forest where raccoons can change the number of stripes on their tails depending on the problem. Some teachers, like Ms. J., usually write problems for each child, but not all teachers do. Because all problems can be solved in a variety of ways, teachers find that only a few problems can occupy the entire class for a day. The following list presents a set of problems that Dyanne van den Heuvel, a second-grade teacher, constructed for her children as she was reading her class the book *The Berenstein Bears and Too Much Junk Food* (Berenstein, S., & Berenstein, J., 1985).

1.  Sister Bear used to weigh fifty-five pounds. Then she ate too much junk food, and now she weighs seventy-one pounds. How many pounds did she gain?

2.  Brother Bear weighed just the right amount for his height. Then he ate too much junk food and gained twenty-four pounds. Now he weighs ninety pounds. How much did he weigh to begin with?

3.  If Brother Bear weighed eighty-four pounds, and he weighed thirty-seven pounds more than Sister Bear, then how much would Sister Bear weigh?

4.  Papa Bear weighed twenty-one pounds more than Brother Bear and Sister Bear combined. If Brother Bear weighed forty-five pounds and Sister Bear weighed thirty-one pounds, then how much would Papa Bear weigh?

5.  While the bears were getting back in shape, Mama kept track of how much weight they lost. Brother Bear lost twenty-three pounds. Papa Bear lost forty-seven pounds more than Brother Bear lost. How many pounds did Papa Bear lose?

6.  Sister Bear was a little "chubby," as Mama Bear put it. Then she began to eat healthier food and exercise more. After one month she had lost eleven pounds. Then she weighed sixty pounds. How much did she weigh when she was "chubby"?

7.  Write your own problem about the Berenstein Bears and their exercise program.

Problem solving is not limited exclusively to word problems. For example, children invent their own ways to solve multidigit number problems. The following solution shows the thinking of a child in a CGI classroom as she added two three-digit numbers, 248 and 176, to solve a word problem:

> Well, 2 plus 1 is 3, so I know it's 200 and 100, so now it's somewhere in the 300s. And then you have to add the 10s on. And the 10s are 4 and 7 . . . well, um, is you started at 70, 80, 90, 100. Right? And that's 4 100s. So now you're already in the 300s because of the (40+70). But you've still got one more 10. So if you're doing it: 300 plus 40 plus 70, you'd have 410. But you're not doing that. So what you need to do then is add 6 more onto 10, which is 16. And then 8 more: 17, 18, 19, 20, 21, 22, 23, 24. So that's 124. I mean 424.

### An Expansive View of Children's Mathematical Knowledge

CGI teachers believe that all children know something about mathematics and that, as teachers, they need to consider and use their children's mathematical knowledge in planning instruction and in making decisions during instruction. CGI teachers realize that they need to continuously learn about their children's mathematical knowledge and thinking as it is developing. They continually assess what each child can do, formally through individual interviews and informally as part of ongoing classroom discourse when children solve problems. During classroom discourse, the teacher typically encourages the children to solve a problem any way they wish. Then the teacher asks individual children how they solved the problem and listens carefully to each child's explanation. Teachers' knowledge of the organized framework of problem types and related solution strategies helps them understand and keep track of individual students' thinking as well as the kinds of problems a student can solve.

*A Limiting View of Children's Knowledge: The Case of Ms. W. and Adam.* To clarify what we mean when we say that CGI teachers have an expansive view of children's knowledge and that they use their understanding of what children know to build on children's thinking, we first describe a teacher who takes a limiting view of her children's mathematical knowledge. In the following example, Ms. W.'s limited view of Adam's knowledge leads her to miss opportunities to use that knowledge to help other students learn (Lubinski, 1989):

*Ms. W.:*  [Writes on the board]
     35
   +35

*Ms. W.:*  Now, who can add this for me? Adam.

*Adam:*  70

*Ms. W.:*  How did you get that?

*Adam:*  Well, I knew that 3 and 3 is 6, so 30 and 30 is 60. And 5 and 5 is 10, and 60 plus 10 is 70.

*Ms. W.:*  OK. You have the right answer. However, if I did 3 plus 3 is 6, and then I went to 5 plus 5 is 10, and I put that down, Adam, I'd have 610.

*Ms. W.:*  [Writes on the board]
     35
   +35
   ―――
   610

*Ms. W.:*  Is that the right answer?

*Adam:*  No.

*Ms. W.:*  You have the right answer, but how could I do that to show it?

*Adam:*  You could do 5 and 3.

*Ms. W.:*  Well, I can't. They live in different houses.

*Adam:*  You add the 5s and then you add the 3s.

*Ms. W.:*  Well, I'm over here in the 1s' house. What do I have to do? I'll bet, Linda, you remember what I did . . .

In an interview following the class, Ms. W. described her thinking about the above situation as follows: "He [Adam] had a very good way to explain it, but he wasn't explaining that I wanted him to carry the ten. You have so many children who will write down the ten and then go to the tens' column and put down a number there too and come up with a three-digit answer when it should be two. I thought his process—his thinking—was excellent, but he would not have been able to record it. He would have known it was wrong, but he wouldn't have known how to change it."

This episode illustrates that children are capable of sophisticated mathematical thinking. But, like many adults, Ms. W. misses the opportunity to capitalize on a child's thinking because she looks at the problem only from her point of view rather than the child's and attempts to teach (in this case, the carrying procedure) rather than to listen, understand, and facilitate the child's development of mathematical knowledge. However, we cannot be too critical of Ms. W. She was concerned with more than whether Adam had the right answer. She did ask Adam to explain how he got his answer, and she seemed to understand Adam's explanation. Yet she was unwilling to let go of her role as the dispenser of knowledge to try to build on Adam's thinking. Although she expressed a concern that Adam's procedure would result in errors for him or other students, nothing in Adam's response suggests that he could *not* have written his answer correctly. Indeed, many students who had difficulty understanding Ms. W.'s procedure of "carrying the one" may have understood Adam's thinking about the problem and might have been able to solve the problem after listening to him. Ironically, Ms. W. did not seem to recognize that Adam was modeling exactly the kinds of mental computations that are advocated by authors of mathematics education reform documents such as the NCTM Standards (1989, pp. 46–47).

*Expanding Teachers' Views of Children's Knowledge.* Although Ms. W. participated in a CGI workshop, she does not yet take the expansive view of children's mathematical knowledge illustrated by Ms. J. However, Ms. W. is starting to listen to how her students solve problems. This is an important step. Some CGI ideas conflict with central beliefs of many teachers—that teachers are the source of knowledge and that teachers have a responsibility to "cover" all the mathematics content specified in a mandated curriculum. Changing beliefs and attitudes takes time. The CGI workshop alone did not change teachers; teachers changed most when they began to listen and attend seriously to their own students' thinking as the children solved problems. We found that the impact of the CGI approach and the change in teachers' behavior were related significantly to how carefully and closely teachers listened to the ways their children solved mathematics problems.

The research-based knowledge of the problem framework and children's strategies gave teachers a context for thinking about children's knowledge and for helping teachers make sense of their children's thinking. As one teacher said to us, "I've always known that I should ask the children questions that would tell me what they were thinking, but I never knew the questions to ask or what to listen for."

Teachers also have to believe that children's thinking is important. Consider contrasting statements about the role of the teacher and the role of the learner made by the same teacher, before the CGI workshop and a year later, after the teacher had been using her knowledge of the problem types and solution strategies in her classroom. Before the workshop, the teacher asserted that "it is the job of the teacher to make sure that she starts out very basic regardless of the math ability of the children." She saw the student's role as "following directions, to be listening, to be looking at the teacher, to be quiet so that they can absorb" what the teacher is saying. After using CGI for a year, she said the teacher "should be a leader, yet an allower of the children to express their ideas and a listener, so she can find out also what they are able to give her on their own." She asserted that the student "should first be definitely thinking and be thinking about what they do know."

*An Expansive View of Children's Knowledge: The Case of Ms. J. and Billy.* To illustrate the thinking and teaching of a CGI teacher who takes an expansive view of children's knowledge, we return to the classroom of Ms. J., whom we visited earlier. Ms. J. is a first-grade teacher who teaches many disadvantaged children. She took the CGI workshop in the initial year, and since then she has used and built on her knowledge of children's thinking in her mathematics classroom. She has children of all ability levels in her classroom, and she has children who do quite remarkable mathematical thinking in her room. Rather than look at these high-achieving children, we focus here on Ms. J's work with Billy, one of the lowest-achieving children in her classroom. By so doing, we emphasize our belief that all children have knowledge on which teachers might build mathematics instruction. When teachers make instructional decisions that take into account a child's mathematical knowledge, they enable that child to learn more mathematics.

Billy was a disadvantaged child who had arrived in Ms. J.'s classroom in the middle of October, six weeks after school had started. He had not been in school previously that year because of a teachers' strike in the community from which he came. When Billy entered Ms. J.'s first-grade class, he could neither count nor recognize numerals. Ms. J. and the other children helped Billy learn to count objects, first to five and then to ten. Billy learned to count to ten verbally, and when he continued to have great difficulty recognizing numerals, Ms. J. gave him a number line with each number clearly identified. Billy carried the number line with him continuously, and if he needed to know what a numeral looked like, he would count the marks on the number line and know that the numeral written beside the appropriate mark was the numeral he needed. As soon as Billy could count, Ms. J. began giving him simple word problems to solve. On a sheet of paper, she would write a word problem such as, "If Billy had two pennies, and Maria gave him three more, how many would he have then?" (a joining problem with the result unknown). Either Ms. J. or another child would then read the problem to Billy, who would get some counters and patiently model the problem. In this problem, Billy made a set of two cubes and a set of three cubes and then counted all the cubes. Ms. J. would then ask Billy to explain how he got his answer. He would tell her what each set meant, and how he had counted them all and gotten five and then counted up his number line to know what five looked like.

During mathematics class, Billy might solve only two or three of these simple problems, but he knew what he was doing, and he was able to report his thinking so that Ms. J. could understand what he had done. When Ms. J. was sure he understood the simple problems such as the joining and separating result-unknown problems, she moved on to somewhat harder problems and to somewhat larger numbers. She encouraged Billy to make up his own problems to solve and to give to other children. Almost all of Billy's time in mathematics class during the year was spent in solving problems by direct modeling or in making up problems for other children to solve.

When we interviewed Billy near the end of the year, he was solving problems more difficult than those typically included in most first-grade textbooks. Billy had become less reliant on his number line, and he could solve result-unknown and change-unknown problems with numbers up to twenty. Although at that point Billy was not yet able to recall basic arithmetic facts, he nonetheless understood conceptually what addition and subtraction meant, and he could directly model problems to find the answer. Billy was no less proud of himself or excited about mathematics than any other child in the classroom. As he said to the school principal, "Do you know those kids in Ms. J.'s class who love math? Well, I'm one of them."

The case of Billy is true. By the end of first grade, this child, who would have qualified for any program for the disadvantaged, had made progress in learning mathematics, understood the mathematics he was doing, and felt good about himself and about mathematics. In his eyes, and in his teacher's eyes, Billy was a successful learner, and clinical interview data also confirmed his success.

What enabled this success to occur? Although Ms. J. was acknowledged as an expert teacher before she took the CGI workshop, she developed significant new knowledge of and beliefs about children's mathematics learning during the year following the workshop. The knowledge that she developed and used enabled her to work more effectively than ever before with all children, including children like Billy.

## Implications for Compensatory Education

The story of CGI is a story of teachers working with young children, including children who are less advantaged or less advanced in their mathematical knowledge, in a way that enables them to learn mathematics with understanding. It is a remarkable story because it demonstrates the professionalism of teachers who work with children in schools. It shows that when teachers are given access to research-based knowledge that is robust and directly useful in helping them fulfill their perceived roles, they use that knowledge as they teach, and it directly benefits the children with whom they work. To be useful, knowledge needs to be well organized so that teachers can use it on a daily basis as part of their ongoing mathematics instruction. The research-based knowledge on children's problem solving in addition and subtraction proved to be an example of well-organized, robust, and useful knowledge. Once teachers were given access to this knowledge, and they perceived that it helped them to understand their own children's thinking, they used the knowledge in their teaching of addition and subtraction. This knowledge helped teachers think about the mathematical knowledge of each child in their mathematics classrooms and to design mathematics curricula and instruction so that each child could learn. It helped teachers understand the thinking of students who were having trouble learning, as well as the thinking of students who were more advanced in their mathematics learning.

Just as this specific research-based knowledge of children's learning of addition and subtraction was useful to primary teachers in Madison, Wisconsin, and in inner-city Milwaukee, so too should the knowledge be useful for primary teachers elsewhere who teach mathematics in compensatory education programs. This knowledge would provide a new framework for thinking about addition and subtraction problems as well as for thinking about young children's mathematical knowledge and abilities to solve addition and subtraction problems.

In addition to this specific knowledge, which could be used directly in compensatory education in mathematics, our work with CGI teachers suggests three important ideas that are important to consider in developing new approaches to teaching elementary mathematics in compensatory education. These ideas have to do with (1) assessing students' mathematical knowledge and understanding, (2) building on students' informal and formal mathematical knowledge, and (3) constructing curricula and teaching in ways that encourage mathematical thinking and problem solving by all children.

These ideas may seem obvious to some teachers. Indeed, many elementary teachers, including compensatory education teachers, might agree with these ideas and even say they are implementing them in their mathematics teaching. However, we have found that these ideas mean very different things to different people, so it is important to discuss these ideas to gain an understanding of what they mean. Further, teachers need to consider what these ideas might mean for reforming their mathematics teaching in ways that will benefit students who have been served by compensatory education programs.

### Assessing Students' Mathematical Knowledge and Understanding

Most elementary teachers believe that they are teaching for understanding in mathematics (see Cohen & Ball, in press; Peterson et al., 1989), but their definitions of what it means to know and understand mathematics differ substantially from researchers' definitions derived from recent studies of children's mathematics learning. For example, as one rather traditional elementary teacher in California commented when discussing the state-level mathematics reform aimed at teaching mathematics for understanding, "What do they think we've been doing—teaching for *mis*understanding?" (Cohen & Ball, in press). Of course, this teacher's concept of mathematical understanding differed substantially from that of researchers and curriculum reformers. Similarly, in a study of our first-grade teachers' goals and beliefs before the CGI workshop, we contrasted seven teachers who had initial beliefs that were more cognitively based and whose students did well on problem solving with seven teachers who had beliefs that were less cognitively based and whose students did less well on problem solving (Peterson et al., 1989). Cognitively based beliefs reflected strong agreement with the ideas that

- Children construct mathematical knowledge
- Math skills should be taught in relation to problem solving
- Instruction should be sequenced to build on children's development of ideas

- Instruction should facilitate children's construction of mathematical knowledge

Although we found important differences between the less cognitively based teachers and the more cognitively based teachers in their goals, knowledge, beliefs, and reports of how they taught addition and subtraction, as well as in their students' problem-solving achievement, *all fourteen teachers indicated that they placed the greatest emphasis on mathematical understanding,* compared with number fact knowledge and word problem solving. However, all seven cognitively based teachers rated fact knowledge as *least* important when compared with understanding and problem solving, while less cognitively based teachers placed number fact knowledge either *first* (tied with mathematical understanding) or *second,* after mathematical understanding. Thus, even though these teachers differed significantly in their beliefs and in their reports of how and what they taught in addition and subtraction, they all believed and reported that they were teaching for mathematical understanding.

How do teachers know whether a child knows and understands mathematics? To assess students' mathematical knowledge and understanding, most teachers rely on observed student engagement or on students' answers to mathematics problems on tests or worksheets (Ball, in press; Peterson et al., 1989). In contrast, CGI teachers who have changed their ideas of what it means for children to understand mathematics adopt or invent new approaches and techniques for assessing students' knowledge and understanding. These include using whole-class and small-group discourse among children to learn about their mathematical knowledge and thinking, as well as interviewing individual children. CGI teachers are concerned with understanding the processes that children use to solve problems rather than focusing on only whether the answer is correct.

### Building on Students' Informal and Formal Mathematical Knowledge

Before being able to use and build on students' mathematical knowledge in teaching, a teacher needs to realize that *all children know and understand some mathematics.* All too often, teachers focus not on what the student knows and how the student is understanding but on what the child does not know and on how the teacher herself or himself understands the mathematics problem. Like Ms. W., teachers often unwittingly encourage their own way of thinking about a mathematics problem and fail to listen to and try to understand a student's way of thinking about the problem. In contrast, teachers like Ms. J., who take an expansive view of children's mathematical knowledge and understanding, are continually astonished by what children know and understand. Ms. J. showed equal enthusiasm in extolling the virtues of her children's mathematical knowledge regardless of whether the child was one like Billy, who came to first grade with less knowledge and understanding than other children, or one like Cheryl, whose knowledge of division in December of first grade astounded Ms. J., who related to us the following story:

> I was working with Cheryl the other day, and she had twelve cubes in her hand. The problem was Riva had twelve carrots, and she made three carrot cakes. She needed to divide them equally into each cake. And you know, Cheryl had these cubes, and go, go, go—she snapped it off real quick. I said, "How did you get that so quickly?" And she goes, "Oh, you know, the numbers, you know—first there were three. If you put three cakes, three carrots in each cake, and then I had nine. But if I add one more, that would be four." So they [the children] are thinking. It's just so sophisticated. It just seems to come together for them.

### Constructing Curriculum and Encouraging Math Thinking and Problem Solving

Our work suggests that knowledge about children's thinking can be an important influence on instruction and learning. Teachers' behavior can be changed by helping them gain knowledge about children's thinking, and this change in behavior results in better mathematics learning by their students. For CGI teachers, this means doing much more of the following in their teaching of addition and subtraction:

- Posing word problems
- Listening to students' thinking
- Encouraging the use of multiple strategies to solve word problems
- Asking, "How did you get your answer?"

For CGI teachers, their use of textbooks and the way they think about the mathematics curriculum also changes.

***Supplementing the Textbook.*** Although teachers had been told explicitly by the school district administrators that they did not have to use the textbook during the year of the experimental study, only two CGI teachers reported that they did not use the textbook at all that year. Eleven of the teachers reported using all or most of the textbook; the remaining four teachers used the textbook in some way, either as a "backup" or "reinforcer" or for practice. When asked how she used the textbook, the following CGI teacher gave a response that was typical during the first year: "I used it as a resource for getting ideas on how to present material. I used it as practice pages for the kids. It is much less of a Bible than it has been in other years, which was really nice for me. I didn't feel as tied to it." However, when asked, "Did you cover everything in your textbook?" the same teacher responded, "Well, yes, I've covered the objectives in the textbook."

Because CGI is premised on the idea of introducing addition and subtraction within the meaningful context of a wide variety of types of story problems, CGI teachers developed their own materials and supplemented the textbook with word problems. During the first year, CGI teachers admitted that, although they used their textbooks, they omitted whole pages of computation problems, and they took pages out of the textbook and rearranged them. In addition, they also used many word problems that they developed on their own or from supplemental enrichment materials. In describing how she supplemented the textbook, one teacher said she used all the kinds of the problems that she had constructed during the summer workshop. She added, "In fact, some of us said that we'd have loved to spend more time on this and throw out the book and just sit and talk with kids about, 'How would you work this one out? How would you work that one out?' You know, once they [the children] start catching on to those problems, I think that's where our emphasis should be."

*Going Beyond the Textbook.* As teachers developed their ideas about CGI over several years, many teachers ceased using a textbook altogether. Fennema, Carpenter, and Loef (in press) describe the growth and development of one such teacher, Ms. G., over a four-year period as she learned to use children's thinking in her mathematics teaching. During the first year, Ms. G. reported, she used the textbook to guide her mathematics instruction explicitly. By the end of the second year, she began to supplement the textbook and to rely more on her knowledge of children. By January of the third year, Ms. G. used her textbook only as a guide; as the year progressed, she spent more time on story problems, and completing textbook pages became a low priority. At the end of the third year, Ms. G. announced that she had received permission from her principal to teach mathematics the following year without a textbook. During the fourth year, Ms. G. reported that she "never even picks up her textbook." Rather, she constructs her curriculum from her knowledge of the variety of problem types and her children's understanding. She has decided that the textbook is too limiting and does not build on what children know and can do.

Over the course of the four years, the mathematics that Ms. G. taught also changed dramatically. She increased the time she spent teaching mathematics and progressed to including mathematics in other subjects and at other times during the day. Most importantly, problem solving rather than drill became the focus of activity in Ms. G.'s mathematics teaching. For example, she taught place value in relation to ongoing problem solving. Although she consciously planned problems and activities in which children could explore place value ideas, and she had children focus on place value ideas where appropriate, she never taught a formal unit on place value. Rather, she completely integrated the teaching of place value with other mathematics. At the end of the year, she reported that she felt her children understood place value ideas better than any group of children she had taught previously.

During the fourth year, Ms. G. also reported doing multiplication and division work with her children. Previously, she would not have taught multiplication or division to her first-graders because she felt these topics were much too hard. In her teaching of multiplication and division, she described how she bought cookies for the students in her class, and the children had to find out how many cookies were in each package. She had selected the packages of cookies so that each package had a different number of rows of cookies and different numbers in a row. She reported that she posed the problem of "how many were in a row, how many rows, then they had to decide how many cookies there were altogether, and then how many cookies each child would get if I were to divide them up." She stated that "it took us the whole afternoon to do that problem. . . . At the end of the day, then, we did divide the cookies up to see if they were right and to see how many were left over." This example of Ms. G.'s teaching illustrates both her attempt to give her children mathematics problems with real-life meaning and her recognition that her children could do many mathematics problems that she had viewed previously as too difficult for young children.

In sum, over the four years, Ms. G. learned from listening and observing her own students that her children have a lot of mathematical knowledge, and she learned continuously how to use and build on that knowledge in her teaching. Ms. G. continues to learn, as do her children.

## Conclusion

In summary, the CGI approach is characterized by

- Teachers who have a knowledge base for understanding their children's mathematical thinking
- Teachers who listen to their students' mathematical thinking and build on the knowledge they get by listening
- Teachers who use their knowledge of students' mathematical

thinking to think about and develop their mathematics instruction

- Teachers who place increased emphasis on mathematics problem solving and decreased emphasis on drill and practice of routine mathematics skills
- Teachers who provide their students with opportunities to talk about how they solve mathematics problems and to solve problems in a variety of ways
- Classrooms in which students do a lot of mathematics problem solving and describe the processes they use to solve problems
- Classrooms in which students demonstrate increased levels of mathematics problem-solving abilities while maintaining high levels of computational performance

Frequently, the message of compensatory education in mathematics has been one of remediation and compensation for children's lack of mathematical knowledge. Our research with CGI teachers offers a strikingly different message. The message of CGI is that when teachers begin listening to and talking with their children, they come to realize how much more their children know than they had recognized previously. Teachers come to understand that children have a lot of mathematical knowledge on which they can build. When teachers know about children's mathematical knowledge and thinking, they can use it to facilitate children's development of mathematical problem-solving abilities. Teachers can achieve the goals of compensatory mathematics education by focusing on and using their children's mathematical knowledge and thinking in their classroom teaching.

### References

Ball, D. (in press). Reflections and deflections of policy: The case of Carol Turner. *Educational Evaluation and Policy Analysis.*

Berenstein, S., & Berenstein, J. (1985). *The Berenstein Bears and Too Much Junk Food.* New York: Random House.

Carpenter, T. P. (1985). Learning to add and subtract: An exercise in problem solving. In E. A. Silver (Ed.), *Teaching and learning mathematical problem solving: Multiple research perspectives* (pp. 17-40). Hillsdale, NJ: Erlbaum.

Carpenter, T. P., Fennema, E., Peterson, P. L., & Carey, D. (1988). Teachers' pedagogical content knowledge of students' problem solving in mathematics. *Journal for Research in Mathematics Education, 19,* 385-401.

Carpenter, T. P., Fennema, E., Peterson, P. L., Chiang, C., & Loef, M. (1989). Using knowledge of children's mathematical thinking in classroom teaching: An experimental study. *American Educational Research Journal, 26,* 499-532.

Clark, C. M., & Peterson, P. L. (1986). Teachers' thought processes. In M. Wittrock (Ed.), *Handbook of research on teaching* (3rd ed.) (pp. 255-296). New York: Macmillan.

Cohen, D. K., & Ball, D. L. (in press). Relations between policy and practice: A commentary. *Educational Evaluation and Policy Analysis.*

Dossey, J. A., Mullis, I. V., Lindquist, M. M., & Chambers, D. L. (1988). *The mathematics report card: Are we measuring up?* Princeton, NJ: Educational Testing Service.

Duckworth, E. (1987). *"The having of wonderful ideas" and other essays on teaching and learning.* New York: Teachers College Press.

Fennema, E., & Carpenter, T. (1989). *Cognitively guided instruction: A program implementation guide.* Madison: Wisconsin Center for Education Research, University of Wisconsin, Madison.

Fennema, E., Carpenter, T., & Loef, M. (in press). Learning to use children's mathematics thinking: A case study. In C. Maher & R. Davis (Eds.), *Relating schools to reality.* Englewood Cliffs, NJ: Prentice-Hall.

Fennema, E., Carpenter, T. P., & Peterson, P. L. (1989a). Learning mathematics with understanding. In J. Brophy (Ed.), *Advances in research on teaching* (Vol. 1, pp. 195-221). Greenwich, CT: JAI Press.

Fennema, E., Carpenter, T. P., & Peterson, P. L. (1989b). Teachers' decision-making and cognitively guided instruction: A new paradigm for curriculum development. In N. Ellerton & M. Clements (Eds.), *School mathematics: The challenge to change* (pp. 174-187). Geelong, Victoria, Australia: Deakin University Press.

Fuson, K. (1988). *Children's counting and concepts of number*. New York: Springer Verlag.

Ginsburg, H. A. (1983). *The development of mathematical thinking*. New York: Academic Press.

Lampert, M. (1984). Teaching about thinking and thinking about teaching. *Curriculum Inquiry, 16*, 1–18.

Lave, J. (1988). *Cognition in practice: Mind, mathematics, and culture in everyday life*. New York: Cambridge University Press.

Lubinski, C. (1989). *Cognitively guided instruction and teachers' decision making*. Unpublished doctoral dissertation, University of Wisconsin, Madison.

National Council of Teachers of Mathematics (NCTM). (1989). *Curriculum and evaluation standards for school mathematics*. Reston, VA: Author.

National Research Council. (1989). *Everybody counts: A report to the nation on the future of mathematics education*. Washington, DC: National Academy Press.

Peterson, P. L., Carpenter, T. C., & Fennema, E. (1989). Teachers' knowledge of students' knowledge in mathematics problem solving: Correlational and case analyses. *Journal of Educational Psychology, 81*, 558–569.

Peterson, P. L., Fennema, E., & Carpenter, T. (1988/1989). Using knowledge of how students think about mathematics. *Educational Leadership, 46* (4), 42–46.

Peterson, P. L., Fennema, E., Carpenter, T., & Loef, M. (1989). Teachers' pedagogical content beliefs in mathematics. *Cognition and Instruction, 6*, 1–40.

Villasenor, A. (1990). *Teaching the first grade mathematics curriculum from a problem-solving perspective*. Unpublished doctoral dissertation, University of Wisconsin, Milwaukee.

Zucker, A. (1990). Review of research on effective curriculum and instruction in mathematics. In M. S. Knapp & P. M. Shields (Eds.), *Better schooling for the children of poverty: Alternatives to conventional wisdom: Vol. 2. Commissioned papers and literature review*. Washington, DC: U.S. Department of Education.

# COMMENTARY

## *Judith J. Richards*

My reaction to the chapter "Using Children's Mathematical Knowledge" by Penelope Peterson, Elizabeth Fennema, and Thomas Carpenter is based on twenty years of teaching in urban public school systems and on experience as an adjunct faculty member at Wheelock College and as a consultant on projects developing new curricula. For the past seventeen years, I have taught in the Cambridge, Massachusetts, school system. I have taught in the Follow Through Program and for the last eight years have been teaching at the Saundra Graham and Rosa Parks Alternative Public School. The age-integrated classrooms at this K-8 magnet school serve a student body that is ethnically, linguistically, and economically diverse.

This discussion responds to each of the key elements in the Cognitively Guided Instruction (CGI) approach described by Peterson et al., with specific attention to the role of the teacher in an urban classroom. I appreciate the opportunity to play an active role in the development of a new focus for preservice and in-service math education, in the empowerment of teachers in the design and implementation of curriculum, and in fostering an awareness of children's mathematical knowledge and thinking.

The CGI approach is one model for bringing current research in mathematics education into daily classroom practice. This approach is based on the following three principles:

- Teachers must have expansive views of children's mathematical knowledge and thinking.
- The mathematics curriculum must focus on problems solving.
- Teachers must encourage and recognize multiple strategies and solutions for problem solving.

102

I would suggest that this foundation is complete only when a fourth cornerstone is in place:

• The mathematics curriculum must be relevant to the events, daily lives, and rich cultural traditions of *all* our children.

### Children's Mathematical Knowledge

The need for teachers to have an expansive view of children's mathematical knowledge and thinking is the basic premise underlying the construction of the new National Council of Teachers of Mathematics (NCTM) Standards. In fact, the first four standards are Mathematics as Problem Solving, Mathematics as Communication, Mathematical Reasoning, and Mathematical Connections. I believe that these standards are directly embodied in the three key principles of CGI and in the fourth cornerstone suggested above.

*Teachers Need an Expansive View of Both Mathematics and Children's Mathematical Knowledge.* Peterson et al. begin their chapter by acknowledging the skills and understanding that all children bring to a school setting and note that this is not a widely held view among educators—particularly in schools with large populations of poor children. All too frequently, inner-city school math programs consist of rote-learning drill and practice (low-order skills) and either "neglect or de-emphasize the teaching of higher order skills" (Levine, Levine, & Eubanks, 1985).

School-aged children are certainly not empty vessels. As the authors of "Using Children's Mathematical Knowledge" stress, a large amount of recent research and classroom practices address the acceptance of the mathematical knowledge children bring to school. Resnick (1987) has studied the differences between children's out-of-school problem solving and their in-school thinking and suggests that formal mathematics may in fact discourage students from bringing knowledge and intuition to school tasks by stressing memorization and written computation. Children can and do demonstrate problem-solving abilities and mathematical thinking independently of their mastery of school-based algorithms and number facts. Robert Moses's Algebra Project (Silva & Moses, 1990) with urban middle school students and Maggie Lampert's work with multiplication are examples of postprimary implementation of this practice of bringing children's mathematical thinking to bear in classroom mathematics.

In addition to the appreciation of children's mathematical understanding stressed by Peterson et al., teachers need a broader conception of the field of mathematics. My experience as an instructor in the teacher-training program at Wheelock College leads me to believe that teachers must themselves have enhanced knowledge of a broad range of mathematical subject matter, including "the nature and discourse of mathematics, and the role of mathematics in culture and society" (Ball, 1989). They must have experience with a wide range of developmentally appropriate materials and must themselves experience problem solving as learners.

During the first session of my course, "Teaching Mathematics to Young Children," I ask students to start a "working definitions" journal entry called "What Is Math?" Over 95 percent of the students restrict their definition of mathematics to computation and numbers. This is in contrast to the NCTM Standards' decreased attention to early use of symbolic numbers and isolated computation.

We must help teachers in the United States develop a wider view of mathematics. Children throughout many other English-speaking countries call the subject *maths*. I believe that this distinction is significant in the curriculum as well. In my view, some of the most innovative and progressive math educational curricula in the past two decades have come out of England (for example, the Nuffield Series of the 1970s) and, more recently, Australia (for example, the Mathematics Curriculum Teaching Project). The need to bring an understanding of the broad field of mathematics and of children's thinking to teacher training is critical.

The National Science Foundation–supported project Cognitively Guided Instruction appears to embody this position. The teachers who took the CGI workshops seem empowered by the experience. Their testimonies are evidence of enormous growth. The teachers speak of textbooks as resources, but they have realized their own potential to make changes in the order of presentation. Textbooks necessarily have one page before another, a structure that dictates linear learning. Children actually learn naturally in a more geometric fashion, which can be supported only if instructional materials are sequenced flexibly.

*How Do We Know What Children Are Thinking?* Children's *mathematizing* (Freudenthal, 1973) is often hidden and lost forever when they get the wrong answer for the "right reason" (sense making). For example, Xiamara, a sixth-grader, encountered the following problem on a test:

> *Three walls of your room are covered with wallpaper. The fourth wall is 17' by 7'. Wallpaper is $2.99 a square foot. How much will it cost to finish the wallpapering job?*

Xiamara initially came up with the "correct" answer ($355.81), but she found herself in a quandary. She believed that her calculations were correct but also believed that no one could spend that much money wallpapering a room. She doubted her own mathematical competence, and since multiplication with decimals was fairly new to her, she reasoned that she must have placed the decimal point incorrectly. She moved the decimal point one place to the left, rounded her answer to two decimal places, and arrived at the answer $35.58. In a subsequent conversation with her teacher, she was fortunate to have the opportunity to explain *how* she arrived at her answer. She came away from the conversation with a renewed sense of her own arithmetic skills but also with a discouraging belief that school word problems do not have to be sensible, just arithmetically correct.

Xiamara's story also reminds us of the need to find ways to assess children's mathematical knowledge and thinking. Answers on test papers and textbook assignments do not bring us an understanding of children's thinking. The CGI approach, Robert Moses's Algebra Project (Silva & Moses, 1990), and the works of Magdalene Lampert (Lampert, 1990), Leah Richards (L. Richards, 1990), and Constance Kamii (Kamii, 1985) all suggest that teachers should offer and orchestrate lively classroom discourse. By observing and recording classroom discussions, teachers may assess children's problem-solving abilities. Peterson et al. suggest that this practice allows teachers to continuously make curriculum changes during instruction. The teacher may also have an active role in the discourse.

Accepting the existence of children's mathematical knowledge and thinking brings the issue of teachers' expectations to the table. There is tremendous evidence to suggest that teachers' expectations drive the course of classroom curriculum and that teachers' attitudes influence student achievement. These effects are particularly evident when children are labeled "disadvantaged." The research reviewed by Eva Chun (as cited by Hilliard, 1989) describes this "down teaching" in detail. If teachers are to provide opportunities for excellence for *all* students, their expectations must be positive and equitable.

**A Focus on Problem Solving in a Meaningful Curriculum**

A focus on problem solving in the CGI classrooms allows children to be individually challenged and to use higher-level thinking skills and multiple strategies and learning styles. The problems presented are not simply a vehicle for children to practice the algorithms. I was pleased to see classroom descriptions that included the introduction of a small number of problems each day. The research literature suggests that this practice is atypical in the United States, yet is the norm in Japanese classrooms.

The approach used by the CGI teacher described in the paper incorporates two innovative instructional techniques. In the first, the teacher writes a story that uses classroom children's names and that reflects her or his perception of the students' math skills. The second technique involves having children share their strategies for solving equations in a group discussion.

I applaud the first of these techniques as a vast improvement over using traditional textbook word problems and a keyword approach. I would also propose extending this approach to give children an opportunity to author their own stories that describe problems for which arithmetic may be of service. This process also allows for story sharing and peer reactions (Kliman & Richards, 1990). The third-graders in our classroom took the California Achievement Test (CAT) after using this writing/response process for four months. Our children, without any textbook experiences with school-based word problems, did as well as the children in two control classrooms on the problem-solving subtest. Although the sample was too small for quantitative analysis, it might be noted that one difference did occur. All of our students, who speak English as a second language, scored in the "mastery range," while students with similar profiles (including an identical twin) in the control classrooms did not demonstrate mastery in this subtest on the CAT.

The authors' use of children's literature is an exciting idea that is equally successful with older children. Marlene Kliman and Glenn Kliman (1990) describe a wide range of mathematical activities and modeling through the use of Jonathan Swift's *Gulliver's Travels*. Children in our classroom spent a day trying to estimate Gulliver's actual height, armed only with Swift's description of a Lilliputian's size as being equal to the length of Gulliver's six-inch hand. Our children measured all their classmates' hand lengths and heights. They averaged these ratios to predict Gulliver's height—a mere five feet tall. They noted that this "made sense," since they had visited the Salem Witch House and knew that people were of shorter stature in the seventeenth and eighteenth centuries.

I would further encourage teachers to "package" arithmetic situations in the cultural folktales of the children in their classrooms. This practice has allowed children of color to assume leadership roles in diverse (in terms of ethnicity, arithmetic skill, language, family economics, and gender) groups in our classroom. Over a third of the children at the Graham and Parks School are Haitian-American. Traditional Haitian folktales are an integral part of all areas of our classroom curricula. For example, I took a well-known problem concerning the sequence of fillings and pourings with a three-liter and a seven-liter container to achieve exactly five liters and "repackaged" it in the Haitian story of "Teyzen": "Do you remember the story of Teyzen? Well, one day Asefi and her brother Dyesel were going to the spring to get water. Their mother gave them each a calabash. Asefi's calabash held seven liters when it was full. Dyesel's calabash held three liters when it was full. Their mother told them to bring home exactly five liters. Tell about the fillings and pourings that the timoun [children] must do in order to bring home five liters."

If teachers demonstrate respect for children's knowledge and make room for it in their classrooms, they have an opportunity to develop a far richer curriculum. "To become meaningful, a curriculum has to be enacted by pupils as well as teachers, all of whom have their private lives outside school. . . . A curriculum as soon as it becomes more than intentions is embodied in the communicative life of an institution, the talk and gestures by which pupils and teachers exchange meanings even when they quarrel or cannot agree. In this sense, curriculum is a form of communication" (Barnes, 1976, p. 14). Teachers from Eurocentric cultures must maintain high regard for and an understanding of other cultural traditions and styles. The misunderstanding of behavioral style can make it difficult to "establish rapport and to communicate" (Hilliard, 1989).

## Multiple Solutions and Strategies

When problem solving is presented in meaningful contexts, all children are encouraged to bring their own learning styles to the process. Patricia Davidson's work from a neuropsychology perspective suggests that people learn math in one of two distinct styles (related to the functions of the brain's left and right hemispheres). She notes, for example, that style I learners (left cortical hemisphere preference) master formulas and have good recall of number facts (for example, $6 + 8 = 14$), while style II learners have stronger spatial and estimation skills. They usually know the "doubles" facts and might add $6 + 8$ by thinking that $6 + 6 = 12$, and since 8 is 2 more than 6, 2 is added on to make 14. What is particularly interesting about this research in light of the work of Peterson et al. with CGI is that some of the CGI teachers reacted to children that Davidson might call style II learners by remarking that their thinking was "sophisticated" or "abstract." Research indicates that teachers are more apt to be analytical (style I) in their own teaching and learning styles (Dunn & Dunn, 1988).

If these same teachers were to accept only single-answer, single-strategy problem-solving methods, they would lock out a large number of children from opportunities for excellence in mathematics. Peterson et al. also describe a teacher with a limited view of children's knowledge. Ms. W.'s resistance to Adam's mental computation strategy and insistence on a meaningless recipe is, unfortunately, typical of many teachers. In *Young Children Reinvent Arithmetic,* Constance Kamii (1985) details many classroom scenes where children like Adam are encouraged to share multiple strategies for mental arthmetic. Whereas children group numbers in many ways, the practice of adding first the tens and then the ones makes absolute sense. The recording is quite simple; the partial sums are listed and then combined:

$$
\begin{array}{r} 35 \\ +35 \\ \hline \end{array}
$$

$$
\begin{array}{r} 60 \\ +10 \\ \hline 70 \end{array}
$$

During my own childhood, I was taught that the one (and only) way to compute mentally was to imagine a "chalkboard in my mind" and then to "see" the numbers and "carry" as I would with paper and pencil. Unfortunately, the numbers always disappeared before I could finish the calculation. I was convinced that I was not "good at math" and did not reach for advanced work in the field. It was not until much later that I learned Adam's strategy (to add larger units first). This offered me a renewed sense of confidence in my own abilities in mathematics.

While I applaud the new empowerment of teachers in the design of meaningful curricula, I am well aware of the position of power that teachers have always held in the classroom and the need to give status to all children's knowledge and thinking. When teachers and children have different "ways of doing math" (strategies), the teacher's approach is usually regarded as "right" or given greater status. Typically, if children do not understand a teacher's explanation, the teacher raises her or his volume and continues delivering the information in exactly the same way. The teacher's style becomes the normative reference, and many students who are sent to remedial classrooms may simply be "learning differently."

In CGI classrooms, children are encouraged to share their strategies for solving equations. This is reminiscent of Constance

Kamii's studies in Alabama classrooms and Kiyonobu Itakura's Hypothesis Experiment Instruction (HEI) method, a system developed in Japan for the construction of knowledge through discussion and demonstration. I have adapted the HEI method for use in my own classroom (J. Richards, 1990). While I applaud the approach for acknowledging and giving status to diverse strategies, I am concerned about the number of children who actually share their strategies in a large group setting. Teachers must be mindful to bring less-frequent speakers into the discourse.

## Conclusion

We have a reform document in mathematics that is unparalleled in other areas of the curriculum. The NCTM Standards offer a new opportunity to bring about a real change.

The question then becomes, "Where do we start?" If we were able to start (on a national scale) with the teachers of young children, we would still lose almost a generation of children and young adults. It would seem, therefore, that the universities and teachers' colleges need to embrace these changes early in the 1990s if we are to affect the greatest number of classrooms during the next decade. In addition, I would love to see the CGI approaches described in "Using Children's Mathematical Knowledge" become a genuine and integral part of the math classrooms of all children. The framework provided by Chapter 1, Follow Through, and other federal target projects might be a good conduit for beginning this transformation. As individual states review their teacher certification standards, the state boards of education might insist that the key elements of CGI be infused into teacher training for future teachers in undergraduate and graduate programs and for current practitioners in in-service programs. Through CGI, Peterson et al. offer the scaffolding for teachers and children to develop a new curriculum.

## References

Ball, D. L. (1989). *Teaching mathematics for understanding. What do teachers need to know about the subject matter?* Washington, DC: National Education Seminar on Teacher Knowledge.

Barnes, D. (1976). *From communication to curriculum*. London: Penguin Books.

Dunn, R., & Dunn, K. (1988, October). *Presenting forward and backward: Teaching K–8*. Norwalk, CT: Early Years Inc.

Freudenthal, H. (1973). *The first person who used mathematizing: Mathematics as an educational task*. Dordrecht, Holland: D. Reichel.

Hilliard, A., III (1989, January). Teachers and cultural styles in a pluralistic society. *National Education Association Journal, 7* (6), 65–69.

Kamii, C. (1985). *Young children reinvent arithmetic*. New York: Teachers College Press.

Kliman, M., & Kliman, G. (1990). *Life among the giants: Mathematics writing and exploring Gulliver's world*. Newton, MA: Center for Learning Technology, Education Development Center.

Kliman, M., & Richards, J. (1990). *Now that we've done the calculation, how do we solve the problem? Writing, sharing, and discussing arithmetic stories*. Newton, MA: Literacies Institute, Education Development Center.

Lampert, M. (1990). When the problem is not the question and the solution is not the answer: Mathematical knowing and teaching. *American Educational Research Journal, 27* (1), 29–63.

Levine, D., Levine, R., & Eubanks, E. (1985). Successful implementation of instruction at inner city schools. *Journal of Negro Education, 54* (3), 313–332.

Resnick, L. B. (1987). Learning in school and out. *Educational Researcher, 16*, 13–20.

Richards, J. (1990). *Group discussion, influence and learning in science: A teacher's perspective on a Japanese curriculum in U.S. classrooms*. Paper presented at the annual meeting of the American Educational Research Association, Boston.

Richards, L. (1990). Measuring things in words: Language for learning mathematics. *Language Arts, 67* (1), 14–25.

Silva, C. M., & Moses, R. P. (1990). The Algebra Project: Making middle school mathematics count. *The Journal of Negro Education, 59* (3), 375–391.

# 4

# Dialogues Promoting Reading Comprehension

*Annemarie Sullivan Palincsar and Laura J. Klenk*

CONVERSATIONS WITH TEACHERS RESPONSIBLE FOR THE LITERACY IN-struction of elementary-aged students at risk for academic difficulty reveal the extraordinary agenda confronting these teachers. As one teacher indicated, with a mixture of apprehension and exuberance, "I want to engender an enthusiasm for reading and writing; I want to provide the kinds of experiences few of these children have had, that will enable them to have something to write about and provide the background knowledge that will be useful in their reading. And, of course, my job is also to teach all the basics." The demands on this teacher, and all teachers working in classrooms of increasingly heterogeneous learners, are many.

## Tensions in Literacy Instruction

The conflicting demands placed upon teachers reflect a number of tensions that currently attend literacy instruction. We briefly con-

The research reported in this chapter has been supported by PHS Grant 05951 from the National Institute of Child Health and Human Development and OSE Grant G008400648 from the Department of Education. The first author gratefully acknowledges her long-standing collaboration with Professor Ann Brown (University of California, Berkeley) in the research program regarding reciprocal teaching. We also wish to acknowledge the many fine teachers who have contributed enormously to the success of this research program.

sider three of these tensions to set the stage for describing reciprocal teaching—an instructional procedure designed to teach heterogeneous groups of learners, through the grades, how to approach learning from text in a thoughtful manner. Following our description of reciprocal teaching, we will summarize the research investigating its use with at-risk learners. Finally, we consider some of the implications of our research for school change efforts in general.

*Basic Skills Versus Critical Literacy.* Fueled by concerns that American students have failed to maintain the competitive edge in a world economy, the argument is made that educators ought to return to basic skills instruction. For example, *A Nation at Risk* (National Commission on Excellence in Education, 1983) urged that teachers be held accountable for students' achieving minimal levels of competence. In juxtaposition to the "back to basics" movement is the call for critical literacy, or literacy instruction that equips individuals with the tools to engage not only in the cognitive activities of thinking, reasoning, and problem solving but also in the uniquely human activities of reflection, creation, and enjoyment. Integral to the dialogue regarding critical literacy is the tenet that every child has the right to the educational opportunities to achieve this level of literacy—not simply "bright children," "normally achieving children," or the children of majority-culture or middle-class families. Such a movement demands the use of what Hilliard (1988) has referred to as "maximum-competency criteria" (p. 199). This tension gives rise to the question "What is the place of basic skills versus higher-order skills in literacy instruction?"

The greatest problem arising when basic skills are contrasted with higher-order skills in the reading domain is the faulty impression that not all students are entitled to instruction in both sets of skills. In fact, traditionally the trend has been to target basic skills instruction for younger and disadvantaged students while reserving the "higher-order" or reasoning skills for older and more successful students. It is this very practice that gave rise to this particular volume. However, if one maintains that the goal of literacy instruction is to prepare learners who are independent and ready to engage in lifelong learning, then this "tension" between basic and higher-order skills makes little sense. Children, regardless of their age or achievement level, should be taught effective reasoning and the skills to learn from text. Let's consider what these skills might be.

One hallmark of the critical reader is a repertoire of strategies for gaining knowledge from text. These are often called the "meta-cognitive skills of reading" (Brown, 1980). They are the strategies that enable readers to

- Clarify the purposes of reading
- Make use of relevant background knowledge
- Focus attention on the major content of the text
- Evaluate that content to determine whether it makes sense and is compatible with prior knowledge
- Monitor to ensure that comprehension is occurring
- Draw and test inferences

In this chapter we discuss an instructional procedure designed to teach children to engage in the metacognitive skills of reading even before they have acquired the basic skill of decoding. We will make the point that the context in which instruction occurs is as important as identifying the skills to be taught.

*Natural Versus Taught Literacy.* This second tension raises the question "To what extent should literacy instruction be thought of as the transfer of knowledge from teacher to child?" The natural-literacy argument suggests that, given a literate environment, young children will make sense of written language in much the same natural and effortless manner in which they learn spoken language (Phelps, 1988). Supporting the natural-literacy argument is evidence that children exposed to written language begin appropriating the literacy of their culture long before formal schooling. In addition, the natural-literacy tradition helps us to understand the diversity of practices and attitudes toward literacy displayed by children from various ethnic and socioeconomic backgrounds. However, the teacher is left dangling in the natural-literacy argument. Is it the teacher's responsibility to provide a "literacy rich" environment where he or she merely facilitates the activity of fairly autonomous learners? Or should classrooms be places where teachers, through conscious teaching of the means to understand text, enable learners to acquire literacy knowledge and tools? Indeed, Delpit (1988) has argued that the tenets of the natural-literacy tradition unwittingly deny African-American students entry into the "culture of power" by cutting off access to teachers as sources of knowledge. In this chapter we explore how it is possible for both teachers and students to assume active roles in literacy instruction so that students profit from the relative expertise of the teacher and from one another.

*Reductionist Versus Holistic/Constructivist Instruction.* This final tension speaks most directly to the procedural question "In what context should literacy instruction occur?" From a reductionist perspective, the content to be learned is segmented into discrete parts, usually through an analysis of the components of a task. Each component or step is then taught to some level of mastery. In reductionist teaching, little attention is paid to the social interactions among teachers and students, and children generally work alone. Illustrative of a reductionist approach to reading strategy instruction (for example, summarization) would be a lesson in which students are asked to underline an explicit main-idea sentence in a short and simplistic piece of text or to choose one of three titles for a short passage.

Poplin (1988), among others, has argued that a reductionist perspective has been particularly influential in the design of remedial education for children at risk. One alarming outcome of a reductionist approach is the impoverished understanding to which it can lead. We recently interviewed a number of disadvantaged and poorly achieving children in elementary school about what it takes to be a good reader. Typical children's responses were "Get a book, open it up, try to sound out the words," "Get your reading done," and "Something you look at and say the words." Their responses made sense when we observed that the teachers' reading instruction focused exclusively on decoding and seatwork.

The alternative holistic/constructivist perspective urges that tasks be presented in goal-embedded contexts; for example, in reading strategy instruction the goal would be to develop a strategic conception of reading rather than to master a series of steps of a strategy. Furthermore, the goal would be pursued through instruction conducted during meaningful reading of extended text. Finally, there would be many occasions for teacher-student and student-student interaction. The reciprocal teaching method described below was designed to provide students practice in a coherent and meaningful way, using the natural social context of discussion.

## Reciprocal Teaching

Reciprocal teaching is an instructional procedure in which teachers and students take turns leading discussions about shared text. The purpose of these discussions is to achieve joint understanding of the text through the flexible application of four comprehension strategies. Research investigating reciprocal teaching has been conducted over the past eight years by large numbers of teachers working primarily with remedial, special education, and at-risk students in first grade through secondary school.

Reciprocal teaching dialogues are "structured" with the use of four strategies: question generating, summarizing, clarifying, and predicting. The text is read in segments silently, as a read-along, or orally by the teacher, depending on the decoding ability of the students. Following each segment, the dialogue leader (adult or child) begins the discussion by *asking questions* about the content of the text. The group discusses these questions, raises additional questions, and, in the case of disagreement or misunderstanding, rereads the text. The discussion then moves on to a *summary* to identify the gist of what has been read and synthesize the reading and discussion. Once again, the dialogue leader offers the initial summary, and there is discussion to achieve consensus. The third strategy, *clarification,* is used opportunistically whenever there is a concept, word, or phrase that has been misunderstood or is unfamiliar to the group. Finally, the discussion leader generates and solicits *predictions* regarding upcoming content in the text. The members are guided to make predictions based on their prior knowledge of the topic and clues that are provided in the text itself (for example, headings, embedded questions).

The particular strategies practiced in reciprocal teaching were selected for a number of reasons. First, they represent the kinds of strategic activity in which successful readers routinely engage when learning from text (that is, self-testing understanding, paraphrasing while reading, anticipating and purpose setting, and taking appropriate measures when there has been a breakdown in understanding). Second, they provide the occasion for making explicit and visible the mental processes useful for constructing meaning from text. Finally, these strategies support a discussion within an interactive and socially supportive context in which to learn about learning from text.

The following transcript illustrates the role of the strategies in supporting the discussion. Six first-graders, five of whom were at risk for academic difficulty, were participating in this discussion. This was the twenty-seventh day that they had been using reciprocal teaching, and they were reading a story entitled "Black Bear Baby." The majority of the children were not yet decoding at the level the text was written, so their teacher read the text aloud to them.

Since the children have already heard the beginning of the story, their teacher begins by asking:

*Mrs. D.:* Boys and girls, last week we started a story about Black Bear Baby. What would be a good idea to do before we start today?

With this question, the teacher encourages the children to reflect on which strategy would be useful at this point in the reading. Several of the children suggest summarizing and several suggest predicting, since they are accustomed to predicting before they begin reading. The group collaborates on a summary of what has occurred thus far, the children adding the bits they remember while the teacher weaves the bits into a coherent whole. The group is then ready to begin reading. The teacher asks Margo to be the "teacher," the discussion leader.

*Mrs. D.:* [Reading] While the mother bear ate, the cubs romped and tumbled and somersaulted, but most of all they liked to wrestle. Baby Bear hid behind a tree, then jumped out, pouncing on his sister. The bear cubs rolled over and over, growling fiercely. Baby Bear was bigger than his sister, and he began to play too rough. His sister jumped onto a tree trunk and climbed quickly upward.

*Kendra:*   [Clarifying] What's rough?

*Mara:*   Like you say rough texture.

*Mrs. D.:*   Well, that's one kind of rough.

*Robert:*   The other one is like they beat you up.

*Mrs. D.:*   That's another kind of rough. Let me read the sentence and see which one you think it is. If it's the way you feel, the texture, or the beating up part.

In this portion, the teacher, rather than define the word *rough*, invites the children to return with her to the text and use the context of the sentence to clarify the meaning of *rough*. She rereads the appropriate sentence.

*Mara:*   It's the kind he [referring to Robert] means.

*Mrs. D.:*   The punching and hitting, playing too hard. Okay!

Mrs. D. then continues reading. The story goes on to describe how, with all the roughhousing, Baby Bear manages to fall off the tree in which he is chasing his sister and splashes into the cold water below. The paragraph concludes with a description of the mother rescuing and drying off her cub.

*Mrs. D.:*   Now, I gave you a lot of information, so you might want to ask more than one question.

*Margo:*   What did he lay in [in reference to the skunk cabbage leaves in which the cub rests after his spill]?

*Mara:*   It's true you could get an answer, but is that gonna get an answer from more than one people? Probably it's just gonna get an answer from one and there's better questions you could ask.

Mara's comment refers to the discussions that Mrs. D. has been having with the students about thinking not only of questions that ask for details but also of questions that have many answers and get the group thinking and talking.

*Mrs. D.:*  Let's go ahead, though, and answer Margo's question.

*Margo:*  Mara?

*Mara:*  The cabbage leaves.

*Kinata:*  Uh-uh, it wasn't no cabbage leaves.

Kinata is confused here because the text referred to them as "skunk cabbage leaves."

*Mrs. D.:*  Remember what they called it: skunk cabbage. Margo, do you understand what Mara was saying? Can you think of a question that could get a whole bunch of answers?

*Mara:*  Like if you would like to see if everybody's knows what's happening in the story . . . you could ask . . . what's happening in the story here?

*Mrs. D.:*  Let me help a little bit. What are the cubs doing while the mother is away? [Here the teacher models an appropriate question.] That might get a whole bunch of answers.

The children reconstruct the number of things that have occurred since the mother bear left, including Baby Bear's mishap.

*Robert:*  He went bang. He was not real hurt 'cause water isn't hard because water . . . you can land on it and splash around.

*Mara:*  You know it kind of told you what time of year it was because it told you it went "splash," because if it was this time of year [February], I don't think he'd splash in the water, I think he'd crack.

*Margo:* [Summarizing] This part of the story told us about Baby Bear and Sister Bear wrestling.

*Mrs. D.:*  Tell us a bit more; there's an important thing you left out.

The children then add other events that transpired in this part of the story, including the fall and Baby Bear's rescue.

*Mrs. D.:*    Okay, now that's a good summary—and good questions from all of you. You had good ideas. I also like the way we have been clarifying those words. Okay, Travis, you're our next teacher. Have we any predictions we can make at this point?

The children discuss some possible events in the story, such as other trouble that Baby Bear might get into, other ways in which the mother cares for her cubs, and how the cubs grow up.

In addition to illustrating the role of the strategies in reciprocal teaching dialogues, this transcript reveals how the teacher supports the children's engagement in the dialogues. In reciprocal teaching instruction, the teacher assumes many roles:

- Modeling competent use of the strategies for the purpose of constructing meaning and monitoring comprehension
- Engaging in on-line diagnosis of the students' emerging competence with the comprehension activity
- Supporting students' efforts to understand the text
- Pushing for deeper understanding
- Consciously releasing control of the dialogue to the students as they demonstrate the ability to assume responsibility for their own learning

The metaphor of a "scaffold" has been used to capture the role of the teacher in this instruction, providing adjustable and temporary support that can be removed when no longer necessary.

To contrast the nature of the dialogue occurring among first-graders and older students, a second excerpted transcript is provided below. In this discussion, seventh-grade remedial reading students are discussing a paragraph describing the layers of the earth in a passage about the formation of volcanoes. The text concludes, "Below the crust is a large layer called the *mantle*. It is a much heavier layer. The part of the mantle just below the crust is a strange place. Pressure there is very great, and the temperatures are very high."

*Doug:*    [Leading the discussion and summarizing] This told about the second layer of the earth, the one that is under the first one.

*Sara:*   The one under the crust.

*Doug:*   Yeah, the crust. It told about what it is like, like how heavy it is and what the temperature is. My prediction is that they will tell us about the next layer because this picture shows another one, and I'll bet it will be cooler because dirt gets colder when you dig.

*Chris:*   That doesn't make sense to me because, because as it's been goin' down, it's been gettin' hotter.

*Stephanie:*   And heavier, too.

*Chris:*   Pretty soon, we'll get to the gooey stuff, and it's real hot.

*Sam:*   That's the lava.

*Mr. M.:*   Well, let's read on and see who's right in their predictions. What will the next layer be like? Who will be the teacher?

At the seventh-grade level, the students are able to perform more independently of the teacher; they can independently return to the text, as Chris does in this example, to support their ideas. There are more examples at this level of students bringing background knowledge (as Doug does) to the text. Finally, students, like Sara, can assist their peers.

***Preparing Teachers to Use Reciprocal Teaching.*** For many teachers, learning dialogues are a new addition to their instructional repertoires. Hence, a critical step in the implementation of reciprocal teaching has been the preparation of teachers. In collaboration with the teachers with whom we have worked, we found the following procedure useful.

First, the teachers are encouraged to reflect on and discuss their current instructional goals and activities related to improving students' comprehension of text. Similarities and differences between the processes and outcomes of their current programs and reciprocal teaching are highlighted. For example, many teachers with whom we have worked already engage in strategy instruction, but the differences between teaching strategies as isolated skills (for example, teaching summarization by asking children to read brief pieces of text and select the best of three main-idea sentences) and teaching strategies for the purpose of self-regulation in reading (for example, summarizing in one's own words naturally occurring text) need to be discussed and demonstrated. This period of reflection is important; for some teachers, reciprocal teaching initially lacks a degree of face validity. For example, we have had teachers who believe that their first responsibility is to teach decoding. For other teachers, listening comprehension is synonymous with teaching children to follow directions. It is important that teachers reconcile their beliefs with the basic tenets of reciprocal teaching. Otherwise, naturally enough, teachers resist or, at a minimum, experience difficulty with implementation and adapt the program to accommodate the more familiar means and outcomes of instruction.

Following this opportunity for self-reflection, the theory informing the design of reciprocal teaching is introduced. The following points are emphasized:

- The acquisition of the strategies is a joint responsibility shared by teacher and students.
- The teachers initially assume major responsibility for instructing these strategies (that is, the teachers "think aloud" about how they generate a summary, what cues they use to make predictions, how rereading or reading ahead is useful when encountering something unclear in the text) but gradually transfer responsibility to the students.
- All students are expected to participate in this discussion—that is, all students are to be given the opportunity to lead the discussion. The teacher enables the students' successful participation by supporting them in a variety of ways—for example, by prompting, providing additional instruction, or altering the demand on the student.
- Throughout each day of instruction, there is a conscious attempt to release control of the dialogue to the students.
- The aim of reciprocal teaching is to construct the meaning of the text and to monitor the success with which comprehension is occurring.

Staff development continues by showing demonstration tapes, conducting sessions in which teachers role-play reciprocal teaching dialogues, examining transcripts to discuss some of the finer points of the dialogue (for example, supporting the engagement of children in considerable difficulty), and conducting a demonstration lesson with teachers and researchers coteaching. Following these formal sessions, additional coaching is provided to the teachers as they implement the dialogues in their respective settings.

*Preparing Students to Use Reciprocal Teaching.* Introduction of students to reciprocal teaching begins with a discussion regarding its purpose as well as its features (the dialogue structured by the strategies and the taking of turns in leading the discussion). The students are then introduced to each of the strategies with teacher-led activities. For example, questioning is introduced by discussing the role that questions play in our lives, particularly our school lives. The students then generate information-seeking questions about everyday events. This activity permits teachers to evaluate how well their students can frame questions. The students then read or listen to simple informational sentences about which they are to ask a question. Next, the students evaluate questions about short segments of text; and finally, the students generate their own questions from segments of text. A similar sequence of activities occurs for each of the strategies.

These activities are included principally to introduce the students to the language of the dialogues and to provide the teacher with diagnostic information suggesting how much support individual children might need in the dialogue. No more than two days of instruction are spent on introducing each of the strategies in this fashion before beginning the dialogues.

In our research, reciprocal teaching has been implemented with small groups, generally ranging from six to eight students, although junior high teachers have handled groups as large as seventeen. The dialogues have been conducted over a period of twenty to thirty consecutive days. The texts were selected according to the grade level of the students. Typically, the texts were drawn from readers, trade books for children, and content area texts (particularly with middle school students, who often find these texts difficult to learn from).

*Evaluating Reciprocal Teaching Instruction.* The majority of the research on reciprocal teaching has been conducted in reading and listening comprehension instruction by general, remedial, and special educators. Since 1981, when the research program began, nearly three hundred middle school students and four hundred first- to third-graders have participated in this research. The instruction was designed principally for students determined to be at risk for academic difficulty or already identified as remedial or special education students. Typically, the students involved in our research fall below the 40th percentile on nationally normed measures of achievement. The students entering these studies scored approximately 30 percent correct on independent measures of text comprehension. Our criterion for success was the attainment of an independent score of 75 percent to 80 percent correct on four out of five consecutively administered measures of comprehension, assessing recall of text, ability to draw inferences, ability to state the gist of material read, and application of knowledge acquired from the text to a novel situation. Using this criterion, approximately 80 percent of both the primary and middle school students have been judged successful. Furthermore, these gains have been observed to endure for up to six months to a year following instruction (Brown & Palincsar, 1982, 1989; Palincsar & Brown, 1984, 1989).

In the most current reciprocal teaching research, rather than involving an array of unrelated texts, the dialogues were used with primary-grade students to learn simple science concepts related to animal survival themes such as camouflage, mimicry, and protection from the elements. These themes were represented across the texts with which the groups were working. The use of an array of texts related to specific themes permitted the students to acquire and use their knowledge of these themes over time, an opportunity that was not available when the students were using random texts and one that is generally not available in most reading instruction. The students explained and justified their understandings of these themes during the course of the discussions. Twenty days of such discussion led to dramatic improvement in both comprehension processes (as assessed by the independent comprehension measures) and thematic understanding (as assessed by the content of the discussions as well as independent measures of the children's content knowledge). The children were asked to sort pictures of animals into the six themes that had been discussed during the course of instruction. Whereas their initial scoring was based on the physical characteristics of the animals, after the dialogues, the students sorted the animals correctly, by theme, 85 percent of the time. In addition, when presented with a novel example, they could identify the theme and justify how that animal exemplified the theme. Reciprocal teaching enabled the children both to learn a body of coherent and useful knowledge and to acquire a repertoire of strategies useful for learning content on their own.

The practical implications of these outcomes are worthy of note. At the middle school level, remedial reading teachers have reported dismissing larger numbers of students from their caseloads following involvement in reciprocal teaching than in any previous year. At the primary level, teachers have reported that a number of students, whom they had initially regarded as at risk, demonstrated greater knowledge and skill in the dialogues than had been observed previously in the classroom. This observation makes sense when one considers that historically these children seldom had occasion to bring their own knowledge to bear in the classroom or to demonstrate the leadership and helping skills displayed during the dialogues, since instruction was focused almost exclusively on decoding.

Anecdotal evidence of internalization on the part of the primary children is provided by teachers' reports that the children begin to use the strategies employed in the dialogue, unprompted, in contexts other than the listening comprehension lessons. For example, one teacher reported that children engaged in the same discourse during small-group reading and asked for clarifications during whole-class discussions.

Decoding-based curricula for at-risk children have been defended on the grounds that these students, often from economically deprived homes, come to school unfamiliar with the basic skills of decoding. Although we have not systematically collected data on the change in the decoding levels of the students in our research, there is evidence from the very successful Kamehameha Early Education Program that at-risk Native Hawaiian children placed in a heavily comprehension-based program (one-third of instructional time is devoted to decoding, while the remainder is focused on comprehension) show greater gains on both comprehension and decoding measures than students placed in a program emphasizing decoding (Calfee et al., 1981). In our own research, we have observed that as children learn to approach text to learn new information and make meaning of the text, the array of strategies they use to decode words increases to include not only phonemic analysis but also semantic analysis, focusing on determining what words make sense, and schematic analysis, or the use of background knowledge to figure the text out. These are levels of text analysis that provide children with considerable leverage in reading. We are not advocating that decoding instruction be replaced by comprehension instruction; indeed, there is considerable evidence to support the effectiveness of decoding instruction with young children. Rather, we are advocating that when decoding is practiced, it be subordinated to the primary activity of understanding the text.

Before concluding our discussion of the outcomes of reciprocal teaching, we want to address the issue of motivation. It is important to note that the students involved in our research have often been characterized as displaying motivation problems. In fact, particularly at the middle school and junior high levels, teachers initially have expressed concern that the behavior problems in their classes would preclude the use of an instructional procedure like reciprocal teaching. Contrary to their reservations, the teachers later reported that students generally were highly engaged in the discussions and acquired a newfound appreciation for the responsibilities attending the role of teacher (as they assumed the role of dialogue leader). The responsiveness of the students further supports research suggesting that motivation is fostered when students are taught strategies to regulate their own learning activity (Paris & Oka, 1986) and when this instruction is conducted in social contexts that invite and depend on their engagement.

### Implications for Implementation

Virtually each of the instructional models discussed in this volume represents a departure from current educational practice. Therefore, it is necessary to consider how one goes about introducing, implementing, and sustaining interest in alternative approaches to the education of children at risk. In the districts in which we have conducted research, three factors have been successful in providing sustained interest in reciprocal teaching:

- The use of instructional chaining and teacher-peer collaboration for in-service education
- The alignment of instructional objectives with assessment practices
- An array of incentives

Earlier in this chapter we described the initial staff development model that was used to prepare teachers to engage in reciprocal teaching, including the use of teacher reflection, discussion of theoretical underpinnings, demonstration, modeling, role playing, team teaching, and coaching. Instructional chaining refers to the development of a network of teachers throughout the districts in which reciprocal teaching has been investigated. Remedial-reading and general educators who had the longest history with the research projects conducted in-service sessions, often with the research team. In addition, these teachers were available to provide demonstration lessons in their own as well as in others' classrooms. Before the teachers began this work, their principals attended information sessions; they also attended and participated in the in-service activities. In one district, over a two-year period, approximately 150 teachers in twenty-three buildings participated in dissemination efforts (Palincsar, Ransom, & Derver, 1988/1989).

In addition to the initial staff development, the teachers met in peer support groups to discuss the progress of their classes and to engage in joint problem solving regarding the difficulties they encountered. By sharing transcripts of different discussions of the same story, the teachers learned from one another.

Equally important is the compatibility of assessment instruments with program goals. If teachers continue to be held accountable mainly for the teaching of the basic and isolated skills of reading, it is foolhardy to think that real change will occur in the instructional opportunities offered to children at risk. With the leadership of the remedial reading staff, the district in which the majority of reciprocal teaching research has been conducted developed a new reading achievement instrument with a number of items designed to measure comprehension holistically, as well as to measure the four strategies of reciprocal teaching. We have been struck repeatedly by the importance of an alignment between assessment and instructional goals.

Finally, in addition to providing well-deserved official recognition for the hard work of developing and testing new ideas, districts have provided support in the form of release time for in-service sessions and substitutes to encourage classroom visits among teachers.

## Conclusion

In this chapter we have argued that, regardless of their status as decoders, all students need instruction and guided practice in the comprehension activities that are the bases of effective reading. Equally important, all students should be helped to understand that the primary goal of reading is comprehension and that there are manageable and concrete activities that they can master to improve their comprehension.

We have described an instructional procedure that has been successful in improving both the listening and reading comprehension of students at risk. In reciprocal teaching, students are taught four comprehension-fostering and comprehension-monitoring strategies for understanding text. They are taught these strategies in a context that features dynamic interaction between students and teachers as well as among students, a feature shared by all the instructional models presented in this volume. Teacher expertise is applied to on-line diagnosis, instruction, modeling, and coaching at the same time that students are recruited to assume increasing responsibility for their own learning from text.

The following points are central to this paper:

- All students are entitled to literacy instruction that teaches not only the performative activity of reading (decoding) but also the functional, informational, and knowledge-enhancing uses of reading.
- Strategy instruction is a successful means of teaching students how to experience the multiple goals of reading.

- Strategy instruction is best conducted in a context that maintains the integrity of reading activity and provides guided and authentic experiences in reading for meaning.
- Reciprocal teaching is one model of instruction illustrating how children who have yet to master decoding skills can still engage successfully in meaningful learning from text.
- The support that we routinely advocate for students must also be provided to teachers as they learn strategic concepts and approaches to reading.

## References

Brown, A. L. (1980). Metacognitive development and reading. In R. J. Spiro, B. C. Bruce, & W. F. Brewer (Eds.), *Theoretical issues in reading comprehension* (pp. 453–481). Hillsdale, NJ: Erlbaum.

Brown, A. L., & Palincsar, A. S. (1982). Inducing strategic learning from texts by means of informed, self-control training. *Topics in Learning and Learning Disabilities, 2* (1), 1–17.

Brown, A. L., & Palincsar, A. S. (1989). Guided, cooperative learning and individual knowledge acquisition. In L. Resnick (Ed.), *Knowing, learning, and instruction: Essays in honor of Robert Glaser* (pp. 393–451). Hillsdale, NJ: Erlbaum.

Calfee, R. C., Cazden, C. B., Duran, R. P., Griffin, M. P., Martus, M., & Willis, H. D. (1981). *Designing reading instruction for cultural minorities: The case of the Kamehameha Early Education Program.* Carnegie Commission Report (ERIC # ED215039).

Delpit, L. D. (1988). The silenced dialogue: Power and pedagogy in educating other people's children. *Harvard Educational Review, 58,* 280–298.

Hilliard, A. (1988). Public support for successful instructional practices for at-risk students. In Council of Chief State School Officers, *School success for students at-risk* (pp. 195–208). Orlando, FL: Harcourt, Brace, Jovanovich.

National Commission on Excellence in Education. (1983). *A nation at risk: The imperative for educational reform.* Washington, DC: U.S. Government Printing Office.

Palincsar, A. S., & Brown, A. L. (1984). Reciprocal teaching of comprehension-fostering and comprehension-monitoring activities. *Cognition and Instruction, 1* (2), 117-175.

Palincsar, A. S., & Brown, A. L. (1989). Classroom dialogues to promote self-regulated comprehension. In J. Brophy (Ed.), *Teaching for meaningful understanding and self-regulated learning* (Vol. 1). Greenwich, CT: JAI.

Palincsar, A. S., Ransom, K., & Derver, S. (December 1988/January 1989). Collaborative research and development of reciprocal teaching. *Educational Leadership,* 37-40.

Paris, S. G., & Oka, E. (1986). Self-regulated learning among exceptional children. *Exceptional Children, 53* (2), 103-108.

Phelps, L. W. (1988). *Composition as a human science.* London: Oxford Press.

Poplin, M. S. (1988). The reductionist fallacy in learning disabilities: Replicating the past by reducing the present. *Journal of Learning Disabilities, 21* (7), 389-400.

# COMMENTARY

## *Yolanda N. Padron*

For the past ten years I have been working as a classroom teacher, university professor, and researcher in the field of bilingual education. More specifically, I have taught in inner-city bilingual classrooms and have taught preservice and in-service teachers how to work effectively with bilingual students. I have always been particularly interested in improving the education of linguistically and culturally different students, who have traditionally not been successful in schools. In my work with at-risk limited–English-proficient students, one instructional intervention that I have used in the classroom and have also found to be empirically effective in improving the comprehension of text is reciprocal teaching, the instructional approach described in "Dialogues Promoting Reading Comprehension," the chapter by Palincsar and Klenk.

The purpose of this commentary is to evaluate the applicability of this approach for at-risk students. In the first section, the benefits of reciprocal teaching for at-risk classrooms will be discussed. The second part will examine issues that need to be considered when implementing this program with at-risk students.

### Benefits of Reciprocal Teaching for At-Risk Students

Reciprocal teaching is one of the most frequently cited approaches to cognitive strategy training. The procedure takes place in a cooperative instructional environment where the teacher and students engage in a dialogue. In general, studies of reciprocal teaching have found that strategies can be taught successfully to low-achieving students and that, once these are learned, their use increases reading achievement (Lysynchuk, Pressley, & Vye, 1990; Padron, 1985; Palincsar & Brown, 1984, 1985).

Palincsar and Klenk describe three tensions, or issues, that confront the reading instructor:

- Whether to teach basic or higher-order (critical-literacy) skills
- Whether to teach literacy or let it develop naturally
- Whether to employ reductionist or holistic/constructivist instructional approaches

Reciprocal teaching procedures resolve these tensions in ways that are conducive to promoting the improvement of reading comprehension for disadvantaged students, particularly those who are culturally and linguistically different.

Instead of choosing *between* teaching basic and higher-order thinking skills, reciprocal teaching addresses *both* and provides a method for working on higher-level strategies of comprehension before students are fully able to decode. As the authors point out, the text on which comprehension strategies will be practiced may be read aloud by the teacher as an alternative to silent or oral reading by students. This technique can be very useful when teaching students who participate in Chapter 1 programs.

Students participating in compensatory education programs come primarily from culturally and linguistically different backgrounds (Slavin, 1989). Students in these classrooms, therefore, may experience a great deal of difficulty with the language in most texts. Having the teacher read the text provides students with the opportunity to learn the comprehension strategies of asking questions, summarizing, clarifying, and making predictions without having to wait until they learn to decode. In my work with limited–English-proficient students, I have found that the poorest readers tend to benefit the most from this approach (Padron, 1985). Even though these students may need assistance in decoding, they are able to learn comprehension skills while also learning to decode.

As discussed by Palincsar and Klenk, reciprocal teaching resolves the tension between "natural and taught literacy" in favor of active instruction, in which students become actively involved in teaching. I have found this to be an important benefit when implementing the reciprocal teaching procedure. Students not only assume a share of responsibility for learning but also become genuinely concerned with the teacher's role. As students participate in this strategy instruction approach, they acquire an appreciation for the teacher's role through their own experience as dialogue leader (Padron, 1989). I have found that as a result behavior problems are virtually eliminated.

Finally, I think that the most valuable aspect of reciprocal teaching for at-risk students is its use of a holistic/constructivist approach. Lower-achieving students have often been denied the opportunity to learn higher-level thinking skills because schools have applied a reductionist approach in which students must demonstrate mastery of basic or lower levels of knowledge and skill before they can be taught higher-level skills (Foster, 1989). As indicated by Palincsar and Klenk, the reductionist (discrete skills) perspective is particularly dominant in at-risk classrooms. Reflecting the teaching they have received, students tend to think of reading as being a series of distinct parts rather than a process of developing a strategic conception of the meaning of what they are reading.

In interviews with at-risk students, I have found that when they are asked what good strategies for comprehending text are, they comment, "Looking hard at the words," "Saying words over and over again," "Reading slowly [or carefully]." Interestingly, these comments are similar to those reported by Palincsar and Klenk. In interviews with teachers of at-risk students and in classroom observations, I have found that much of reading instruction for these students focuses more on decoding than on comprehension. Understandably, during my research, students have often questioned why they are being asked about what they do to comprehend text. Students in my studies, for example, have stated, "No one has ever asked me how I read," "Our teacher never asks us to think about how we read."

In my work with Hispanic students, I have found that the teacher-student and student-student interaction provided by reciprocal teaching is particularly beneficial. The Hispanic limited-English-proficient students involved in the reciprocal teaching programs in my research looked forward to reading instruction and were more willing to extend the reading period than were students participating in reading taught from a traditional reductionist perspective. Students seem particularly to enjoy the interactive social environment provided by reciprocal teaching.

## Concerns About Meeting the Needs of At-Risk Students

Although studies using reciprocal teaching procedures continue to find positive results (for example, Lysynchuk et al., 1990), few studies have investigated the use of this procedure with culturally and linguistically different students (Waxman, Padron, & Knight, in press; Padron, 1989). In developing strategy instruction for students who participate in Chapter 1 programs, special consideration should be given to cultural and linguistic differences. Students participating in Chapter 1 programs are generally low-ability students from low-income families. These children may be enrolled in migrant and bilingual education programs. Consequently, Chapter 1 programs usually include a disproportionate percentage of black and Hispanic students (Heller, Holtzman, & Messick, 1982; Slavin, 1989). Furthermore, cultural and linguistic differences should be considered because the successful use of some strategies appears to be influenced not only by age and ability but also by cultural differences (Waxman et al., in press). In this section, I will address several issues that need to be considered when implementing reciprocal teaching with at-risk students.

*Cultural Sensitivity.* Prior knowledge plays a powerful role in comprehension and learning. Students participating in reciprocal teaching are asked to make predictions to activate their prior knowledge. Differences in students' prior knowledge are likely to affect the way they respond to instruction (Stein, Leinhardt, & Bickell, 1989). For example, expert comprehenders generally try to relate new material to personal experience (Campione & Armbruster, 1985). Differences in background knowledge or experience due to cultural differences may be an important source of variation for strategy use and outcomes (Steffenson, Joag-Dev, & Anderson, 1979). A student who has no prior knowledge about the topic being discussed may not be able to apply strategies such as summarizing, predicting, or asking questions (Stein et al., 1989).

In a classroom where students not only possess low ability but also have a culturally different background, strategy instruction thus becomes extremely complex. If students are young, have low ability, or are culturally different, they may not be able to tap prerequisite prior knowledge without help and may need more teacher-directed activity to help them accomplish the linkage.

The lack of prior knowledge for some at-risk students, however, can be dealt with by providing reading materials that concern problems universal to all cultures. That is, texts can be provided that address issues to which all students can relate (for example, "protection from the elements"). The most recent reciprocal teaching research, as described by Palincsar and Klenk, uses this kind of universal theme and develops it over a whole series of related texts. In this way, students have the opportunity to develop the background knowledge they need for effective implementation of comprehension strategies.

Another approach teachers can employ is to use culturally relevant texts. Using this kind of material increases the likelihood that students will have needed background knowledge and also addresses a second key issue—student affect. As a result of their lack of success in school, many at-risk students have a low self-concept and come to believe that they are incapable of learning. Consequently, strategy instruction needs to include techniques that address students' affective needs (Coley & Hoffman, 1990). Although reciprocal teaching has generally been conducted with students who are not highly motivated, the program, as described by Palincsar and Klenk, does not address affective variables explicitly. I have concerns about the suitability of a strategy instruction program that does not address self-concept for at-risk students who are culturally and linguistically different.

I would encourage combining reciprocal teaching approaches with the fostering of students' self-concept by incorporating the students' culture into the classroom. This requires providing reading materials that are culturally relevant, meaning that they

- Include ethnic characters
- Deal with universal issues

- Include settings and experiences with which students can
  identify

By incorporating the students' culture in the classroom environment, teachers can help students feel better about themselves
and their place in school.

*Teacher Training and Reciprocal Teaching.* From the
teachers' point of view, reciprocal teaching procedures are very demanding. Teachers of children who are at risk are presented with a
complex classroom situation. First, teachers must diagnose students'
needs, discriminating the strategies that they do know from those
that they do not know or use inappropriately. In addition, teachers
in these classrooms must deal with different cultural backgrounds.
In many instances, teachers also have to address different levels of
language proficiency. The variety of languages found in these classrooms and the difficulty of assessing the students' level of proficiency
can make diagnosis of strategies difficult. It is easy to confuse lack
of language proficiency with the absence of an appropriate comprehension strategy. Diagnostic instruments to help teachers readily
diagnose students' strategy use need to be developed.

Coupled with the difficulty of diagnosis is the fact that the
majority of instruction in Chapter 1 programs tends to be delivered
by instructional specialists outside the regular classroom setting.
Although these specialists tend to have a higher educational level
than the regular classroom teacher, they also tend to have less experience (Archambault, 1989). In my experience with teachers who
teach in at-risk classrooms, I have found that novice teachers are
often overwhelmed by the complexity of their classroom. To deal
with this complex classroom environment, teachers tend to "problem minimize"—that is, to redefine their goals in a way that reduces
the amount of effort required. Problem minimizing may be more
likely in classrooms where students are disadvantaged and/or culturally and linguistically different. For example, if students have
not been exposed to some of the experiences or prior knowledge
required by the content, teachers may problem minimize by deciding not to teach the content or teaching the content only to "those
who know." As a result, there may be an overemphasis on repetition

of content through drill and practice (Knapp & Shields, 1990; Lehr & Harris, 1988; Levin, 1987).

The manner in which teachers were trained is another important key to the success of reciprocal teaching. Palincsar and Klenk describe extensive in-service preparation for reciprocal teaching in which teachers were exposed to the variety of approaches used in the program (for example, modeling, coaching, role playing, discussions). This is extremely important in training teachers to implement reciprocal teaching, since many teachers have not been exposed to strategy training procedures. Furthermore, as indicated by Palincsar and Klenk, many teachers do not believe that strategy instruction is beneficial, particularly for low-achieving students. Teacher preparation may need to address teachers' beliefs that these students are not able to benefit from strategy instruction. I have encountered teachers who have commented, "This type of instruction may be fine for high-ability students but not for my low-ability students." Demonstration of the effectiveness of strategy instruction for low-ability students is needed to motivate these teachers to make the effort to acquire and practice reciprocal teaching techniques.

Finally, teacher training in the implementation of reciprocal teaching must be carefully orchestrated. Palincsar and Klenk point out that for many teachers reciprocal teaching is a new and different approach from anything that they have been exposed to in their teacher preparation programs. Teachers, for the most part, have been trained with the direct instructional approach in which the teacher has a dominant role. Reciprocal teaching calls for teachers to assume a very different, "coaching" role.

Training teachers who teach at-risk students in a reciprocal teaching procedure may require more than training in how to implement strategy instruction. I have suggested that teachers also receive instruction on how to address the cultural and linguistic differences represented in their classrooms. For example, teachers may need to participate in cultural awareness programs. In this type of training, teachers can be provided with information about the students' cultures. Learning about these cultures can help eliminate some of the stereotypical beliefs that linguistically and culturally different students cannot learn.

## Conclusion

This commentary has addressed several issues in the use of reciprocal teaching with at-risk students. First, the suitability of the program for at-risk students was addressed. Considering the evidence of the positive effects that reciprocal teaching has had in increasing students' reading comprehension, this procedure appears to be a promising one for use with at-risk students.

The research on cognitive strategies strongly suggests that the approach can provide a useful technique for enhancing reading comprehension of at-risk students. Giving students models of appropriate cognitive reading strategies and practice in applying them can help students become better readers. Postponing instruction in the use of cognitive reading strategies may mean that children develop habits that will make later comprehension instruction difficult (Wilson & Anderson, 1985).

Second, the suitability of reciprocal teaching for at-risk populations was assessed. The teaching approach appears thoroughly compatible with efforts to incorporate students' culture in the classroom and to foster positive self-concepts. However, these issues have been given little attention in many implementation efforts. To make reciprocal teaching more appropriate for disadvantaged students, cultural sensitivity and carefully structured staff development procedures are crucial.

In conclusion, further research is needed in designing instructional programs that address not only the cognitive needs of low-achieving students but also their self-concepts. Such instruction would help ensure that students not only acquire an acceptable level of achievement but also develop the attitudes and thinking skills that are necessary for academic success.

## References

Archambault, F. X. (1989). Instructional setting and other design features of compensatory education programs. In R. E. Slavin, N. L. Karweit, & N. A. Madden (Eds.), *Effective programs for students at risk* (pp. 220–263). Boston: Allyn & Bacon.

Campione, J., & Armbruster, B. (1985). Acquiring information from texts: An analysis of four approaches. In J. Segal, S. Chipman, & R. Glaser (Eds.), *Thinking and learning skills: Relating instruction to research* (Vol. 1, pp. 317–359). Hillsdale, NJ: Erlbaum.

Coley, J. D., & Hoffman, D. M. (1990). Overcoming learned helplessness in at risk readers. *Journal of Reading, 33* (7), 497–502.

Foster, G. E. (1989). Cultivating the thinking skills of low achievers: A matter of equity. *Journal of Negro Education, 58,* 461–467.

Heller, L., Holtzman, W., & Messick, S. (Eds.). (1982). *Placing children in special education: A strategy for equity.* Washington, DC: National Academy of Sciences Press.

Knapp, M. S., & Shields, P. M. (1990). Reconceiving academic instruction for the children of poverty. *Phi Delta Kappan, 71,* 753–758.

Lehr, J. B., & Harris, H. W. (1988). *At risk, low-achieving students in the classroom.* Washington, DC: National Education Association.

Levin, H. M. (1987). Accelerated schools for disadvantaged students. *Educational Leadership, 44* (6), 19–21.

Lysynchuk, L., Pressley, M., & Vye, N. (1990). Reciprocal teaching improves standardized reading comprehension performance of poor comprehenders. *The Elementary School Journal, 90,* 470–484.

Padron, Y. N. (1985). *Utilizing cognitive reading strategies to improve English reading comprehension of Spanish-speaking low-achieving students.* Unpublished doctoral dissertation, University of Houston.

Padron, Y. N. (1989, April). The effect of strategy instruction on bilingual students' cognitive strategy use in reading. Paper presented at the annual meeting of the American Educational Research Association, San Francisco.

Palincsar, A., & Brown, A. (1984). Reciprocal teaching of comprehension-fostering and comprehension-monitoring activities. *Cognition and Instruction, 1,* 117–175.

Palincsar, A., & Brown, A. (1985). Reciprocal teaching: A means to a meaningful end. In J. Osborn, P. Wilson, & R. C. Anderson (Eds.), *Reading education: Foundations for a literate America* (pp. 299–310). Lexington, MA: Lexington.

Slavin, R. E. (1989). Students at risk of school failure: The problem and its dimensions. In R. E. Slavin, N. L. Karweit, & N. A. Madden

(Eds.), *Effective programs for students at risk* (pp. 3–19). Boston: Allyn & Bacon.

Steffenson, M., Joag-Dev, C., & Anderson, R. (1979). A cross-cultural perspective on reading comprehension. *Reading Research Quarterly, 15,* 10–29.

Stein, M., Leinhardt, G., & Bickell, W. (1989). Instructional issues for teaching students at risk. In R. E. Slavin, N. L. Karweit, & N. A. Madden (Eds.), *Effective programs for students at risk* (pp. 145–194). Boston: Allyn & Bacon.

Waxman, H. C., Padron, Y. N., & Knight, S. L. (in press). Risks associated with students' limited cognitive mastery. In M. Wang, H. Walberg, & M. Reynolds (Eds.), *Handbook on special education.* Oxford: Pergamon.

Wilson, P., & Anderson, R. (1985). Reading comprehension and school learning. In J. Osborn, P. Wilson, & R. Anderson (Eds.), *Reading education: Foundations for a literate America* (pp. 319–328). Lexington, MA: Lexington.

# 5

# Teaching Writing to Students at Risk for Academic Failure

*Mary Bryson and Marlene Scardamalia*

IN NORTH AMERICA, WRITING IS INCREASINGLY LIKELY TO BE CONCEP-tualized as a learning tool that should constitute an integral part of the school curriculum at each stage in a student's development. Willinsky (1990) refers to this view of writing as "the new literacy" and suggests that this pedagogical model represents a major shift from the way that educators have traditionally defined and implemented writing instruction. One might venture to say that in enlightened educational environments, students are encouraged to "write to learn" through a set of intellectual activities that integrate curricular strands rather than to "learn to write" as an isolated practice engaged in for its own sake. Writing to learn is about composing texts in rich social contexts for personally defined goals—texts that actively involve students in coming to terms with saying something meaningful, irrespective of whether the particular task involves constructing a reflective argument, telling a story, composing a poem, or describing something interesting to a pen pal.

Needless to say, any specific discussion of "writing" means calling attention to a restricted range of activities and the resulting products, both of which vary considerably across cultures and historical periods (De Castell & Luke, 1983). In this chapter, we focus on a particular kind of writing that we refer to as "epistemic," the object of which is both to inquire into a particular topic and to familiarize and/or to persuade one or more readers of the fruits of an investigation. Such tasks might include descriptive, opinion, or informative types of assignments. Evidence abounds that there is a huge gap between current pedagogical intentions with regard to epistemic writing and their execution in classroom instruction (Applebee, 1981). In a similar vein, large-scale evaluation of students' writing indicate that, by secondary school, only a minority of normally achieving learners acquire a level of expertise in written composition that extends beyond functional literacy (Kirsch & Jungeblut, 1986).

For students deemed "at risk for academic failure" (for example, learning disabled, minority, or poor children), the picture is even more bleak. Writing instruction for chronic low achievers typically focuses on techniques for remediating so-called basic skills such as spelling, grammar, and handwriting. A central assumption made by many educators of low-achieving students is that the acquisition of so-called low-level text production skills is a necessary prerequisite to the acquisition of composing skills associated with writing as a powerful tool for personal learning, such as problem-solving strategies and rhetorical knowledge. A direct consequence of this "bottom-up" approach to writing instruction is that the achievement gap increases as students move through school, and at-risk learners become progressively more disadvantaged because of a systematic lack of instruction in the higher-order skills that underlie epistemic writing. Accordingly, a more equitable and socially conscious use of the term *at risk* would be to characterize those learning environments that are at risk of failing to provide a substantial proportion of students with equitable access to an empowering and successful educational experience.

In this chapter, we outline the cognitive concomitants of an expert model of writing as "knowledge transforming" and a novice model of writing as "knowledge telling." This account provides a theoretical framework for a consideration of the particular needs of at-risk writers and the pedagogical implications that stem from an approach to writing that emphasizes the significance of agency in expert writers and, therefore, the importance of developing students' rhetorical competence, providing dynamic social contexts, and providing explicit cognitive supports for novice writers. We elaborate on the general instructional implications by describing two specific intervention studies from our research program. The main goal of both the M.U.S.E. (Monitoring Understanding and Strategic Execution) and the CSILE (Computer-Supported Intentional Learning Environments) programs is to foster agency in immature learners through the provision of cognitively based instruction in, modeling of, and support for the construction of knowledge-transforming types of composing strategies.

In concluding, we will reflect on the sociocultural implications that stem from shifting control of the learning process from teacher to student. We also discuss the significance of key features of our specific model of composition instruction for accomplishing a wider goal—namely, the development of an empowering pedagogy for at-risk learners.

### Writing as Problem Solving: Insights from Novice and Expert Models of Composing

Commonsense wisdom suggests that, for novices and experts alike, written composition is a difficult and complex task. Perhaps writing is so demanding because it is a complex task best addressed as a problem-solving endeavor (that is, with a well-regulated application of strategies, subskills, and appropriate knowledge) but is, in essence, a task in which no problem is given. (An earlier version of the description of these models appeared in Bryson, Bereiter, Scardamalia, and Joram, 1991.) The theme, story line, or argument must be constructed by the writer through cycles of deliberate knowledge-building sessions. Research on thinking during composing, however, suggests that experts' writing problems are qualitatively distinct from those faced by novices.

Thinking-aloud protocols analyzed in research on the composing processes of expert writers (Flower & Hayes, 1980) reveal a tremendous investment of mental effort in the elaboration, coordination, and execution of complex goals and subgoals, such as how to shape content for a particular audience, how to express conceptual intentions in the language of prose, or how to construct a catchy title. In stark contrast, novice writers' thinking-aloud protocols reveal that, given a writing assignment, they set to work and proceed directly toward their goal in a forward-acting manner. False starts and uncertainties as to how to proceed are rare. The most common difficulty faced by novice writers is knowing what to do when they run out of things to say about a given topic (Bereiter & Scardamalia, 1987).

To view writing as problem solving, therefore, is to view it in a somewhat paradoxical light. That is, not all writers view composition as a task that requires the kind of effortful and strategic use of cognitive resources that we commonly associate with problem-solving processes. The paradox can be largely removed by adopting the premise that expert and nonexpert writers are solving different problems. This premise is reasonable because of the ill-structured nature of writing problems. In particular, the goal in writing tasks is usually defined in only general terms, leaving the specification up to the writer. Consequently, writers who are ostensibly engaged in carrying out the same assignment can be pursuing radically different goals.

We have found it useful in our research on writing instruction to describe the thinking processes that characterize novices and experts using two contrasting models of composing (for more details, see Scardamalia & Bereiter, 1985). The "knowledge-telling" model avoids many of the problems of writing and, even for relatively young writers, makes efficient use of highly practiced skills. The "knowledge-transforming" model contains a dynamic that tends to escalate the complexity of writing problems. It is important to note that there are, undoubtedly, many models of composing in addition to the two that we have chosen to describe. Our goal here is to highlight clear differences in the underlying mental operations that appear to be accessible to immature, as compared with mature, writers. The fundamental purpose for including a section on the ways in which novice and expert writers seem to think during composing is to provide a theoretical foundation for our instructional recommendations.

*Knowledge Telling as a Problem-Reducing Strategy.* Novice writers, whose thinking-aloud protocols show little or no evidence of planning or concern about main ideas or form, start writing almost instantly and proceed about as rapidly as they can move the pencil. According to the knowledge-telling model (Bereiter & Scardamalia, 1987), novice writers follow a procedure that enables them to reduce the problems of writing to a routine procedure for "telling what one knows about the topic" (Scardamalia & Bereiter, 1986, p. 792). According to this model (see Figure 5.1), knowledge tellers, once provided with a writing assignment (for example, "Is television a good influence on children?"), begin automatically to retrieve knowledge using two kinds of cues. Topic identifiers (for example, "television shows," "good aspects," and "children") serve as cues that prime associated concepts. Discourse knowledge provides a second type of cue. For instance, a writer whose concept of an opinion essay consisted of "say what you believe about the question and give reasons" would use "say what you believe" and "reasons" as retrieval cues, which, in combination with topic identifiers, would be used to retrieve from memory ideas relevant to defending an opinion about children and television. Knowledge tellers typically transcribe information as it is called up from long-term memory, or in short-circuit "think-say" cycles, rather than transforming it to fit rhetorical and more broadly based content goals.

Exhibit 5.1 is a segment of a sixth-grade student's thinking-aloud protocol (from a study conducted by Paris, 1986) and illustrates the forward-moving nature of knowledge telling in response to general topic and discourse structure cues. (Content statements are italicized.)

The overall picture of the composing process exhibited by this sixth-grade writer during thinking aloud is characteristic of the kinds of content-based thinking typically manifested by novice writers as predicted by the knowledge-telling model. The predominant activity is generating topic- and genre-appropriate content. The knowledge teller does not represent the task of composing as a goal-directed one in which epistemological and rhetorical problems must be jointly resolved. Rather, the novice writer's greatest difficulty seems to be that of accessing a sufficient quantity of relevant knowledge to satisfy length and genre requirements. Problem-solving episodes are infrequent in knowledge tellers' thinking-

**Figure 5.1. Structure of the Knowledge-Telling Model.**

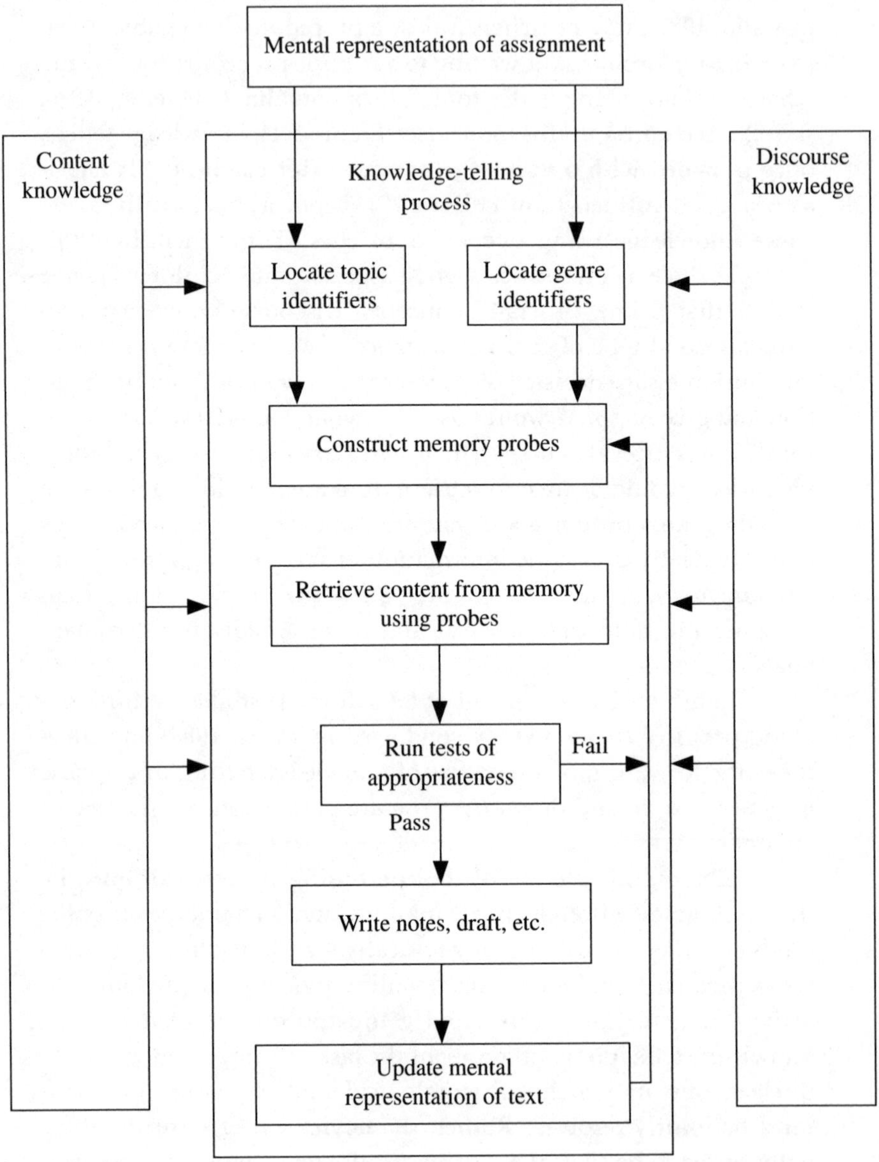

*Source:* Bereiter & Scardamalia, 1987.

**Exhibit 5.1. Segment from a Novice Writer's Thinking-Aloud Protocol.**

---

*I think it is good and bad for children to watch television because I like the cartoons and some sad movies.*

*But I like good movies that come on TV because they are good to watch.*

*But usually it is good to watch comedy shows because they are very funny.*

*They keep you laughing almost every time you watch them.*

*It is good to watch interesting movies.*

*Interesting shows like "Young and the Restless," "All My Children," and "General Hospital" . . . because it's sometimes exciting.*

*But pay TV has some very good movies like* Splash, Police Academy, Romancing the Stone.

*But sometimes I watch sports.*

*My favorite sport is baseball.*

*I like football, but not that much.*

*I hate golf and tennis and all the other stuff except soccer.*

*But I usually watch wrestling at my friend's house because it's kind of exciting, and I like the way they fight.*

---

aloud protocols because the task routine manages to bypass content-related as well as rhetorical problems.

***Writing to Learn, or Expert Composing as Knowledge Transforming.*** There are numerous testimonials from writers indicating that writing itself plays an important role in the development of their understanding (Murray, 1978). Henry Miller suggested that "writing, like life itself, is a voyage of discovery." In a recent interview, Sam Shepard said, "The great thing about writing is that in the course of going after it, it teaches you something. You start out thinking you know something about it, but then you discover you hardly know anything. And the more you do it, the more things begin to inform you about where you're going" (Sessums, 1988, p. 78). Likewise, Robert Frost reported that "I have never started a poem whose end I knew. Writing a poem is discovering."

Scardamalia and Bereiter (1985) have described the expert writer's composing processes as a dialectical interplay between content problems (what to say) and rhetorical problems (how to say it). These authors argue that expert writing involves successfully managing the coordination of both kinds of problems. Content problems are problems of the writer's own knowledge and beliefs and rhetorical problems are problems related to achieving the writer's purposes. Exhibit 5.2, a segment from an expert writer's thinking-aloud protocol (adapted from Paris, 1986), illustrates how a writer wrestles with both kinds of problems and how the two kinds of problems interact. (Content statements are italicized.)

In the knowledge-transforming model of expert writing (see Figure 5.2), problems arising in the "rhetorical space" are often translated into problems requiring solution in the "content space." New decisions arrived at in the content space also create new problems in the rhetorical space, and so on in a dialectical fashion. The result often will be that by the end of the composing process, both

**Exhibit 5.2. Segment from an Expert Writer's Thinking-Aloud Protocol.**

---

So, I'm looking for examples of programs that could be argued . . . that could be argued were good influences on children.

Now I know I already don't believe this, but *"Sesame Street" comes to mind as a possible good influence.*

And I find myself trying to work it out.

So I'm going to say . . .

I'm making up two columns here . . . and just trying to respond to my own thought processes.

*"Sesame Street" jumped to mind as a good influence.*

So I guess what I need is three columns here. . . . I need a column just for the specific and the example. And I can work back and forth between columns.

*"Sesame Street" is good because it could be argued that it educates.*

*And it educates in a specific way . . . giving children basic information, ABCs, etc.*

But immediately when I say it's a good influence, I have reservations about it.

Now I'm just trying to clarify for myself the reservations about it. . . .

---

**Figure 5.2. Structure of the Knowledge-Transforming Model.**

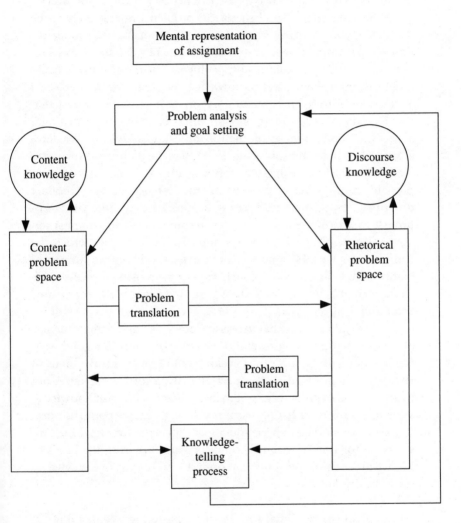

*Source:* Bereiter & Scardamalia, 1987.

the writer's ideas and the nature of the written product have evolved in unexpected ways—hence the experience of writing as discovery.

Solving content and rhetorical problems interactively is the distinctive characteristic of the knowledge-transforming model of writing. Thinking-aloud protocols generated by expert writers suggest that significant composing problems emerge from this back-and-forth interplay between knowledge and goals. As we described at the beginning of this section, expert writers often suggest that they experience a profound sense of "discovery," or "new learning," as a direct consequence of their composing activities. We have argued elsewhere (Bryson et al., 1991) that the dialectical processes that underlie a knowledge-transforming approach to composing are probably responsible for the learning that can occur as a by-product of writing. In contrast to "writing as dialectic," a more linear approach to writing (such as is often recommended in composition textbooks) would settle all the content issues first, after which the composition would be planned and carried out in a straightforward manner. But, as we have noted, expert composing processes are characterized by recursion, so that planning keeps being reactivated throughout.

It would appear that access to knowledge and verbal fluency, although incorporating several necessary conditions for good writing, are not sufficient for the development of an expertlike mode of writing. The most difficult aspect of writing for the novice is not to gain access to knowledge but to know what to do with knowledge so as to transform a list of disconnected facts into a powerful idea, an evocative story, or an elaborate conceptual structure. Thus, instruction for novice writers should focus on fostering the kinds of higher-order thinking skills that underlie epistemic, or knowledge-transforming, writing.

### General Instructional Implications: Fostering a Shift from Knowledge Telling to Knowledge Transforming

We have described two different composing models: writing as a form of knowledge telling and as a process of knowledge transformation. We used the categories of "novice" and "expert" to differentiate between immature and mature writers. However, this kind of analysis raises the question of how a student might best be facilitated in making a shift toward a more advanced kind of composing. We do not want to be satisfied with having "labeled" a student but would like to make use of these models to promote more "expertlike" thinking in novice writers.

Results from instructional studies conducted by members of the Ontario Institute for Studies in Education (OISE) Writing Research Group (for an overview, see Bereiter & Scardamalia, 1987) suggest that several factors are involved in enhancing expertlike composing, as follows. We describe each component separately and discuss how it was incorporated into the design and evaluation of a specific writing environment called M.U.S.E. M.U.S.E. was designed to teach tenth-grade normally achieving and reading-disabled students strategies for sustaining independent reflective inquiry during the composition of argument-type texts (Bryson, 1989).

In the assessment study of the M.U.S.E. environment, our subjects were thirty-one students in two tenth-grade classes—one for normally achieving students and one for severely reading-disabled students. The intervention for students in the experimental group included strategy-based instruction, modeling of expertlike thinking, and procedural facilitation. The intervention for students in the control group involved instruction in the structural features of good arguments (beliefs and reasons on both sides, facts/descriptions/examples, and conclusions). There were ten instructional sessions for students in both groups over a five-week period. Sessions were seventy minutes long. Posttest texts written by both normally achieving and reading-disabled experimental students were rated as significantly more reflective and structurally more complex than those written at pretest. Likewise, posttest analyses of control students' texts and thinking-aloud protocols revealed no gains as a result of instruction in the structural features of good arguments.

Below we describe the major theoretical principles driving the design of M.U.S.E. and the way in which each principle has been applied.

### Explicit Strategy-Focused Instruction

Analyses of experts' thinking during composing reveal that they are using specific higher-order strategies to permit an active and effortful approach to writing. These strategies can be made explicit and taught directly to novice writers to foster a more expertlike approach to composing. Novice writers seem to lack these "heuristics for writing"—that is, executive strategies for making use of what is already known to extend current knowledge. For example, Scardamalia, Bereiter, and Steinbach (1984) taught reflective writing strategies to sixth-grade students and included instruction in a simplified version of dialectical reasoning. This was explained to students as "a matter of trying to 'rise above' opposing arguments by preserving what is valid on both sides" (p. 181). Posttest results revealed that the experimental students' compositions were rated as significantly more reflective than those generated by control-group students. In an intervention study aimed at fostering expertlike revision strategies, Scardamalia and Bereiter (1983) taught students to stop after composing individual sentences in order to execute a routine of evaluating generated text, diagnosing problems, choosing a tactic, and carrying out any revision decided on. Results revealed that students' revisions improved significantly from pre- to posttest in terms of both the kinds of thinking exhibited during composing and the rated quality of texts.

Teaching expertlike strategies to novice writers probably is not sufficient to bridge the gap between knowledge-telling and knowledge-transforming composing behaviors. Purposive skilled writing seems most likely to be learned in dynamic social contexts that provide elaborate support for and modeling of expertlike composing. Nonetheless, some kind of instruction in expertlike thinking processes during composing is probably a necessary component of an instructional program.

*M.U.S.E. Application.* Students received instruction in a set of reflective operations as well as in strategies for argument construction. The strategies were divided into two main categories:

- Problem-solving strategies: (1) plan, (2) identify confusions, and (3) notice opportunities for new learning
- Verbal-reasoning strategies: (1) build an argument, (2) challenge its assumptions, (3) elaborate statements, (4) search for additional ideas, and (5) put it together

*Procedural Facilitation*

To foster more complex kinds of thinking in novice writers, it has proven critical to provide students with support for carrying out more demanding kinds of thinking. Scardamalia and Bereiter (1986) suggest that

> in procedural facilitation, help is of a nonspecific sort, related to the students' cognitive processes, but not responsive to the actual substance of what the student is thinking or writing. Help consists of supports intended to enable students to carry out more complex composing processes by themselves. . . . It can do little good to direct students' attention to their goals for composition if they are not consciously able to represent such goals. There is substantial evidence that procedural facilitation can increase the level of sophistication of the composing processes students carry out within the limits imposed by the kinds of mental representations they construct [p. 796].

*M.U.S.E. Application.* To take over some of the information-processing load imposed by presenting students with a wholly new set of thinking strategies during argument construction, we provided "thinking prompts" for each of the target strategies. Prompts took the form of sentence openers printed on cards. For example, a student who had decided to get some help to challenge an argument in favor of a particular resolution could get a "challenge" prompt, such as, "Yes, I can understand the argument, but what about . . ." or "A person who would be affected negatively by my argument could say that . . ." Students were encouraged to incorporate the sentence openers into their thinking during argument construction.

*Modeling Thought*

Expertlike thinking during writing is usually invisible to students, who typically are able only to view finished products that reveal none of the cognitive activities behind their composition. Modeling expertlike thinking during composing has proven to be a powerful instructional technique for helping novices to acquire more effective kinds of writing strategies.

*M.U.S.E. Application.* Significant portions of the instructional sessions in the evaluation study of the M.U.S.E. environment were devoted to the modeling of expertlike composing strategies, first by the instructor and then by students. This provided novice writers with the opportunity to witness and then to practice a higher level of argument construction than we had observed at pretesting.

The M.U.S.E. study provides us with an example of the kind of learning environment that can encourage novice writers to engage in a kind of thinking during composing that is closer to our expert model—a model of writing-to-learn processes. In this study, a cognitively based analysis of students' thinking during composing suggested that both normally achieving and reading-disabled students tended to conceptualize writing tasks in terms of telling what they knew about a particular topic, rather than thinking of writing as an opportunity to reflectively challenge their preconceptions.

The posttest results suggest that it is possible to foster reflective problem solving during composing by providing immature writers with a combination of strategies instruction and a supportive, socially collaborative environment. Novice writers need to learn how to think as "real" writers do—that is, in relation to a given writing task, to conceptualize and deal with interesting problems whose resolution during composing affords possibilities for discovery.

The results from our M.U.S.E. study offer potentially valuable insights into the kind of instruction that can effectively foster expertlike thinking in students who are least likely to demonstrate strategic control over composition processes. Clearly, the particular problems faced by students deemed at risk for academic failure are not necessarily comparable to those faced by students labeled as having a learning disability. However, Ysseldyke, Algozzine, Shinn, and McGue (1982) found negligible psychometric differences between groups of students identified as learning disabled and low achievers. In fact, all such labels probably have much more to do with institutionally constructed procedures for categorizing and streaming students who appear to have serious difficulties with schoolwork than with genuinely distinct categories of individuals. Thus, it is plausible to infer that instruction that was successful in improving learning-disabled students' written products and in enhancing their composing processes might also be valuable for students at risk for academic failure.

### Specific Implications for Writing Instruction with At-Risk Students

To date, studies of so-called novice writers have typically used normally achieving school- or college-age students to construct models of immature composing strategies (for example, Scardamalia & Bereiter, 1986; Flower & Hayes, 1980). This practice raises a question concerning the suitability of such models for understanding the particularly intransigent problems exhibited by students at risk for academic failure.

Traditionally, educators have used a deficit model to conceptualize the writing problems presented by so-called educationally disadvantaged, underprepared, or basic student writers. This approach focuses on the inability of at-risk students to cope with the demands of literacy tasks as they are constituted within conventional, mainstream educational environments. Remediation usually consists of breaking down complex writing tasks, such as composing a persuasive letter, into two levels of ability that are structured linearly from lower-level, or "basic," skills like spelling and punctuation to higher-level, or more demanding, intellectual processes like synthesis or critical analysis. The main assumption here is that students need to acquire facility with basic skills before they can tackle the intellectually more demanding aspects of complex tasks. Writing instruction for at-risk students that is designed using a two-level approach to curriculum sequencing effectively prevents at-risk students from receiving instruction in higher-order thinking skills because they spend almost all their time attempting to master the basics. As Griffin and Cole (1984) suggest:

The widespread use of this educational strategy has, where proper management techniques are used, brought children up to grade level on "the basics" but failed to boost them into the higher-order activity. Widely discussed as the 3rd–4th grade watershed, the heavy focus on level 1 skills seems to help children do only what they were trained to do in a rote way; there is no "transfer" of the achievement up into the "higher level" of learning. A number of minority children get stuck at level 1: They are not exposed to practice with activities at higher levels of the curriculum when they do not demonstrate mastery of the "basics." This failing is then attributed to the children's own lack of ability for the "higher" skills, which they were neither tested on nor taught [p. 207].

There is no good reason for assuming that at-risk students are uniquely disadvantaged in the domain of higher-order thinking or that remediation in basic skills will help them to become better writers. A more plausible assumption is that educationally prepared students come to school having learned more than unprepared students about the kinds of literate uses of language that schools validate.

Accordingly, we might wish to think of at-risk students as novice writers who are uniquely unfamiliar with the conventions of standard written English and who develop, with a cumulative record of in-school failure, dysfunctional coping strategies that interfere with the acquisition of more sophisticated composing processes (see Hull & Rose, 1989; Perl, 1979; Rose, 1980).

Studies of literacy instruction offered in Chapter 1 programs reveal that typically students at risk for academic failure receive (1) less classroom reading instruction than nonparticipants and (2) teaching that concentrates on basic, or low-level, skills rather than on higher-order thinking strategies (Allington & Franzen, 1989). This kind of inequitable pedagogy increases the achievement gap over time between the haves and the have-nots in a purportedly democratic educational system.

Students who are underprepared for dealing with the kinds

of literacy tasks that are the mainstay of traditional schooling require intervention on several different levels, as discussed below.

*Learning Literate Uses of Language.* Sociolinguistic studies provide a growing body of evidence that at-risk students lack experience with the uses of language that characterize academic literacy (Heath, 1983; Shaughnessy, 1977). French sociologist Pierre Bourdieu has argued that unless the exclusionary aspects of language are explicitly attended to in educational contexts, literacy instruction serves to entrench or "reproduce" existing social inequities (Bourdieu & Passeron, 1977). Epistemic writing, as we have described it in this chapter, demands a certain relationship to language that can exclude students who have either a low socioeconomic or a minority cultural background. As Hull and Rose (1989) have argued, underprepared students need to learn a wholly new, unfamiliar, and intimidating kind of language to express themselves as writers in academic composition tasks. These authors suggest that at-risk students benefit from opportunities to imitate and to practice using kinds of discourse with which they are unfamiliar. Accordingly, it seems likely that basic writers would benefit from instruction in the kinds of literate uses of language, or genres, that characterize academic writing.

*Making Visible the Invisible: Providing a Window on Expertlike Thinking.* The foundation of epistemic writing is the subordination of text-making activities to learning goals. Expertlike writing involves deliberate, reflective, strategic kinds of thinking directed toward extending the cutting edge of one's own competence by representing and solving problems that require the generation of new knowledge. This complex web of higher-order thinking processes is "in the head" and hence largely invisible to the immature writer, who sees only a polished finished product. As Collins, Brown, and Newman (1990) suggest, "Standard pedagogical practices render key aspects of expertise invisible to students. In particular, too little attention is paid to the processes that experts engage in to use or acquire knowledge in carrying out complex or realistic tasks. . . . Few resources are devoted to higher-order problem solving activities that require students to actively integrate and appropriately apply subskills and conceptual knowledge" (p. 2).

Evidence from cognitively based instructional studies in diverse domains suggests that low-achieving students benefit from opportunities both to model and to practice and appropriate expert-like thinking skills. A key factor in studies that have provided encouraging results in teaching higher-order thinking to low-achieving students has been the provision of some kind of support, or "scaffolding," during the learning of a new approach to a familiar task. The traditional model of learning, which focuses on the activities of a decontextualized learner who develops toward states of increasing autonomy, essentially independently of any social network, has largely been supplanted by a model that features learning as a distinctively social process wherein responsibilities are negotiated, or "distributed," between two or more individuals. The provision of cognitive scaffolds for immature learners ensures that students at different levels of expertise have access to the kinds of support required for functioning at an optimal level.

***Fostering Active Engagement in Learning Through Writing.*** Dewey (1916), Whitehead (1929), and more recent authors (for example, Bereiter & Scardamalia, 1990; Collins et al., 1990) have condemned the way in which conventional educational environments manufacture meaning for pupils by presenting learners with ready-made knowledge in isolation from any kind of meaningful context and by artificially motivating students using some variation of the "carrot and stick" method. Clearly, writing activities that are not engaged in for any particular communicative or epistemological purpose are unlikely to result in active engagement of higher-order thinking processes. As Vygotsky (1978) suggested, "Teaching should be organized in such a way that reading and writing are necessary for something. If they are used only to write official greetings to the staff or whatever the teacher thinks up, then the exercise will be purely mechanical and may soon bore the child; his activity will not be manifest in his writing and his budding personality will not grow" (p. 117).

***Voices, Visibility, and Empowerment for At-Risk Students.*** Students who are labeled "at risk for academic failure" undoubtedly constitute a diverse group, including students whose cultural heritage is not consistent with the sociocultural context of mainstream schooling as well as students who are unable to achieve acceptable levels of literacy for a variety of causes, none of which allow one to advance a deficiency model of underachievement. It seems important, therefore, to suggest that we undoubtedly need to expand our notions about what counts as "literacy." We need to question and to deconstruct the kinds of arbitrary constraints that historically have tended to exclude minority students from effectively participating in school-based literacy activities. Griffin and Cole (1984) conducted an intervention study with minority students in which learners wrote to pen pals and composed rap texts in collaborative sessions using microcomputers. The overlap between the genres used in this study and the students' linguistic background resulted in high levels of engagement and considerable effortful, strategic thinking during composing.

Likewise, majority-culture educators need to recognize that our texts, lectures, and instructional programs have tended, historically, to take up a lot more "space on the shelves" than has the work of minority-culture educators. As Lisa Delpit (1988) argues, "The dilemma is not really in the debate over instructional methodology, but rather in communicating across cultures and in addressing the more fundamental issue of power, of whose voice gets to be heard in determining what is best for poor children and children of color. Will black teachers and parents continue to be silenced by the very forces that claim to 'give voice' to our children?" (p. 296). Minority-culture education theorists (for example, Lee, 1991; Reyes, in press) are critical of the indiscriminate uses of majority-culture pedagogical strategies with minority-culture students and have described the characteristics of learning environments that are likely to be more empowering for "at-risk" students.

### Literate Cultures Accessible to At-Risk Students

Identification of the knowledge-telling and knowledge-transforming strategies has made it possible to predict results from instructional interventions (Bryson, 1989; Scardamalia & Paris, 1985) and suggests radically different procedures for instruction. If the goal of schooling is knowledge reporting, then the knowledge-telling strategy has considerable advantages. It is fast and efficient, and it provides teachers with a quick look at what students know. However, if the goal is knowledge advancement—as the knowledge-transforming approach suggests it should be—then a knowledge-building culture must be put in place. The focus must be on advancing knowledge, not just on carrying out a process approach to writing. M.U.S.E. simulates more literate cultures through use of procedural facilitations and instructional interventions that give students access to knowledge-transforming operations and models of expert performance. The broader challenge is to provide long-term social supports for such processes.

We believe that new knowledge media will be instrumental in providing higher levels of agency for children in knowledge building (Scardamalia & Bereiter, 1991, in press; Scardamalia, Bereiter, McLean, Swallow, & Woodruff, 1989). There should be benefits for all students, with unique advantages for students at risk. Our prototype system is known as CSILE—Computer-Supported Intentional Learning Environments. It is a networked, hypermedia environment, with writing, illustrating, reading, and commenting as integral processes. A communal database is the centerpiece of the system, and students are engaged in the social construction of knowledge in areas of science, history, social studies, art, and so on. Students are authors of public-domain material and are engaged in interchanges that help them elaborate ideas and build knowledge. Simple searching and commenting features provide access to one another's contributions, and students are encouraged to work collaboratively. The emphasis is on knowledge advancement rather than writing.

The environment is designed to be accessible to epistemologically naive students as well as to students who are barely able to produce text. The environments are seductive, bringing students into increasingly sophisticated social and knowledge networks. For example, a student may produce a simple graphical note, which may look like a scribble to other people but which the child wants to preserve. Thus comes the challenge of storing the note, so a label is needed—perhaps just an arbitrary letter or two. Once the note is stored, simple search routines enable the student to retrieve it. The student does not even have to recall the label but simply must recognize it from a list of entries. This same list gives the student an overview of what others are doing, and through simply placing a cursor on a label the student can retrieve her or his own notes or view notes of others. The student can then browse the database and even copy into personal space parts of notes generated by others and use these as building blocks for subsequent notes. Each step is relatively easy and rewarding. We have found that the notion of labeling a note, having it disappear, then being able to retrieve it is not simply fun—it is a real boon to early literacy. Students come to realize that it is easier to find a note if they label it effectively; further, others are more likely to find it helpful. Each note is stored automatically with the author's name and can be retrieved by searching author fields. Accordingly, even the youngest of students soon learn to read the names of their peers. Through these simple mechanisms they are brought into contact with notes more sophisticated than they themselves can produce, or possibly even read, and are provided with models of work across a wide spectrum of ability levels. Thus they get ideas for future notes. They are also able to link notes to organizing frameworks and thus become part of a group contributing notes within some more comprehensive framework. As coauthors, they are party to more complex ideas than they produce on their own.

The collaborative context established for knowledge building in CSILE has led to the use of comments as an important means of communication. When a comment is linked to a note, the author is notified. This provides a rewarding and motivating context for student interchanges. Less able students engage in commenting as much as the more able students, and the more and less able students interact with each other. We have been struck with the quality of students' commentary. Over time, and with teacher support, we see increasing numbers of entries with the following types of helpful input: "I've been reading about that too, and you provided some information that is new to me. Here is some information that I hope will help you." "Would you finish the story soon so I'll know if it's going to have a sad ending please. Keep up the good work." "I really like your note but I just have one question. . . ." "I have read most of your notes and find them very well written and interesting."

"Maybe you could find out if . . . and add it to one of your notes."
"I like your story because. . . ." As models of effective commentary
are found in the database, such activity is taken up by increasing
numbers of students. At first, the lower-achieving students copy
phrases like those presented above, adding little input of their own.
But as comments are addressed to them and as they receive notes in
return for ones they send, they get drawn more deeply into interchanges, with increasingly more self-generated material.

To date, results relevant to the use of CSILE by at-risk students include the following: (1) There are no significant differences
in number of contributions to the database from students in the
lower versus the upper half of classes. This suggests an equal sense
of commitment and ownership on the part of all users. (2) In the
most collaborative model of use of the system, the students in
the lower and middle performance ranges (as assessed by scores on
the Canadian Test of Basic Skills) gain more relative to the highest-
achieving students. At the same time, CSILE students at each ability
level—low, middle, and high—gain more than do control students
of comparable ability levels. Overall, classes supported by this computer environment show significant advances on achievement tests
(language subtests) relative to control students. (3) All students engage in substantial reading and writing activities on a daily basis
as they build the databases. (4) Students at different ability levels
interact effectively with one another.

In interpreting these results, it is important to appreciate that
the classes in which CSILE is being tested are in a middle-class
neighborhood. Although the lower-achieving students may be performing several years below grade level, they are still advanced relative to students whose lives are characterized by poverty and their
disabling circumstances. Also, the proportion of lower-achieving
students in each class is relatively low, comprising at most one-third
of the class. Thus, one might say that CSILE has not been used with
the most at-risk students, and to the extent that it has, the effects are
moderated by the presence of such students in low proportions.
This may be true, but we do not think that it detracts from our main
point. The problem we face is that of creating knowledge-building
cultures. We have tried to show how a literature culture can be
created with epistemologically naive students. Where it succeeds,

students at all ability levels are drawn into a common enterprise. Because the medium is computer based, we can link students in diverse locations, which means we can link at-risk students with students where a cooperative knowledge-building culture has already taken hold. We believe that the culture would spread, and we take results from the M.U.S.E. experiments to support this conjecture. We know already from the M.U.S.E. experiments that students with severe learning disabilities benefit substantially from access to higher-order knowledge operations. It seems reasonable to assume that the benefits would increase as we weave these kinds of activities into the social fabric of classrooms.

## Conclusion

Clearly, we need to devote serious attention to the question of how to help children who come to school poorly prepared for the kinds of literacy activities that predominate in traditional educational environments. To date, the focus of Chapter 1 literacy instruction has been on the provision of direct instruction in basic reading skills to the virtual exclusion of teaching higher-order comprehension/interpretation skills as well as expertlike composing skills. It seems that the pedagogical emphasis in instruction for at-risk students needs to shift from a hierarchical model of students as receivers of meaning to a dialectical model that enables the reversal of traditional emphases in instruction for at-risk learners from a focus on content knowledge and basic skills to a focus on rhetorical competence and agency in the construction of meaning. To this end, our main recommendations concerning the design of cognitively based writing instruction might be summarized as follows:

- Provide students with opportunities for imitating, practicing, appropriating, and modifying a wide variety of discourse forms.
- Make overt the covert cognitive activities that underlie expertlike composing by encouraging teacher- and student-directed modeling of thinking aloud and discussion of specific problem-solving strategies.
- Maintain attention to cognitive goals that involve learning and the transformation of knowledge through the writing process,

in addition to text-based goals that pertain to satisfying specific task requirements.

- Provide support for distributed learning in a dynamic social context by including collaborative writing sessions and by structuring the learning environment so that everyone is both a teacher/learner and a reader/writer.

- Provide support, or cognitive scaffolding, for the acquisition of more powerful forms of thinking during composing, by structuring learning experiences that allow novice writers to practice new skills without being overwhelmed.

- Facilitate student-based ownership of an emergent learning agenda by encouraging students to set personally meaningful goals for writing and by ensuring that a genuine audience is available for children's texts.

- Identify the particular sociocultural biases that constrain traditional school-based definitions of literacy and expand notions of what counts as "writing" so that minority students' linguistic heritage is not excluded.

## References

Allington, R. L., & Franzen, A. M. (1989, May). School response to reading failure: Chapter 1 and special education students in grades 2, 4, and 8. *Elementary School Journal, 89,* 529–542.

Applebee, A. (1981). *Writing in the secondary school: English and the content areas.* Urbana, IL: National Council of Teachers of English.

Bereiter, C., & Scardamalia, M. (1987). *The psychology of written composition.* Hillsdale, NJ: Erlbaum.

Bereiter, C., & Scardamalia, M. (1990). Intentional learning as a goal of instruction. In L. B. Resnick (Ed.), *Knowing and learning: Issues for a cognitive science of instruction.* Hillsdale, NJ: Erlbaum.

Bourdieu, P., & Passeron, J. (1977). *Reproduction: In education, society and culture.* Newbury Park, CA: Sage.

Bryson, M. (1989). *Cognitive supports for composition: Fostering reflectivity in the processes and the products of reading disabled and normally achieving adolescent student-writers.* Unpublished doctoral dissertation, University of Toronto, Canada.

Bryson, M., Bereiter, C., Scardamalia, M., & Joram, E. (1991). Going beyond the problem as given: Problem solving in expert and novice writers. In R. Stumberg and P. Frensch (Eds.), *Complex Problem Solving.* Hillsdale, NJ: Erlbaum.

Collins, A., Brown, J. S., & Newman, S. E. (1990). Cognitive apprenticeship. In L. B. Resnick (Ed.), *Knowing and learning: Issues for a cognitive science of instruction.* Hillsdale, NJ: Erlbaum.

De Castell, S., & Luke, A. (1983). Defining "literacy" in North American schools: Social and historical conditions and consequences. *Journal of Curriculum Studies, 15,* 373–389.

Delpit, L. (1988). The silenced dialogue: Power and pedagogy in educating other people's children. *Harvard Educational Review, 58* (3), 280–298.

Dewey, J. (1916). *Democracy and education.* New York: Macmillan.

Flower, L., & Hayes, J. R. (1980). The cognition of discovery: Defining a rhetorical problem. *College Composition and Communication, 31,* 21–32.

Griffin, P., & Cole, M. (1984). New technologies, basic skills, and the underside of education: What's to be done? In J. A. Langer (Ed.), *Language, literacy, and culture: Issues of society and schooling.* Norwood, NJ: Ablex.

Heath, S. B. (1983). *Ways with words.* Cambridge: Cambridge University Press.

Hull, G., & Rose, M. (1989). Rethinking remediation. *Written Communication, 6* (2), 139–154.

Kirsch, I. S., & Jungeblut, A. (1986). *Literacy: Profiles of America's young adults* (Report No. 16-PL-02). Princeton, NJ: Educational Testing Service.

Lee, C. (1991, April). *Big picture talkers/words walking without masters: The instructional implications of ethnic voices for an expanded literacy.* Paper presented at the annual meeting of the American Educational Research Association (AERA), Chicago.

Murray, D. M. (1978). Internal revision: A process of discovery. In C. R. Cooper & L. Odell (Eds.), *Research on composing.* Urbana, IL: National Council of Teachers of English.

Paris, P. (1986). Goals and problem solving in written composition. Unpublished doctoral dissertation, York University, Canada.

Perl, S. (1979). The composing process of unskilled college writers. *Research in the Teaching of English, 13,* 317–336.

Reyes, M. de la Luz. (in press). A process approach to literacy using dialogue journals and literature logs with second language learners. *Research in the Teaching of English.*

Rose, M. (1980). Rigid rules, inflexible plans, and the stifling of language: A cognitivist analysis of writer's block. *College Composition and Communication, 32* (1), 65–74.

Scardamalia, M., & Bereiter, C. (1983). The development of evaluative, diagnostic and remedial capabilities in children's composing. In M. Martlew (Ed.), *The psychology of written language: Developmental and educational perspectives.* London: Wiley.

Scardamalia, M., & Bereiter, C. (1985). The development of dialectical processes in writing. In D. Olson, N. Torrance, & A. Hildyard (Eds.), *Literacy, language and learning.* Cambridge: Cambridge University Press.

Scardamalia, M., & Bereiter, C. (1986). Research on written composition. In M. Wittrock (Ed.), *Handbook of research on teaching.* New York: Macmillan.

Scardamalia, M., & Bereiter, C. (1991). Higher levels of agency for children in knowledge building: A challenge for the design of new knowledge media. *The Journal of the Learning Sciences, 1* (1), 37–68.

Scardamalia, M., & Bereiter, C. (in press). Schools as knowledge-building communities. In S. Strauss (Ed.), *Human development: The Tel Aviv annual workshop: Vol. 7. Development and learning environments.* Norwood, NJ: Ablex.

Scardamalia, M., Bereiter, C., McLean, R. S., Swallow, J., & Woodruff, E. (1989). Computer-supported intentional learning environments. *Journal of Educational Computing Research, 5* (1), 51–68.

Scardamalia, M., Bereiter, C., & Steinbach, R. (1984). Teachability of reflective processes in written composition. *Cognitive Science, 8* (2), 173–190.

Scardamalia, M., & Paris, P. (1985). The function of explicit discourse knowledge in the development of text representations and composing strategies. *Cognition and Instruction, 2* (1), 1-39.

Sessums, S. K. (1988, September). Sam Shepard: Geography of a horse dreamer. *Interview,* 72-80.

Shaughnessy, M. P. (1977). *Errors and expectations: A guide for the teacher of basic writing.* New York: Oxford University Press.

Vygotsky, L. S. (1978). *Mind in society: The development of higher psychological processes.* Cambridge, MA: Harvard University Press.

Whitehead, A. N. (1929). *The aims of education.* New York: Macmillan.

Willinsky, J. (1990). *The new literacy.* New York: Routledge.

Ysseldyke, J. E., Algozzine, B., Shinn, M. R., & McGue, M. (1982). Similarities and differences between low achievers and students classified learning disabled. *Journal of Special Education, 16,* 73-85.

# COMMENTARY

## Harvey A. Daniels

As a former Chicago public school teacher and now as codirector of the Illinois Writing Project, I have been concerned with the teaching of writing to minority, disadvantaged, at-risk, inner-city students for over twenty years. Right now, I am working with a team of talented teacher-consultants in conducting an ambitious multiyear, citywide staff development project on writing instruction, an in-service program that is unfolding alongside the wider— and widely hailed—school reform efforts here in Chicago. In running this project, my colleagues and I are working in schools of at-risk children every day, trying to help them and their teachers with the challenge of writing. Because I am so thoroughly immersed in the perplexing adventure of helping teachers teach writing, I find Bryson and Scardamalia's chapter stimulating and welcome.

Bryson and Scardamalia provide strong empirical support for a major shift in the instructional strategies typically used to teach writing to at-risk students. Their research further discredits the skills-oriented curriculum that still prevails in so many public schools, especially those serving poor and minority students. Instead, Bryson and Scardamalia's work affirms the emerging "process" paradigm of writing instruction, which calls for "scaffolded" classrooms where students acquire higher literacy, not through decontextualized skill and drill but through long-term modeling, instruction, and collaboration. And although Bryson and Scardamalia's research agenda is cognitive and their methodology is experimental, their findings are largely harmonious with those of other researchers who have focused more on social interaction, using qualitative research methods (Graves, 1983; Heath, 1983). Indeed, one very happy contribution of the chapter is to solidify the emerging professional consensus about what sort of composition instruction is likely to work for students at risk—and, indeed, for students in general (Farr & Daniels, 1986). Among the key classroom strategies that their paper underscores, endorses, or recommends are the following:

- Students should spend less time on subskill activities and much more time composing whole original pieces of writing. This means providing ample daily writing time, which can be scheduled by reallocating the time currently spent on separate lessons in grammar, usage, spelling, handwriting, vocabulary, and the like.
- Students should select and develop their own topics for writing rather than merely writing to whole-class, teacher-made prompts.
- Teachers should write along with their students, talking about their own planning, decision-making, and problem-solving strategies, thereby providing transparent demonstrations of how writers work.
- Teachers should schedule regular one-to-one writing conferences with students, since this structure provides the kind of scaffolded interaction that is most powerful in teaching writing.
- When teachers give students feedback on their writing, they need to focus more on coaching the writing process and helping the writer think through rhetorical problems, rather than on identifying errors. It is actually more helpful for teachers to be a sounding board for writers than for teachers to give them advice.
- Classrooms should be full of social interaction around writing, with children coauthoring pieces, doing research in teams, sharing drafts aloud with the whole group, and helping each other revise in small peer editing groups.
- Above all, teachers of at-risk students need to believe that their children can write—believing in the power of their kids' language and the validity of their experience. At-risk children can and will write if provided the kind of rich, supportive, interactive, scaffolded classroom that Bryson and Scardamalia describe.

In our current in-service project in Chicago, these are precisely the strategies, activities, and attitudes that we are trying to help teachers embrace as they return to their students in regular inner-city classrooms, in Chapter 1, and in other special programs. And when teachers do implement this new kind of instruction, we often see dramatic results as these at-risk, overdrilled kids are freed to write and their teachers shift from correcting to coaching. These classrooms experience a writing boom. Children show a burst of fluency, productivity, and pride. Walls become covered with lavishly illustrated stories, poems, reports, posters, and cartoons. Letters fly out of classrooms, through the building, into the community, and around the country. Students keep journals filled with responses to books they are reading, as well as accounts of personal experiences, and they exchange these with other readers and writers. Homemade books are "published," catalogued, and shelved in the school library alongside the books of other authors of children's literature. Kids report that writing time is their favorite part of the school day; teachers testify that if an assembly or other schedule change impinges on writing time, the students rebel. Teachers also report, with delighted surprise, that these kids can really write after all and sometimes shake their heads with regret over past years of teaching when they did not even invite kids to write. Primary teachers often report that students learn phonics so effectively through inventing their own spellings that much less reading time is required for direct instruction in the sound-symbol relationships.

The overall message of Bryson and Scardamalia's chapter, as validated through our experiences with teachers and children in Chicago, is this: At-risk kids need time to write, they need encouragement and coaching, and they need to believe in themselves as writers. Other, more privileged children have plenty of other family and community experiences that invite them to "join the literacy club." But for these at-risk children, we must be absolutely sure that school invites them into the circle of writers. This can be accomplished with amazing speed and effectiveness, if teachers change their instructional roles and practices in the key ways Bryson and Scardamalia have outlined in their paper.

### Reactions, Concerns, and Suggestions

Bryson and Scardamalia are unusually realistic about the politics of literacy, schools, and change. They begin at the beginning by facing the worst-kept secret of American schools: that students considered "at risk" are almost invariably offered the most mechanistic, lowest-level curriculum, and that this pattern locks poor and minority students in at the lowest levels of achievement throughout the school. Bryson and Scardamalia quite rightly turn the "at-risk" catchphrase around from a blame-the-victim euphemism to a critique of schools: It is *schools* that are at risk—at risk of failing students by depriving them of experiences that might actually work.

Later in their chapter, Bryson and Scardamalia raise the complementary political point that prevailing American definitions of literacy are narrow and highly discriminatory. "Mainstream" people label as "illiterate" communities of their fellow citizens who in fact use language, literacy, and print in very complex but divergent ways. The families and communities of "at-risk" students are filled with powerful and elegant uses of language and literacy, just as are all human communities. The fact that these communities are socioeconomically isolated from the mainstream culture naturally perpetuates these differences, and public schooling, at its most insidious and ironic, penalizes such variety.

The theoretical centerpiece of the paper is Scardamalia's familiar construct of two polar-opposite kinds of writing—knowledge transforming, or epistemic, versus knowledge telling. The epistemic category presents a highly idealized view of what expert writers do: subordinating task assignments to "overarching goals for learning and the transformation of current knowledge." A skeptic might ask Bryson and Scardamalia, "Well, how many term papers or business reports actually do offer (or can ever offer) such grand personal-growth possibilities?" In contrast, plenty of real-life writing tasks clearly fall into the disvalued "knowledge-telling" category and yet pose tremendously interesting cognitive problems. In reality, most writing tasks offer various degrees of knowledge telling and transforming, and a continuum model would certainly be more palatable to most everyday writing teachers.

What Bryson and Scardamalia *do* contrast very effectively here is whether writing is planned or not. Expert writers have access to rhetorical planning strategies and have ways of balancing content and rhetorical concerns as the composing goes on; inexpert writers typically do not. To a great degree, the chapter is about metacognition: The two think-aloud samples included show one youngster whose planning consists only of possible sentences for the text and one "expert" writer who talks almost exclusively about his own thought processes. The main contrast lies in composition-planning strategies: Expert writers have them and can use them when possible, whereas inexperienced writers lack them and lack the metacognitive awareness to use them.

Bryson and Scardamalia show strong faith that such planning strategies can be mastered through "direct instruction," faith evidenced both in their repeated use of the phrase itself and in such research strategies as handing experimental students revision-prompting cards ("Yes, I can understand the argument, but what about . . . ?"). These aspects of the M.U.S.E. program appear to show a lingering faith that higher-order cognitive operations can simply be planted in children by clear-cut, immediate, and simple interventions. And while the reported research results suggest that M.U.S.E. students retained enough of the target planning behaviors to pass posttests with significant improvements, no improvements against the control groups or over any longer term were reported.

Bryson and Scardamalia's faith in direct instruction is matched by a lack of attention to collateral, unconscious, or incidental learning in the development of writing ability. Since this sort of learning is the primary mechanism by which human beings acquire their native *oral* language—and because writing is another language function—one should expect that these indirect learning processes would play an important if not predominant role in learning to write. Along these lines, there is no discussion in the description of M.U.S.E. of students' *reading* experience as a source of implicit information about higher-order composition. Similarly, Bryson and Scardamalia seem to think that the only writers who possess planning strategies are those who can verbalize them for think-aloud researchers. This is an alluring but unsupported assumption. Most bicycle riders cannot verbalize their riding either, but most of them get around the block, and some are champions. Many effective writers plan writing *by* writing; they find their direction and plan their text structure in the act of trying out directions, sentence by sentence. Undoubtedly, these writers are engaged in a reciprocal internal dialogue between content and form concerns, making long-range text-level plans, but they are doing it outside of awareness. Indeed, such a writer might be almost helpless to explain to herself or anyone else how the writing got planned and done. And yet we need not classify such a writer as lower on a developmental totem pole of expertness. Still, to be fair, Bryson and Scardamalia do not rely only on "direct instruction" in writing behaviors. They also respect and draw on theorists who argue for diffuse explanations of language learning. Further, their M.U.S.E. program included many elements that, if implemented consistently, would indeed facilitate plenty of such incidental learning.

Still, in these hectic days of school reform, the use of the term *direct instruction* is potentially misleading, since this term has been adopted and aggressively "trademarked" by the defenders of a behaviorist approach that Bryson and Scardamalia explicitly reject. I think what they mean to endorse, and what would serve their case better, is something more like *direct experience*—Bryson and Scardamalia want students to have an active, direct immersion in certain target activities. They aim not to reinforce the transmission model of teaching but rather to assert that higher-order learning comes from active, guided practice in a supportive social context.

### Classroom Connections

Too often, researchers need to call on the services of translators, popular writers, colleges of education, or school in-service programs to make their findings useful to classroom practitioners. Because Bryson and Scardamalia's research essentially validates and strengthens the emerging "process" paradigm of writing instruction, ample resources are already in place to help teachers follow the guidance this work offers. It is worth taking a minute to outline specifically how such help is available.

Bryson and Scardamalia offer three main recommendations to teachers: teach planning strategies, provide procedural facilitation, and serve as a model of a writer at work. Although Bryson and Scardamalia might not be totally delighted by every translation, their main recommendations are endorsed and explicated in many of the most widely read pedagogical books for teachers—works by Graves (1983), Calkins (1986), Atwell (1987), Romano (1987), and

Zemelman and Daniels (1988). All strongly recommend modeling, calling for teachers to write often with their students, to offer pupils a window into the work and the thinking of an expert writer at work. Graves suggests that teachers offer occasional "think-aloud" or "compose-aloud" sessions, during which they vocalize their thought processes while composing on a blackboard or overhead, giving students a chance to hear some of that internal dialogue between content and rhetoric that Bryson and Scardamalia so strongly recommend.

Bryson and Scardamalia recommend "procedural facilitation," a kind of "nonspecific support related to the student's cognitive processes but not responsive to the actual substance of what the student is thinking or writing." Donald Graves (1983) teaches teachers to engage student authors in "process conferences" in which they ask students questions related to procedures, not content. "What are you working on? Where are you in the piece? What kinds of problems are you facing? What kind of help do you need to move on from here? What are you going to do next?" More generally, Zemelman and Daniels (1988) have described the entire role of the teacher in process writing instruction as a matter of "facilitation," tracing the term back to its origins in group dynamics and humanistic psychology.

Note that the above approaches to modeling and facilitation are also specifically focused on helping students *plan* their writing, learning to consciously (and unconsciously) balance content and rhetorical concerns. This theme of developing higher-order, strategic planning—working and thinking like a "real" writer—pervades the "process" pedagogical literature. One outstanding example is Nancie Atwell (1987), who warns teachers about the danger of allowing students to work on only content during revisions—in Bryson and Scardamalia's terminology, this would mean remaining at the "knowledge-telling" level of composition. To counteract this tendency and push students up the cognitive ladder, Atwell recommends conferences in which the student begins not by sharing selections but by formally paraphrasing the paper and identifying its current problems.

## Conclusion

Bryson and Scardamalia's work in the M.U.S.E. project, as well as the several earlier studies they cite, provides strong support for the emerging consensus that so-called process writing is the best hope for at-risk students. Happily, we need not wait for classroom translations of Bryson and Scardamalia's recommendations, because they are already in wide professional circulation in books, journals, and face-to-face workshops. Indeed, there is a strong, ongoing national movement to implement the key ideas that Bryson and Scardamalia endorse. What is needed is the time and the money to continue the process of nurturing a paradigm shift, which may well take another generation. Perhaps most importantly, Bryson and Scardamalia have reminded the community of professional educators once again that so-called at-risk students do not need a segregated curriculum: What works for them is what is best for everyone.

## References

Atwell, N. (1987). *In the middle: Writing and reading with adolescents.* Portsmouth, NH: Heinemann.

Calkins, L. (1986). *The art of teaching writing.* Portsmouth, NH: Heinemann.

Farr, M., & Daniels, H. (1986). *Language diversity and writing instruction.* Urbana, IL: National Council of Teachers of English.

Graves, D. (1983). *Writing: Teachers and children at work.* Portsmouth, NH: Heinemann.

Heath, S. B. (1983). *Ways with words: Language, life and work in communities and classrooms.* Cambridge: Cambridge University Press.

Romano, T. (1987). *Clearing the way: Working with teenage writers.* Portsmouth, NH: Heinemann.

Zemelman, S., & Daniels, H. (1988). *A community of writers: Teaching writing in the junior and senior high school.* Portsmouth, NH: Heinemann.

# 6

# What Schools Can Do
# to Improve Literacy Instruction

## *Robert Calfee*

MANY CHILDREN LEAVE AMERICAN SCHOOLS WITHOUT THE LITERACY skills to thrive in our society. Societal demands for competence in thinking and communication have increased, and fewer families have the resources to teach their children the "school game." The challenge facing the nation's schools has been extensively documented. Knapp and Shields (1990a) note that "we often teach the children of poverty *less* than they are capable of learning," while Williams, Richman, and Mason (1987) report the consistent finding that a *schoolwide* effort is essential to effective compensatory education for at-risk students.

What can *schools* do to improve literacy instruction? Schools are the crucial ingredient for several reasons. We might urge families to read more to children, but such entreaties will have little influence on current societal realities. We might search for new instructional treatments for at-risk students, but piecemeal remediation has had little lasting influence. We might increase the pressure on students and teachers (by using higher standards, tougher selection criteria), but coercion is at cross-purposes with American education and does not work anyway.

The option sketched in this chapter builds on two propositions:

- *Critical literacy,* a conception of reading and writing as high-level competency in using language as a tool to solve problems and to communicate, is the core curriculum for elementary education. Unlike prevailing notions of basic skills, critical literacy provides an "engine" advancing effective education throughout all domains of knowledge and skill.
- *The school as a community of inquiry,* building on the concept of critical literacy, can transform the school from an "assembly line" into a team of professionals working to assist all students in realizing their full potential. The same model works for both the classroom and the faculty meeting.

This chapter connects three "buzzwords" now swirling through the myriad currents of American education: students at risk for school failure, the whole-language movement, and restructuring. Each theme encompasses a vital set of issues. The aim of this chapter is to show how a reformulation of reading and writing in the elementary grades can integrate these three themes. Its message is that critical literacy can serve as the centerpiece for empowering teachers and administrators as full-fledged professionals. When the school staff practices what it preaches, when every sermon promotes the effective use of language for thinking and communicating, the school is more likely to nurture student achievement. The synergistic effect of the two propositions is likely to be greatest for schools serving large proportions of students at risk for academic failure. These youngsters, more than middle-class children, depend on the school for challenge and direction; and these schools, more than middle-class schools, depend on the vigor and competence that comes from genuine professional interaction.

This chapter describes the concept of a schoolwide approach to the literate use of language. I begin with anecdotes arising from my experience with two correlated programs, Project READ and the Inquiring School, which have been implemented in elementary and middle schools throughout the country. Project READ, the first stage of the process, is a staff development program for helping classroom teachers to create a literate environment, a setting where the literate use of language permeates the entire school day. In the second stage, the Inquiring School, the literate-environment model extends to encompass the entire school.

### Stories from School

What you have to do with a story is, you analyze it; you break it into parts. You figure out the characters, how they're the same and different. And the plot, how it begins with a problem and goes on until it is solved. Then you understand the story better, and you can even write your own [first-grader, Los Angeles].

We started our play by finding a theme, something really important to us personally. A lot of us come from broken homes, so we made the play about that. We did a web [a semantic "map"] on HOME; that gave us lots of ideas. Then we talked about how things are now and how we would like them to be. It's pretty lonely when you don't have a daddy, or maybe not even a mommy. So the play began with nothing on the stage, and one of us came out, sat down, and said "My life is broke." We thought that would get the theme across. It worked pretty good [second-grader, Los Angeles].

We thought about your suggestion—start in September with vocabulary strategies, then narrative in October, and pick up exposition and decoding after the winter break. But the team wasn't happy: "That will take the whole school year. We can move faster if we work together." They came up with the idea of four cadres, one for each component, everyone a specialist. It was great—by December, every part of the program was in place somewhere in the school [teacher, San Francisco Bay Area elementary school].

Several of us tried the program—it combines whole language with the skills our kids need. And it worked! My third-graders were a disaster last year, and now look at their projects. They think they can do anything, and all of them made tremendous growth in reading and writing—and motivation. But we don't have the principal's support; it's hard to find time to team with one another; and the district takes our in-service days. I like the program, but it's not affecting the school as a whole [teacher, San Francisco Bay Area].

It's depressing. After our success in integrating reading and writing, test scores up, students writing like crazy—then the new superintendent cuts money for staff development. Our principal is supportive, and we will keep the program alive at this school; I'm meeting just this afternoon with a new teacher to plan and observe. But our links to other schools are gone. Last spring this program topped the district wish list—as a write-in! But I don't know what will happen now [teacher, Sacramento].

Tales like these are familiar to anyone who has worked directly with schools, especially those serving children from poor communities, in which demands are heavy and resources are slim. The stories have two morals. First, they demonstrate that students from at-risk backgrounds can become fully literate; they can acquire the capacity to use language to think and to communicate at the highest levels. Accomplishing this goal calls for a unified effort from the earliest grades onward. Second, the effort requires of teachers and administrators the same advanced level of literacy in dealing with one another as colleagues. This step calls for *fundamental change*, for *restructuring* of the institution. The process begins in the classroom, but it becomes self-sustaining only as it encompasses the entire school.

My story of an approach to such change begins in an unlikely setting, a school with no obvious problems.

### Another Tale: Project READ

In 1980 I visited San Jose's Graystone Elementary School. In classrooms, students moved through the routines of the basal reader, following the neatly printed daily schedule, the class arranged in three groups by ability, one working with the teacher and the other two intent on their assigned worksheets. The scene was familiar to me, similar to my experiences in elementary schools from south-central Los Angeles to Silicon Valley.

Like most series in the past quarter century, the basal readers at Graystone employed a behavioral-objectives design. The program took shape as a series of stages (Chall, 1983), beginning with decoding skills (phonics), then fluent oral reading of words and sentences, and finally "real stories." The design introduced each objective in turn, then practiced, reinforced, and assessed it. The guiding assumption was that "practice makes permanent." The teacher's role was to ask questions from the manual, which included the correct answers. The routines were not especially challenging for these students, but standardized achievement scores were high, and parents were satisfied.

The times were changing, however. Several teachers had moved away from the basal primer toward children's literature. Others had taken workshops in "process writing"; they were experimenting with student journals that gave children opportunities to write about personally relevant experiences—spelling didn't count. A few teachers returned from conventions excited about a new approach, "whole language." Although not quite sure about the details, they were intrigued. The principal was encouraging the staff to look into an integrated reading-writing curriculum. These images of possibilities were fuzzy, and the faculty were wary: "If it ain't broke, don't fix it."

I shared my impressions with the staff, the "good news" as well as concerns. Somewhat to my surprise, the teachers invited me back for a second discussion. They posed challenging questions: "What does research say we ought to be doing in reading and writing?" "What reading series would you recommend?" "How *do* kids learn to spell?" "What about children with dyslexia and learning disabilities?" The teachers continued the dialogue for several reasons: genuine interest in the issues (the school was well regarded by parents and the district and could afford risks), dissatisfaction with boring routines (even basal advocates found the lessons lifeless), and informed leadership (for the principal, curriculum and instruction were the heart of the enterprise).

As a novice at staff development, I often made naive recommendations. "Maybe if you were familiar with findings from cognitive learning, linguistics, and rhetoric, you could see how to integrate reading and writing with materials you already have—like library books." The teachers were cautious, even skeptical: "Doesn't sound very practical. We can't do a lesson with one library book; we need sets of thirty." "Seems like a lot of work, designing new lessons every night. Where will we find the time?" I replied that theory could be quite practical and that students might learn more if they did more of the work. I assumed that, given sound and simple concepts, classroom teachers would make good instructional decisions. My previous experiences with teacher-proof packages had convinced me of the futility of that approach, and I believed that the principal could support the initial stage of change, even though it called for a major shift in teachers' decision making.

*Summer Institute: Discovery Learning.* The meetings led to plans for a week-long summer institute, a collaborative enterprise between our Stanford team and the Graystone faculty. In-service workshops typically handed teachers routines and recipes; I cautioned the staff that I could recommend principles and procedures from research, but that they were the experts in practice.

We designed the institute around integration of reading and writing, but our plans soon encompassed the entire language arts spectrum. We included psycholinguistic concepts and methods from rhetoric (Booth, 1989), with concrete examples from a teacher familiar with "language experience" techniques (Ashton-Warner, 1963). A kindergarten teacher showed how storybooks could support the emergence of literacy in young children *before* they mastered phonics. A fourth-grade teacher described her "bootleg" drama program; her practice was to move students quickly through the basal readers, so her students had the spring to write and produce their own plays. The teachers stressed the importance of spending time reading to students, encouraging discussion, and supporting creative activities like compositions and presentations.

Some teachers asked, with concern, "When do you teach

'reading'?" A crucial insight into this question came from the realization that literacy was a matter of *mode* more than *medium,* that the literate person has acquired a distinctive style of language use, whether reading or speaking, writing or listening (Horowitz & Samuels, 1987; Tuman, 1987; Olson, 1989). When first-graders contrast the characters of Swimmy and Frederick (Lionni, 1985), they are learning literate ways of thinking, even though the teacher may handle the mechanics of reading and writing. Teachers began to question the "no pain, no gain" philosophy; perhaps a reading lesson could promote growth in literacy even if it was enjoyable.

From the institute emerged a curriculum framework that linked oral language development with the technology of print. Our group agreed that students needed to learn skills, which took shape not as piecemeal objectives but as advanced-level *structures* and *strategies* for handling topics and texts. The basic building blocks came from rhetoric, which students usually encounter in high school and college, if at all: concepts such as character and plot, semantic maps and compare-contrast matrixes. Some teachers worried whether low-ability students could handle these abstractions; my recommendation was to experiment—try the strategies and see how they work.

Translation and simplification of the research ideas were important. For instance, "semantic map" is a mouthful for kindergartners. The underlying concept is simple; any topic of moderate familiarity can be diagrammed as a small set of nodes that organize the details. The result looks like a spiderweb (see Figure 6.1, top panel); *web* is a workable label for young children. The *strategy* for producing a web *structure* is relatively simple. The teacher asks students to free-associate to an everyday word like *fish,* writes their reactions on the board in clusters, and then asks them to justify each cluster. The middle panel of Figure 6.1 shows a second, more demanding strategy. Here the teacher records the responses in a list, and students then have the job of devising clusters that make sense to them.

A second rhetorical structure, the compare-contrast matrix, is shown in the bottom panel of Figure 6.1. Processing demands in this strategy are greater than for the web; the student must hold two or more topics in mind, while simultaneously considering dimen-

**Figure 6.1. "Semantic Map": Examples of Web and Weave.**

Web

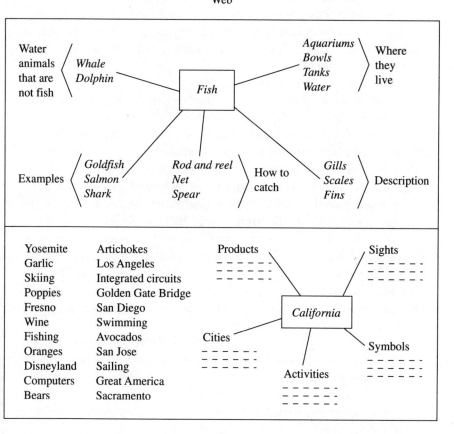

Weave

| Charlotte | Wilbur |
|---|---|
| Sharp | Fierce |
| Clever | Scheming |
| Lived by her wits | Brutal |
| Trapper | Bloodthirsty |

sions on which the topics are similar or different. We called this structure a *weave,* a label familiar to most kindergartners. One strategy for constructing a weave begins with a pair of webs: "What words do Charlotte and Wilbur use to describe Charlotte in *Charlotte's Web?*" From these two collections, students arrange the words into a matrix.

*First-Year Aftermath: New Discoveries.* In September, after the summer institute, Graystone teachers proceeded to implement the ideas. They were generally pleased with the results. They found that the structures and strategies allowed students at all grade levels to "compose" complex but coherent texts, given some instructional support and an occasional transcriber. Teachers discovered that kindergartners as well as fifth-graders, low-achieving "robins" as well as the "cardinals" in the high group, had greater potential than teachers thought. They were impressed with changes in student interest and interaction. They found themselves shifting roles from possessors of knowledge to orchestrators of learning. The high-level routines supported cooperative learning and tutoring; the suggestion to "web" a topic allowed a student team to generate a multitude of ideas with minimal guidance.

The Stanford team had emphasized the importance of metacognition (thinking about thinking) and metalinguistic awareness (talking about language) during the institute (Garner, 1987; Palincsar & Brown, 1984). Metalearning leads children to apply what they have learned in one setting to a novel situation; they are more likely to transfer knowledge and skills when they are explicitly directed to look beyond the limits of the initial learning (*meta* is Greek for *beyond*). Salomon and Perkins (1989) refer more simply to "highroad" transfer, which depends on reflection as well as practice.

The Graystone teachers took on this challenge and began to create *metainstructional* lessons, in which students shared responsibility for setting the purposes and outcomes of a task. This shift in emphasis was accidentally fostered through classroom observations of the Stanford staff, who asked students, "What are you doing? Why are you doing it?" These questions tapped metaawareness, providing useful feedback about program effectiveness, but teachers also saw the questions serving an important function during teaching and learning. Students often knew more than teachers expected (Peterson, Clark, & Dickson, in press). Fulghum (1990) comments, "To answer the question, 'How do children learn?' I asked them. They know. They have not been hanging around a closet for six years waiting for school so they could learn" (p. 90).

Evaluation of the first year of Project READ (Calfee & Henry, 1986) showed positive outcomes on standardized measures of student achievement. Teacher morale was high, and Graystone began to attract visitors from other district schools. The next year the program was recommended by the administration to six inner-city schools in the district. We soon discovered the meaning of "institutional support." The new schools served student populations we would label today as at risk, but we came to doubt that the children were the problem. In classrooms that adopted critical-literacy strategies, improvement in student achievement was sudden and dramatic (by achievement we meant children's competence in reading and interest in writing, not standardized scores). But the schools were overburdened with conflicting programs, time and resources for staff development were sparse, and staff expectations and vision were eroded by years of frustration.

The second year was instructive for us. On the one hand, we were encouraged by the outcomes for students whose home and family backgrounds were quite different from the Graystone neighborhood. On the other hand, institutional barriers to program implementation were daunting. As years have gone by, I have realized that the second year taught us a significant lesson about improving literacy instruction for schools serving the children of the poor: Improving problem solving and communication at the *school* level was essential to sustain problem solving and communication in classroom practice.

## Basic Principles of Critical Literacy

The Graystone project sprang from dissatisfaction with existing practice and the search for a workable alternative to prevailing approaches in language arts instruction. We—the Graystone faculty and the Stanford team—were neither radicals nor romantics. On the one hand, we had to rely on existing resources and materials (California's tax-limitation initiative had passed four years previously). On the other hand, we had to keep in mind the realities of accountability, including standardized tests.

We began by rethinking the reading-writing curriculum. In 1980, this term meant textbooks or scope-and-sequence charts. We moved away from this definition and turned back to the original meaning of *curriculum* as a *course* of study. A young person entering high school requires full command of the language to handle the challenges of secondary education and life thereafter. It was this shift in perspective that took us from a view of reading and writing as "basic skills for handling print" toward the concept of *critical literacy:* the capacity to use language in all its forms as a tool for problem solving and communication.

This change in conception may appear subtle, but the implications are substantial. Phonics is no longer the gateway to literacy but part of a tool kit. Student discussion is no longer ancillary to instruction but an essential constituent. Comprehension is not satisfied when students give simple answers to literal questions but only as they can reconstruct the text and connect it to personal experience. Composition is no longer an optional activity inserted when convenient but a crucial counterpart to comprehension from the earliest grades onward. The conception foreshadowed the current emphasis on whole-language approaches to literacy (Goodman, Smith, Meredith, & Goodman, 1987; Weaver, 1988), which emphasize purpose and meaning in all facets of language arts instruction.

The curriculum of critical literacy builds on five principles:

- The rhetorical techniques that support critical literacy can be taught from the earliest grades onward.
- Although students vary widely in the experiences they bring to the classroom, the potential for linguistic, cognitive, and metacognitive growth is remarkably constant for children of varying backgrounds.
- The key to effective development of intellectual potential is the acquisition of effective organizational strategies.
- In the school setting, the foundation for practical realization of

the first three principles is a fundamental change in the design of the daily lesson.

• Literacy for tomorrow's students requires them not only to read and write but also to possess an explicit understanding of how language operates for thinking and communicating.

The first of these principles comes from *rhetoric,* a set of techniques found in college composition texts and "how to communicate" seminars. Psychologists have applied the techniques in recent years to study structures of knowledge, such as story grammars and expository patterns (Calfee & Drum, 1986; Orasanu, 1986). These methods are generally judged as too advanced for any but the most able students, and then only in the later grades. We thought that the techniques could be interpreted to mesh with the capacities of kindergartners, not because we were "pushy" but because we thought that children at all grades would find the techniques both challenging and helpful in reading and writing.

The second principle emphasizes the *constancies* in human thought and language (Calfee & Nelson-Barber, in press). Educators observe individual differences among students; they are less tuned to noticing similarities. For instance, all kindergartners enter school as full-fledged language users; they have a rich vocabulary store organized in semantic networks, and they can use story schemas to talk about cartoons and fairy tales (Applebee, 1978). They do not realize that they possess such rich resources, however; they are not strategic about learning or performance, and they lack a metalanguage for talking about knowledge and language. They also vary enormously in the match of their experiences and styles with the conventions of schooling. Nonetheless, and despite observed variations, every child has the basic intellectual potential to achieve the goal of critical literacy.

The concept of common intellectual potential is especially important for enhancing the education of children at risk for academic failure. As Graham (1987) has pointed out, today's elementary curriculum is a fixed track, where every student must leap the same hurdles wearing the same uniform. A youngster lacking conventional knowledge and skill must run the race barefoot and with bound ankles. A deeper understanding of the reading-writing curriculum can open the way for students' experiences and styles to serve as bases for acquiring the tools of literacy.

Despite decades of research showing results to the contrary, breakdowns in communication are still attributed to student deficits. For instance, a recent newsletter for practitioners twice quoted teachers in despair over children who entered school "not knowing their colors" (*NEA Today*, 1990, pp. 3, 29). Colors and color names are acquired early, usually by two or three years of age, by virtually all children in all cultures. What is it about instructional practice that stifles children's capacity to express themselves in the classroom about such simple matters (Heath, 1983)? Knowledge of story structures has equal validity whether gained from children's memories of folk stories from the mountains of Oaxaca, the jungles of Cambodia, or the most recent episode of Teenage Mutant Ninja Turtles, whether applied to an expurgated basal text, a prizewinning piece like *The Polar Express* (Van Allsburg, 1985), or a tale from *The People Could Fly* (Hamilton, 1985). The fundamental principle is to draw on what children *do* know as a foundation for learning.

The third principle addresses the issue of *organization* in human thought. The human mind has virtually infinite potential to store experience in long-term memory, but the attentional capacity of short-term memory is quite limited (Calfee, 1981). Hence the KISS principle—"keep it simple, sweetheart." This description of the human mind holds for virtually every person, regardless of age, intelligence, or socioeconomic level. To be sure, some children grow up in homes that surround them from the earliest years with experiences that help them make sense of the world's complexities. More to the point, children from middle-class homes learn the routines that are the bread and butter of the typical school day. They play "animals, vegetables, and minerals" (a simplifying strategy), and they even play "school" (responding to silly questions where the asker already knows the answer).

The KISS principle has intuitive appeal, but "simple ain't easy." In fact, simplicity is a scarce commodity in today's schools. The reading curriculum is often a chaotic collage of bits and pieces (Knapp & Shields, 1990a, 1990b). Lessons lack any sense of purpose or connection to personal experience. Pull-out programs add to the turmoil. Tests appear out of the blue, sometimes during a student's first week in a new school.

The critical-literacy curriculum builds on the concept of "chunks." The mind can handle about half a dozen distinctive pieces of information (chunks) at any given time. This principle applies to both students and teachers. Selecting workable units is the key to effective use of intellectual resources. Hence the question: What can serve as the foundational elements of an integrated language-literacy curriculum? In Project READ we shaped an answer around the linguistic analysis of spoken language into *phonology, semantics,* and *discourse.* Counterpart building blocks—decoding and spelling within phonology, vocabulary and concept formation within semantics, comprehension and composition of narrative and expository texts within discourse—provided a simple set of benchmarks for deciding what to teach from kindergarten onward (Calfee & Drum, 1986).

We found it possible to divide each component into a few "subchunks" with accompanying graphic structures and instructional strategies. The decoding-spelling strand, for instance, breaks along two dimensions: language origin and level of analysis. English is a historically rich language, with layers from Anglo-Saxon, Romance, and other sources. Spelling patterns at each layer have distinctive features at both the letter-sound and morphological (word-part) levels (Balmuth, 1982). In kindergarten, the word-part strand leads children to examine compound words from Anglo-Saxon: "You know *doghouse* and *raincoat,* what do you think about *rainhouse* and *dogcoat?*" In sixth grade, students can explore Romance combinations: "See what you can make from these prefixes, roots, and suffixes; *inter-, bi-; -nation-, -system-; -al, -ness.*" Some combinations are real, while others have not yet entered the language. The curricular goal in both instances is to engage students in unpacking complex words. The instructional strategy gives students basic building blocks and the task of "making your own words." The result is X-ray capacity to see the elements in *peregrinations* and to write *nononsenseness* with confidence (as no-non-sense-ness). Children for whom Spanish is the first language gain an advantage from their familiarity with the Latinate pattern (prefix-root-suffix), which is less well known to native English speakers (Henry, Calfee, & Avelar La Salle, 1989).

The fourth principle centers on *lesson design*. Basal lessons are typically a composite of curricular objectives and scripted activities. Lesson design in Project READ follows two criteria: (1) clarity of curricular goals and (2) dependence on students' collective experience to achieve the goals. The first criterion is supported by the lesson *opening* and *closing*, the second criterion by the *middle* activities.

In the opening and closing, the teacher briefly lays out the content, process, and structure of the lesson. The content is the topic, process is the means of analysis, and structure is the picture that synthesizes. The middle activities then lead students to explore the topic, with the teacher as facilitator.

Here is an example. A first-grade class starts a lesson on food. The topic is familiar but has opportunities for problem solving and communication; grocery stores and menus both entail categorization (Barton & Calfee, 1989). The teacher begins, "We all know something about food; let's see what's on your mind. We'll do this by webbing; let's first find out what you know about the topic, and then we'll organize the information. What comes to mind when you think about 'food'? I'll write your ideas down."

This brief presentation is the opening; it states the topic (food), identifies the process (free associations and clustering), and lays out the structure (a web).

The move to the middle was quick: "What comes to mind . . . ?" The teacher's request for associations is genuine and opens the way for discussion. The move to structure is equally direct. Once students have generated a collection of associations, the next step is to cluster the array: "How can we can bunch the words?" The emphasis throughout the lesson is on students' thoughts rather than on extracting correct answers. The lesson employs commonplace content to assist students in acquiring high-level structures and strategies of broad applicability. The latter components provide the basis for "high-road" transfer (Salomon & Perkins, 1989; Calfee, Avelar La Salle, & Cancino, in press), as students discuss application of the structures and strategies in situations that go beyond the specifics of the lesson.

*Explicitness* is the fifth curriculum principle. Rhetorical devices like the topical net, along with explicit labels (webbing), allow students to talk about language and thought. Questions are open-ended and probe for explanations. "What comes to mind when you think about food?" is an authentic question, more so than "What goes with ice cream?" Equally important, any answer is an opportunity for the student to make public her or his reasoning. "Pickles and peanut butter! What an unusual combination. How did you come up with that?" Our natural response is to react to weird answers with strained expressions. When a teacher acknowledges the unusual nature of an answer and then probes for the underlying reasoning, virtually any response becomes a creative exercise. This strategy extends the theme of metacognition to all interactions and transforms playful impulses into metainstructional exchanges.

## The Inquiring School

*After the Honeymoon.* Initial results from READ were encouraging, as measured by student performance and teacher morale, both quantitatively and qualitatively (Calfee, Henry, & Funderburg, 1988). But Graystone was a "rich folks" school—what is the connection with advancing the achievement of children at risk for school failure? The answer reflects ten years of experience since Graystone, during which we have explored the same concepts in the inner cities of San Jose, Los Angeles, Pittsburgh, Omaha, and New York as well as rural sites near Sacramento and Santa Cruz, California. Initial efforts at extending the program were frustrated by institutional barriers: lack of time, limited resources, overburdened agendas, well-intended but disconnected top-down programs, and frustration from years of experience with miracle cures.

We persisted with the READ experiment, nonetheless, simplifying strategies, fine-tuning structures, building the network of colleagues. Within five years, READ workshops had been held in more than two dozen sites around the country, many in collaboration with model schools. Classroom observations convinced us that low-achieving elementary students were indeed capable of handling advanced concepts, that their background was not a major barrier to development of high-level skills. Teachers frequently expressed surprise at the talents of these "disadvantaged" students.

For instance, in New York City, in a webbing lesson on the concept of *weather,* a student gave *volcano* as an associate. Pressed to explain, he referred to a newscast of a volcanic eruption in the South Seas that darkened the skies around the globe. His teacher commented, "This student is junior-high age, but he hasn't passed the standards test. I thought his problem was deficient language and experience—and motivation. But now I know that he watches the TV news, he understands it, and he connects it to his personal experiences. I'm astounded!"

In a school serving families from tenements on New York's Lower East Side, a first-grader listed creatures in Lionni's *Swimmy:* a crab, a jellyfish, and a "snaky thing" (an eel). The teacher commented, "Normally I would have corrected her: 'Not a crab; what was it [a lobster]?' But I thought, this child arrived from Puerto Rico only a year ago. She may not know the concept of crustaceans, but she sees the connections. Her 'wrong answer' tells me more than the 'right one' about her ability."

Both examples illustrate the importance during metainstruction for teacher reflection on the meanings of student discourse— the value in encouraging students to say what is on their mind, reinforcing their efforts, and turning any answer into an opportunity to explore student thinking.

Nonetheless, five years of efforts to expand the program had left us with a mixed message: some remarkable successes, a few memorable disappointments, and frequent uncertainties. The successes correlated with school-level indicators of effective schooling (Brookover, 1982; Purkey & Smith, 1985): strong leadership, clear goals, and emphasis on student learning.

The "flavor" of effectiveness was different in successful READ schools, however. Strong leadership meant time spent in classrooms and with teams of teachers. Clear goals meant sustained emphasis on improved reading and writing instruction over two or three years rather than a collage of programs. The goals were conceptual rather than operational. Teacher reactions were as important as student performance. Student learning included test scores (standardized measures showed statistically significant upward trends in READ sites), but more consequential were the quality of student writing and discussion, students' capacity to explain what they were doing and why, and the morale and togetherness of the teaching staff. In a school where READ was working, displays of student work in classrooms, the hallways, and the teachers' lounge were convincing evidence; the enthusiasm and articulateness of the faculty about student progress were compelling (Whittaker, 1990; Whittaker, Wolf, & Wong, 1989). One principal, asked how to evaluate READ, replied that she would bring a group of students into her office, select a literature book from her shelf, and ask them to analyze the story. She was confident about this approach, even though it was less objective than placement in the basal reader or mastery of district competencies.

## The Aha! Experience

Once the teachers had reading and writing in place, we saw the need for other changes. After we "chunked" the bits and pieces, after we found ways to connect to students' experience rather than going through the textbook—then we realized how disjointed our categorical programs were. And so we spent faculty meetings redesigning Chapter 1, bilingual ed, special ed, and so on. We actually made a "weave," a matrix—what is our present situation, and where do we want to be in six months? What worked with kids worked for us! Now the whole day is together for teachers and students. A lot of work, but it really brought the staff together [principal, Los Angeles].

In 1983–1984, during a visit to Glazier Elementary School in southeast Los Angeles, I observed a situation that led me to rethink the potential of the READ concept. The event is summarized in the anecdote above, which describes the decision by the Glazier staff to integrate categorical programs into the regular program. Glazier served students from a poor neighborhood, for many of whom English was a second language. At the principal's initiation, the faculty began to explore a "schoolwide" program—this concept is now embodied in Chapter 1 legislation, but in 1983-1984 it was a radical idea. By springtime, instruction at Glazier was virtually seamless; the staff had designed and implemented a program without pull-out routines, ability grouping, or any other stigma associated with categorical programs serving at-risk students.

It suddenly came to me that the Glazier situation exemplified Schaefer's (1967) concept of the school as a center of inquiry:

> [W]e can no longer afford to conceive of the schools simply as distribution centers for dispensing cultural orientations and information. . . . The intellectual demands upon the system have become so enormous that the school must become more than a place of instruction. It must become a center of inquiry—a producer as well as a transmitter of knowledge. . . . Not only our need for new knowledge but also our responsibility for the intellectual health of teachers suggests that schools should be conceived as centers of inquiry. [Where once] a commitment to learning throughout adult life was a necessity for a minority. . . , it is now a requirement for everyone who would not be a mere slave to the society he serves. . . . [The school must be the model] of an institution characterized by a pervasive search for meaning and rationality in its work . . . , [and students] similarly encouraged to seek a rational purpose in their studies [pp. 1-5].

The Glazier experience was remarkable, not only for the school's accomplishments (which were impressive) but also for the process that characterized the effort. The principal's explanation was exquisitely simple: "We use the same techniques in faculty and team meetings that we teach students in the classroom. Webbing and weaving help our students solve problems and communicate with one another. No reason why we grownups can't benefit from the same approach."

In May 1984, the school was a visitation site for the International Reading Association convention in Los Angeles. The busload of teachers and administrators that roamed through classrooms heard a common technical language and educational purpose from principal, teachers, and students. They saw variety in the style and quality of the program and heard a few complaints. For instance, a fourth-grade boy said he preferred worksheets: "Now I have to do a lot more thinking and talking." Although the young man's complaint was earnest, his reflectiveness (as well as the quality of his writing project) suggested that he was prospering under the new regime.

In the years since Glazier, my colleagues and I have explored the concept of the Inquiring School in numerous contexts (Calfee, in press). The basic idea is simple: Students are more likely to acquire critical literacy if the practice pervades the entire school. The argument also works in the other direction: Restructuring the elementary school depends on the effective use of language for the problem solving and communication that should be at the heart of the reading-writing curriculum from the earliest grades onward.

This motif sometimes emerges naturally: the principal emphasizes a literate style of discourse throughout the school, the resource specialist initiates team meetings or study groups, and the school faculty take collective responsibility for shaping the program (as in the third anecdote at the start of the paper). Spontaneous events like these are rare and easily snuffed out, however, especially in schools under fire because of low student achievement.

*Creating the Inquiring School.* The critical question, of course, is how to develop an Inquiring School by design rather than serendipity. Our experience over the past few years suggests that the task is possible and that the key is to begin with a focus on curriculum and instruction, the heart and soul of elementary schooling (Bean, Zigmond, & King, 1990; Heisinger, 1988; Whittaker, 1990). Hence, we generally advise a school to develop a READ cadre at the outset and then move toward a schoolwide effort after a year's experience with the techniques.

What are the characteristics of an elementary school that distinguish it as an Inquiring School? The first ingredient is the presence of a few clearly articulated goals about the educational purpose of the school and the techniques used to achieve those goals. Whether a visitor asks principal, teachers, students, secretary, or custodian, everyone responds with the same message.

A second ingredient is summarized by KISS; the concepts, practices, and technical language of the school all support the attainment of this small number of distinctive and overarching goals, all centered around a common thematic purpose. Rather than the collages of routines and programs that are so commonplace in today's schools, all the pieces fit together into a coherent package.

The third ingredient is a problem-solving stance by the entire community. Research shows that low-achieving students tend to attribute success to luck and failure to lack of ability (Dweck & Leggett, 1988); I suspect that the same pattern holds for organizations as well as individuals. In the Inquiring School, the group takes charge of problems; here is where critical literacy plays a key role by facilitating communication.

Our design for supporting development of the Inquiring School model is still in the early stages, but we have identified three components that seem critical: (1) effective small-group processes, (2) techniques for self-study and evaluation, and (3) individual efficacy. Our focus here is on the adults in the school, but again it seems that success in these three areas is likely to have an impact on students as well as staff.

The reasoning behind these three items is as follows. First, if teachers are to break through the isolation that pervades schooling today, they need a set of formal routines for working as a team. Our approach is to build on the lesson-design methods from READ as a model for planning and conducting effective meetings. Second, once teachers have techniques that foster collaboration, they can benefit further from systematic methods for problem solving; from recent studies, "teachers as practical researchers" seems to us a promising direction. Finally, the advantages of the Inquiring School model entail cost to the individual, and it is important to show individuals how to "recharge their batteries" and to handle the tensions between leadership and collaboration.

We have given the most attention thus far to the first item on the list, small-group process, because it flows naturally from the READ lesson design. In planning a problem-solving meeting, whether for the entire school faculty or between two teachers in a peer-coaching session, it makes sense to consider the opening, middle, closing, and follow-up of the session and to think about the processes for analyzing the problem and the structure for framing the solution. The explicit connection between the classroom and the school can be an immediate and powerful demonstration of the long-term value of the techniques of critical literacy. Webbing, for instance, works well to draw out kindergartners, but it serves adults equally well under the fancier label of *brainstorming*.

It is important to make these connections explicit rather than to rely solely on intuition. The usual assumption is that educated adults are naturally adept at working together; in fact, it is a demanding human endeavor. Summer institutes and workshops provide teachers with opportunities to practice communication and decision-making techniques (Saphier, Bigda-Peyton, & Pierson, 1989). Anyone who has conducted workshops knows the enormous outpouring of teacher talk. Unless guided, however, these exchanges remain at an informal level of discourse. By explicit rehearsal of group problem-solving techniques, school teams gain expertise that sustains the skills when they return to the schoolhouse, where team spirit can be dampened by day-to-day commonplaces. Our institute agenda explicitly addresses such issues as when the first team meeting will be held, what the agenda will be, and how the quality of the session will be monitored.

We have given less attention to the other two Inquiring School elements mentioned above. It has been suggested that *internal program evaluation* complement mandates imposed from above, that teachers and administrators take initiative as researchers (Cochran-Smith & Lytle, 1990). The benefits from this shift in perspective can be substantial. As teachers acquire a taste for working in a professional collaboration, they (re)discover the value of teamwork (Duckworth, 1987; Lampert, 1984; Rosenholtz, 1989). They learn to reflect on their own learning and development (Peterson, 1988; Zeichner & Liston, 1987). Strengthening *individual efficacy and leadership* is supported by several writers (Covey, 1989; Cuban, 1988), usually as a sidelight to the more important work of the school. We are currently exploring connections between this element and the concepts of critical literacy—language plays a critical role in self-awareness and self-confidence. In the Inquiring School model, teachers are routinely expected to demonstrate their craft and explain their reasoning, both of which are powerful catalysts for professionalization (Richert, in press, a, in press, b).

## Final Lessons: Application in At-Risk Settings

The proposition that poor children should receive literacy instruction of equal challenge to that provided students from more affluent backgrounds permeates this paper. The READ/Inquiring School model turns topsy-turvy several assumptions and practices for education of the disadvantaged by doing the following:

- Instruction based on rote repetition ("They can't handle abstractions") is displaced by student activities that encourage independent thought and collaborative teamwork.
- A piecemeal curriculum is supplanted by purposeful projects built around student experience and aimed toward transcendental outcomes (for example, the meaning and responsibilities of democracy).
- Standardized assessment is complemented by performance on genuine projects (for example, the second-grade production of "Broke" described earlier).
- The school faculty, isolated and fearful of higher-ups, frustrated by student "failure" and disinterest, turns with renewed expertise and vigor to the task of education.

My experiences over a decade in dozens of schools have left me with two lessons, both noted earlier but worth repeating. First, *virtually all students* are capable of a level of critical literacy that allows them to thrive as adults. Moreover, *virtually all teachers* have the intellectual and motivational capacity to support students in achieving this goal.

The second lesson is that a supportive school context is essential to realizing these goals. Schools serving children from disadvantaged neighborhoods face barriers of significant proportions, ranging from bureaucratic intrusions to skeptical expectations. Success depends on the curriculum materials, the techniques for instruction, the organizational arrangements, the principal's leadership style—and the financial resources available to the school. But none of these elements is as critical, in my opinion, as the substance and style of faculty interactions. When these interactions mirror the tenets of critical literacy, then the foundation exists for student success, for a schoolwide community of inquiry. Then teachers will fully realize their potential as a collective of intelligent, creative, and caring individuals. Then the hurdles of poor communication, low morale, and limited resources can be surmounted by teachers who reflect the highest standards of the professional vision that attracted them to schooling in the first place.

## References

Applebee, A. N. (1978). *The child's conception of story*. Chicago: University of Chicago Press.

Ashton-Warner, S. (1963). *Teacher*. New York: Bantam Books.

Balmuth, M. (1982). *The roots of phonics: A historical introduction*. New York: McGraw-Hill.

Barton, J., & Calfee, R. C. (1989). Theory becomes practice: One program. In J. Flood, D. Lapp, & N. Farnham (Eds.), *Content area reading-learning: Instructional studies*. Englewood Cliffs, NJ: Prentice-Hall.

Bean, R., Zigmond, N., & King, C. (1990). Changes in reading teachers' teaching practices and explanatory capabilities. Paper presented at the annual meeting of the American Educational Research Association, Boston.

Booth, W. C. (1989). *The vocation of a teacher: Rhetorical occasions 1967–1988*. Chicago: University of Chicago Press.

Brookover, W. (1982). *Creating effective schools*. Holmes Beach, FL: Learning Publications.

Calfee, R. C. (1981). *Cognitive psychology and educational practice*. In D. Berliner (Ed.), *Review of educational research*. Washington, DC: American Educational Research Association.

Calfee, R. C. (in press). The Inquiring School: Literacy for the year 2000. In C. Collins (Ed.), *Reading and writing in the twenty-first century*. Hillsdale, NJ: Erlbaum.

Calfee, R. C., Avelar La Salle, R., & Cancino, H. (in press). Critical literacy as the foundation for accelerating the education of at-risk students. In H. Levin (Ed.), *Accelerating the education of at-risk students.* New York: Falmer Press.

Calfee, R. C., & Drum, P. A. (1986). Research on teaching reading. In M. C. Wittrock (Ed.), *Handbook of research on teaching* (3rd ed.). New York: Macmillan.

Calfee, R. C., & Henry, M. K. (1986). Project READ: An in-service model for training classroom teachers in effective reading instruction. In J. V. Hoffman (Ed.), *Effective teaching of reading: Research into practice.* Newark, DE: International Reading Association.

Calfee, R. C., Henry, M. K., & Funderburg, J. A. (1988). A model for school change. In S. J. Samuels & P. D. Pearson (Eds.), *Changing school reading programs.* Newark, DE: International Reading Association.

Calfee, R. C., & Nelson-Barber, S. (in press). Diversity and constancy in human thinking: Critical literacy as amplifier of intellect and experience. In E. H. Hiebert (Ed.), *Literacy for a diverse society.* New York: Teachers College Press.

Chall, J. S. (1983). *Stages of reading development.* New York: McGraw-Hill.

Cochran-Smith, M., & Lytle, S. L. (1990). Research on teaching and teacher research: Issues that divide. *Educational Researcher, 19* (2), 2–11.

Covey, S. R. (1989). *The seven habits of highly effective people.* New York: Simon & Schuster.

Cuban, L. (1988). *The managerial imperative and the practice of leadership in schools.* Albany: State University of New York Press.

Duckworth, E. (1987). *"The having of wonderful ideas" and other essays on teaching and learning.* New York: Teachers College Press.

Dweck, C. S., & Leggett, E. L. (1988). A social-cognitive approach to motivation and personality. *Psychological Review, 95,* 256–273.

Fulghum, R. (1990, September, special issue). A bag of possibles and other matters of the mind. *Newsweek, 116* (28), 88–92.

Garner, R. (1987). *Metacognition and reading comprehension.* Norwood, NJ: Ablex.

Goodman, K. S., Smith, E. B., Meredith, R., & Goodman, Y. (1987). *Language and thinking in school: A whole-language curriculum.* New York: Richard Owen.

Graham, P. A. (1987). *Achievement for at-risk students.* Unpublished manuscript, Faculty of Education, Harvard University, Cambridge.

Hamilton, V. (1985). *The people could fly: American Black folktales.* New York: Knopf.

Heath, S. B. (1983). *Ways with words.* Cambridge, MA: Cambridge University Press.

Heisinger, C. (1988). *Opening doors for children at risk: Report to Metropolitan Foundation.* Unpublished manuscript. School of Education, Stanford University, Stanford, CA.

Henry, M. K., Calfee, R. C., & Avelar La Salle, R. (1989). A structural approach to decoding and spelling. In S. McCormick & J. Zutell (Eds.), *Thirty-Eighth yearbook of the National Reading Conference.* Chicago: National Reading Conference.

Horowitz, R., & Samuels, S. J. (1987). *Comprehending oral and written language.* San Diego, CA: Academic Press.

Knapp, M. S., & Shields, P. M. (1990a). *Better schooling for the children of poverty: Alternatives to conventional wisdom: Vol. 1. Summary.* Washington, DC: Office of Planning, Budget and Evaluation, U.S. Department of Education.

Knapp, M. S., & Shields, P. M. (Eds.). (1990b). *Better schooling for the children of poverty: Alternatives to conventional wisdom: Vol. 2. Commissioned papers and literature review.* Washington, DC: Office of Planning, Budget and Evaluation, U.S. Department of Education.

Lampert, M. (1984). Teaching about thinking and thinking about teaching. *Journal of Curriculum Studies, 16,* 1-18.

Lionni, L. (1985). *Frederick's fables: A treasury of favorite stories.* New York: Pantheon Books.

*NEA Today.* (1990, September). Are you going back to a restructured school? *NEA Today, 9* (1), 4-5.

Olson, D. R. (1989). Literate thought. In C. K. Leong & B. S. Randhawa (Eds.), *Understanding literacy and cognition.* New York: Plenum Press.

Orasanu, J. (Ed.). (1986). *Reading comprehension: From research to practice.* Hillsdale, NJ: Erlbaum.

Palincsar, A. S., & Brown, A. L. (1984). Reciprocal teaching of comprehension-fostering and monitoring activities. *Cognition and Instruction, 1,* 117–175.

Peterson, P. L. (1988). Teachers' and students' conditional knowledge for classroom teaching and learning. *Educational Researcher, 17* (5), 5–14.

Peterson, P. L., Clark, C. M., & Dickson, W. P. (in press). Educational psychology as a "foundation" in teacher education: Reforming an old notion. *Teachers College Record.*

Purkey, S. C., & Smith, M. S. (1985). School reform: The district policy implications of the effective schools literature. *The Elementary School Journal, 85,* 352–389.

Richert, A. E. (in press, a). Teaching teachers to reflect: A consideration of program structure. *Journal of Curriculum Studies.*

Richert, A. E. (in press, b). Case methods and teacher education: Using cases to teach teacher reflection. In R. Tabachnik & K. Zeichner (Eds.), *Issues and practices in inquiry-oriented teacher education.* London: Falmer Press.

Rosenholtz, S. J. (1989). *Teachers' workplace: The social organization of schools.* New York: Longman.

Salomon, G., & Perkins, D. N. (1989). Rocky roads to transfer: Rethinking mechanisms of a neglected phenomenon. *Educational Psychologist, 24,* 113–142.

Saphier, J., Bigda-Peyton, T., & Pierson, G. (1989). *How to make decisions that stay made.* Alexandria, VA: Association for Supervision and Curriculum Development.

Schaefer, R. J. (1967). *The school as a center of inquiry.* New York: Harper & Row.

Tuman, M. C. (1987). *A preface to literacy.* Tuscaloosa: University of Alabama Press.

Van Allsburg, C. (1985). *The polar express.* New York: Houghton Mifflin.

Weaver, C. (1988). *Reading process and practice: From socio-linguistics to whole language.* Portsmouth, NH: Heinemann.

Whittaker, A. (1990). Implementation, reflection, and revision: The cycle of collaboration. Paper presented at the annual meeting of the American Educational Research Association, Boston.

Whittaker, A., Wolf, S., & Wong, I. (1989). The inquiring school: Staff development and evaluation through collaboration. Paper presented at the annual meeting of the American Educational Research Association, San Francisco.

Williams, B. I., Richmond, P. A., & Mason, B. J. (Eds.). (1987). *Designs for compensatory education.* Washington, DC: Research and Evaluation Associates.

Zeichner, K. M., & Liston, D. P. (1987). Teaching student teachers to reflect. *Harvard Educational Review, 57,* 23–48.

# COMMENTARY

## Edys S. Quellmalz

My response to the schoolwide programs described to promote literacy in at-risk students draws on twenty-five years of experience in education, including teaching English and history at a low-income junior high school in the Los Angeles Unified School District; directing curriculum development projects in reading, composition skills, art, and higher-order thinking skills; and teaching courses in cognitive and instructional psychology, critical thinking, and the design of assessment instruments at Stanford University. In my current position as director of the Region F Chapter 1 Technical Assistance Center, I have worked with state and local education agencies in nine western states to address their needs in Chapter 1 curriculum and evaluation issues. From these experiences, I have developed a strong awareness of the complexity of school change; I have also maintained the conviction that we can, and must, improve the schooling of disadvantaged students.

Developing the literacy skills of students considered at risk presents a formidable challenge. Many of these educationally disadvantaged students suffer the twin problems of poverty and low academic achievement. To help these students catch up to the achievement levels of their peers, compensatory education programs historically have used a range of in-class and pull-out models to supplement instruction. Partly in response to the education reform movement's call to restructure and improve schools, the current Chapter 1 regulations permit use of Chapter 1 funds to develop schoolwide projects for at-risk students. Designers of these programs are seeking guidance for changes in the structure and methods of their Chapter 1 programs.

204

In "What Schools Can Do to Improve Literacy Instruction," Robert Calfee describes two programs he has developed. His Project READ and the Inquiring School embody research-based strategies that Chapter 1 practitioners could well incorporate in the design of schoolwide projects. As the reactor to Calfee's paper, I will highlight key elements of his programs and examine their link to components of Chapter 1 schoolwide projects. I will examine the research-based strategies in his and other schoolwide and literacy projects, then propose what else we need to know or do to plan and implement programs that will improve the literacy development of disadvantaged youth.

## What Are Schoolwide Projects?

Schoolwide projects are school-site attempts to apply the general elements of restructuring in a particular context. Restructuring may involve changes in organization, curriculum, instruction, and assessment. Key characteristics include school-site authority and decision making, redefinition and combinations of staff roles, redesign of curriculum and instruction to promote higher-order thinking, and thoughtful assessment of student achievement. Some restructured schools may radically reorganize the entire school structure, program, staff, and accountability systems; others may concentrate on redesign of fewer components. To provide a context for evaluating Calfee's programs, I describe some other prominent schoolwide efforts below.

A number of projects provide examples of attempts to redesign the entire school program. The organizational, curricular, and assessment components of these programs provide a backdrop for viewing applications of effective practice and the relationship of Calfee's Project READ and the Inquiring School to them.

The School Development Program introduced by James Comer of Yale University has focused for fifteen years on the achievement of inner-city children. His project, now implemented in a range of school districts throughout the country, addresses all aspects of the school structure. The program includes a governance and management team, a mental health team, and curriculum and staff development activities. Schools following the Comer model have been evaluated extensively with the finding that student achievement increases (Haynes, Comer, & Hamilton-Lee, 1988). Another restructuring program, Project Zero at Harvard University, is examining a series of pilot projects designed around the theory of multiple intelligences advanced by Howard Gardner. He proposes that at least seven distinct intellectual capacities—linguistic, musical, logical-mathematical, spatial, bodily kinesthetic, interpersonal, and intrapersonal—are used to approach problems. The programs combine in-depth school project work with extended exploration and apprenticeship in the community (Brickley & Gardner, 1990).

Henry Levin of Stanford University recently has advanced his concept of Accelerated Schools. In pilot projects in several states, school staff and community collaborate as a management team to create a central vision for the school and plan strategies to coordinate staff development, curriculum and instruction, parent involvement, and community services. The programs emphasize language; some employ Calfee's Project READ (Levin, 1987).

As in Calfee's projects, literacy forms the centerpiece of two other programs. Robert Slavin of Johns Hopkins University has developed the Success for All program based on his research with disadvantaged students. Key ingredients are intensive, early prevention and intervention, frequent assessment, and family support teams. Initiated primarily as a highly structured reading program, the project is being expanded to other subjects as well (Madden, Slavin, Karweit, & Livermon, 1989). In a state-initiated effort, the Arkansas Department of Education has developed the Multicultural Reading and Thinking (McRAT) project as an interdisciplinary program designed to improve students' higher-order thinking strategies as they apply to reading and social studies. The administrative, staff development, instructional, and evaluation components of the program have been implemented for five years in districts across the state (Quellmalz & Hoskyn, 1988).

Although these established restructuring programs evolved from different origins, they share elements essential to the success of any schoolwide effort. Schools seeking to design a schoolwide project for compensatory education should examine closely the effective procedures reported by these and Calfee's projects.

## Organizational Elements of Schoolwide Projects

The practitioner seeking guidance on how to change organizational elements of the school will find some information in various sections of Calfee's chapter. Calfee describes the organizational features of his programs as *strong leadership,* exhibited by time spent in classrooms with teams of teachers; *focus on a few simple, conceptual goals* sustained over two or three years; *integration of categorical programs* into the core curriculum; and adoption of *critical literacy as the process for professional interaction* about school goals, change strategies, and outcomes. Calfee repeatedly emphasizes that Project READ and the Inquiring School propel changes in the school structure with critical-literacy strategies such as the weaving and webbing activities described for classroom reading and writing instruction. Calfee writes that these techniques are used by school faculty as tools to consider ways to revamp staff development, curriculum planning, instructional strategies, and assessment of student success. Although the procedures are not detailed in his paper, Calfee references recent attempts to document team decision making and internal evaluation. He also mentions plans to develop strategies for individual development and for leadership. He emphasizes, however, that the style and substance of critical-literacy communication strategies promote reflective professionalism and empower a schoolwide community of inquiry.

Calfee's programs differ in their origins from many of the other efforts described above. His programs developed as "bottom-up" *curriculum* projects that focused on strategies for organizational change and support only as they became necessary. Other restructuring programs have begun as "top-down" *organizational change efforts,* with curriculum as only one component.

The research base for the organizational elements necessary to restructure the entire school program includes and goes beyond Calfee's descriptions. The research suggests that critical aspects of organizational change are

- Strong leadership
- Clear goals
- Collaborative involvement of all school staff in plan development, implementation, and evaluation
- Reconsideration of staffing patterns
- Provision of time and resources for collaborative planning, staff development, and reflection
- Reconsideration of class and staff schedules

The research also indicates that the change process requires extended time.

Some restructuring programs, such as Comer's and Levin's, include school-based governance teams to develop a unity of purpose and feeling of empowerment in the school. Leadership and collaboration of the teams lead to development of clear goals. Calfee's recommendation that the goals be few and conceptual meshes with my experience with the Arkansas and Chapter 1 projects. When schools attempt too many changes, the change efforts may lose focus and coherence. Too often, staff development plans present brief one-shot presentations that are not elaborated by extended sessions or by in-class modeling and feedback.

*Staff Development Requirements.* Alternative strategies for rescheduling class and staff time are not often documented. Staff development may take place on pupil-free days; during scheduled staff, grade-level, or department meetings; or during weekends or summers. Teachers may team teach, allowing one or more to be released. District or school administrators may relieve teachers so they can meet to plan and coordinate Chapter 1 and regular classroom assignments or engage in peer coaching or observations. Extensive staff development is a critical component of successful schoolwide programs. We would like to see specific ways that various schoolwide programs arrange for precious time for staff development.

*Requirements for Developing Chapter 1 Schoolwide Programs.* Chapter 1 schoolwide projects require a three-year effort, in recognition of the time required to implement substantive changes in schools. The federal regulations require staff, parental, and student involvement in the project-planning process. The regulations also require that the plan describe the results of a comprehensive needs assessment, goals to meet the needs, strategies for addressing the needs, uses of funds, training for parents and staff, and development and implementation of accountability measures. Content of the goals, staff development, materials, and measures are left to the individual schools.

### Redesigning the Curriculum

The Calfee projects have formulated an integrated language program with rhetorical structures and their components as the basic building blocks for studying topics, concepts, and strategies in literature and other subject areas. Narrative and expository discourse structures form the basis of lesson and unit design.

Cognitive research has tended to support the effectiveness of approaches in which students develop organized schemata or categories of information to capture the key concepts and strategies in a discipline. Coverage of isolated, discrete bits of information is eschewed in favor of integrated knowledge structures. The recommendations are to pursue depth, not breadth, thereby promoting more advanced skills within and across disciplines. Furthermore, projects are encouraged to develop student's metacognitive skills (skills in regulating their own thinking). The metainstructional lessons in Project READ stress self-consciousness about reading strategies, a recommended metacomprehension goal for developing strategic readers.

*Curriculum Approaches in Schoolwide Projects.* Other restructuring projects resemble Calfee's programs in drawing on these research recommendations. The Key School, part of Gardner's Project Zero, has restructured the entire curriculum. Students work on extended projects during the morning hours, then explore extensions of the concepts and skills they have learned by going to community activities and apprenticeships in the afternoon. The Arkansas McRAT project teaches four higher-order thinking strategies—analysis, comparison, inference, and evaluation—within the context of studying literature and other rhetorical structures as well as other cultures. The McRAT project also focuses on students' meta-cognitive skills by asking students for explanations of how they use explicit reasoning strategies and of how they would transfer the strategies to another topic, subject area, or practical application.

Other restructuring efforts address changes within particular disciplines rather than across the entire school. Whole-language approaches are of this type, as are history/social science and science approaches stressing extended treatment of fewer topics. California's literature-based language arts framework, which integrates literacy strategies with the study of original texts, is another example.

*Requirements for Disseminating Innovative Curricula.* To understand how schoolwide projects for at-risk students might revise, integrate, or coordinate curricula within and among disciplines, we need examples of the scope and sequence charts, curriculum plans, and model assignments the projects are using. Moreover, whether a schoolwide project team decides to adopt, adapt, or design curriculum reform, time must be provided for planning, staff development, and reformulation of units. These curricular reforms are based on cognitive theories of learning, which stress very different principles from those of behavioral learning theory, on which the basic skills movement and early compensatory education programs were founded. Teachers must experience significant shifts in their knowledge of, and commitment to, these new paradigms.

### Research-Based Instruction in Schoolwide Projects

*Research-Based Instructional Techniques.* The critical-literacy strategies used in Calfee's Project READ teach students the major discourse structures and techniques for comprehending them. Lesson design involves attention to the content, processing strategy, and structure for representing important concepts. For example, the "web," a semantic map, and the "weave," a compare-contrast matrix, provide pictorial representations of the relationships among words and ideas. The lessons also encourage student discussion, explanation, and transfer of their strategies.

The instructional components of Project READ draw on sound reading research. Comprehension research has provided evidence that comprehension is improved by building on students' background knowledge, attending to the structure of the type of material to be read, and reflecting on ideas and relationships in the text. The charting tools tap the visual modality and help students to organize and "see" the relationships among an often confusing sea of words.

Other projects have used charts, outlines, and other techniques to provide "scaffolding" for students' comprehension and composition. For example, visual-mapping techniques such as story mapping, character mapping, Venn diagrams, and charts for evaluating the pros and cons of issues are central components of the McRAT project. Studies of writing programs also have found such forms of visual mapping to be important tools for helping students to plan and structure the ideas in their stories and essays.

The effectiveness of interactive instructional models such as cooperative learning and reciprocal teaching is demonstrated in extensive research. Cooperative learning and tutoring are mentioned briefly as components of Project READ. Students discuss structures and concepts of their reading; they help and challenge each other. These kinds of interactive activities, stressed in programs such as Slavin's Success for All, are sharp departures from the stereotypical "drill and kill" worksheets characteristic of earlier generations of Chapter 1 programs.

***Accommodating Individual Differences in Schoolwide Literacy Programs.*** Effective instructional strategies for teaching reading comprehension help students not only to understand at a surface level what they have read but also to interpret and critique it. Schoolwide projects are based on the premise that instructional strategies that are effective for all students will help students who would have had additional instruction in the Chapter 1 program. Since a major goal of Chapter 1 is to promote students' advanced skills, schoolwide projects do not require differentiated instruction or materials for Chapter 1–eligible students. Nor, for that matter, do current Chapter 1 regulations prohibit supplemental tutoring for

Chapter 1 students on the same assignments and materials originating in the regular classroom.

The emphasis on advanced skills for Chapter 1 students is accompanied by recommendations for direct comprehension instruction in core literature requiring sustained reading and thinking. Assistance with basic skills, such as decoding or the vocabulary required to read the book, may come during a sustained reading lesson. Similarly, assistance with the mechanics of writing may come in the context of the student's final editing process, after peer conferencing and revision of early drafts to clarify ideas and streamline coherence.

Given the long-overdue call for elimination of "drill and kill" seatwork on low-level literacy skills, we have little systematic evidence about whether special strategies are necessary or useful for promoting more advanced skills in educationally disadvantaged students. For example, all students are likely to benefit from the visual-mapping techniques, but some students may need the visual mapping and scaffolding at greater levels of detail or longer. Work in student teams during webbing and weaving activities or during literary interpretation may require more structure or assistance when Chapter 1 students are involved. Models and strategies for literacy instruction for compensatory education students are sorely needed.

## Assessment and Evaluation

Evaluations of the Calfee project are described only generally rather than in terms of the tests and assessment instruments used and the specific gains achieved. "Competence in reading and interest in writing, not necessarily standardized scores," are mentioned as some forms of the data. Although these projects seem to have been more consistently and closely evaluated than most restructuring and literacy programs, we need more detail to judge the effectiveness of these and other programs. If the quality of student writing and discussion has improved, systematic ways of describing and evaluating the improvements should be reported.

A major difficulty for designers of Chapter 1 programs is that innovative programs seldom analyze achievement of Chapter 1 students separately from achievement of all students, although many of the projects have included Chapter 1 students.

*Requirements for Assessment in Chapter 1 Schoolwide Programs.* Assessment and evaluation requirements are central components of government-funded compensatory education programs. In the Chapter 1 regulations, schoolwide projects must not only document achievement gains but also prove that the Chapter 1 students' achievement is greater than it would have been if the usual Chapter 1 service delivery model had continued. Therefore, standardized assessment and systematic evaluation are essential for Chapter 1 schoolwide projects.

The federal Chapter 1 National Reporting Standards require documenting achievement gains in basic and advanced skills. For reading programs, the comprehension subtest of a nationally normed reading test is an acceptable measure of advanced skills in reading. In language arts programs, a nationally normed language arts test that measures the program's basic and advanced skills is acceptable for national reporting.

Chapter 1 programs are encouraged, too, to use multiple measures to assess student growth and to specify performance standards for growth in terms of desired outcomes. Therefore, compensatory programs that consider additional measures of reading comprehension and basic skills appropriate and necessary should, indeed, use them.

*Alternative Measures of Student Achievement.* Some test publishers are developing nationally normed tests that assess comprehension of longer texts. Other likely candidates for alternative measures are the reading, writing, and integrated literacy assessments used in the regular classroom. These may include tests developed by the district, other criterion-referenced tests, writing assessments, and teacher-made tests. Portfolios of student work also may serve as formal or informal measures of progress. If the portfolios of literacy activities are meant to serve as formal assessments, however, they need to have consistent structure, content, and evaluative criteria across classrooms and schools. More informal, but instructionally useful, assessments may include portfolios of assignments in progress, drafts of writing assignments, copies of reading or learning logs, and other records of progress in literacy development. Tapes and checklists of students' reading and speaking fluency may be considered.

Experts in literacy research agree that the multiple-choice format can tap only limited aspects of reading and writing competence. Clearly, multiple interpretations are a hallmark of the literacy-based curriculum; writing must be assessed by evaluation of actual writing samples. Districts have the authority to supplement assessment of Chapter 1 reading programs with alternative assessment formats specified in terms of other desired outcomes. Districts also have the authority to specify what constitutes substantial progress toward the desired outcomes. Currently, a number of districts are experimenting with portfolio assessments. Writing assessments have achieved acceptance if they have been developed to meet standards of technical quality.

Once again, educators committed to improving the literacy achievement of at-risk students need models of assessments deemed appropriate for measuring the goals of integrated literacy programs. Furthermore, policymakers concerned with improving the quality of Chapter 1 evaluations need evidence that alternative assessment formats meet reasonable standards of technical quality and thus can provide credible, useful evidence about the effectiveness of literacy programs for at-risk students.

## Summary

The schoolwide projects to improve literacy instruction for students at risk described by Robert Calfee represent state-of-the-art strategies for teaching literacy. I have attempted to identify the strategies of Calfee's and other literacy or restructuring efforts that seem most relevant for the design of Chapter 1 schoolwide projects emphasizing literacy. I also have noted the research-based aspects of literacy and restructuring efforts that might be useful for designers of literacy programs for at-risk youth to try. Finally, I have described information we still need to seek and models we need to see in order to understand better how to tailor general research findings to improve the literacy of educationally disadvantaged students. In looking back on the last twenty-five years of compensatory education, I must conclude that we have come a long way, but we also have a long way to go.

### References

Brickley, D., & Gardner, H. (1990). A school for all intelligences. *Educational Leadership, 47* (7), 33–36.

Haynes, N. M., Comer, J. P., & Hamilton-Lee, M. (1988). The school development program: A model for school improvement. *Journal of Negro Education, 57* (1), 34–44.

Levin, H. M. (1987). New schools for the disadvantaged. *Teacher Education Quarterly, 14* (4), 60–83.

Madden, N. A., Slavin, R. E., Karweit, N. I., & Livermon, B. J. (1989). Restructuring the urban elementary school. *Educational Leadership, 46* (5), 14–18.

Quellmalz, E. S., & Hoskyn, J. (1988). Making a difference in Arkansas: The Multicultural Reading and Thinking Project. *Educational Leadership, 46,* 52–55.

# 7

# A Cognitive Apprenticeship for Disadvantaged Students

*Allan Collins, Jan Hawkins, and Sharon M. Carver*

HISTORICALLY, THERE HAS BEEN A GREAT DIVIDE BETWEEN EDUCA-
tion for the advantaged (including, for example, Latin and geometry) and training for the disadvantaged (for example, vocational
education). As education has become universal, we have extended
education for the advantaged to more and more of the population,
though with limited success and in watered-down form. But it is
difficult for most students to understand why they should be reading *Macbeth* and learning to multiply fractions, when there is no
obvious call for such knowledge in any life they can imagine for
themselves. And there is increasing resistance among students to
being force-fed an education that seems irrelevant to their lives.

   Our argument in this chapter is that the changing nature of
work in society (see, for example, Zuboff, 1988) provides a potential
meeting ground where education for the advantaged and disadvantaged can come together in a curriculum in which the educational
tasks reflect the future nature of work in society. Work is becoming
computer based and, at the same time, requires more and more
ability to learn and think. Hence, a curriculum built around tasks

This work was supported by the Center for Technology in Education under
grant number 1-135562167-A1 from the Office of Educational Research and
Improvement, U.S. Department of Education, to Bank Street College of
Education.

that require learning and thinking in a computer-based environment will make sense to both advantaged and disadvantaged students and will educate them in ways that make sense for society at large.

Only in the last century, and only in industrialized nations, has formal schooling emerged as a widespread method of educating the young. Before schools appeared, apprenticeship was the most common means of learning. Even today, many complex and important skills, such as those required for language use and social interaction, are learned informally through apprenticeshiplike methods— that is, methods involving not didactic teaching but observation, coaching, and successive approximation.

The differences between formal schooling and apprenticeship methods are many, but for our purposes, one is most important: in schools, skills and knowledge have become abstracted from their use in the world. In apprenticeship learning, in contrast, skills not only are continually in use by skilled practitioners but also are instrumental to the accomplishment of meaningful tasks. Said differently, apprenticeship embeds the learning of skills and knowledge in their social and functional context. This difference has serious implications for the design of instruction for students. Specifically, we propose the development of a new "cognitive apprenticeship" (Collins, Brown, & Newman, 1989) to teach students the thinking and problem-solving skills involved in school subjects such as reading, writing, and mathematics.

## Traditional Apprenticeship

To foreshadow those methods and why they are likely to be effective, let us first consider some of the crucial features of traditional apprenticeship (Lave, 1988). First and foremost, apprenticeship focuses closely on the specific methods for carrying out tasks in a domain. Apprentices learn these methods through a combination of what Lave calls observation, coaching, and practice or what we, from the teacher's point of view, call modeling, coaching, and fading. In this sequence of activities, the apprentice repeatedly observes the master and his or her assistants executing (or modeling) the target process, which usually involves a number of different but interrelated subskills. The apprentice then attempts to execute the process with guidance and help from the master (that is, coaching). A key aspect of coaching is the provision of scaffolding, which is the support, in the form of reminders and help, that the apprentice requires to approximate the execution of the entire composite of skills. Once the learner has a grasp of the target skill, the master reduces (or fades) participation, providing only limited hints and feedback to the learner, who practices by successively approximating smooth execution of the whole skill.

## From Traditional to Cognitive Apprenticeship

Collins et al. (1989) proposed an extension of apprenticeship for teaching subjects such as reading, writing, and mathematics. We call this rethinking of learning and teaching in school *cognitive apprenticeship* to emphasize two issues. First, the method is aimed primarily at teaching the processes that experts use to handle complex tasks. Where conceptual knowledge and factual knowledge are addressed, cognitive apprenticeship emphasizes their uses in solving problems and carrying out tasks. That is, in cognitive apprenticeship, conceptual knowledge and factual knowledge are exemplified and practiced in the contexts of their use. Conceptual knowledge and factual knowledge thus are learned in terms of their uses in a variety of contexts, encouraging both a deeper understanding of the meaning of the concepts and facts themselves and a rich web of memorable associations between them and the problem-solving contexts. We expect this dual focus on expert processes and learning in context to help solve current educational problems.

Second, *cognitive apprenticeship* refers to the focus on learning through guided experience in cognitive skills and processes rather than physical ones. Although we do not wish to draw a major theoretical distinction between the learning of physical skills and the learning of cognitive skills, there are differences that have practical implications for the organization of teaching and learning activities. Most importantly, traditional apprenticeship has evolved to teach domains in which the process of carrying out target skills is external, thus readily available to both student and teacher for observation, comment, refinement, and correction, and bears a rel-

atively transparent relationship to concrete products. The externalization of relevant processes and methods makes possible such characteristics of apprenticeship as its reliance on observation as a
primary means of building a conceptual model of a complex target
skill. The relatively transparent relationship, at all stages of production, between process and product facilitates the learner's recognition and diagnosis of errors, on which the early development of self-
correction skill depends.

Applying apprenticeship methods to largely cognitive skills
requires the externalization of processes that are usually carried out
internally. Given the way that most subjects are taught and learned
in school, teachers cannot make fine adjustments in students' application of skill and knowledge to problems and tasks, because
teachers have no access to the relevant cognitive processes. By the
same token, students usually do not have access to the cognitive
problem-solving processes of instructors as a basis for learning
through observation and mimicry. Cognitive research has begun to
delineate the cognitive processes that comprise expertise, which
heretofore were inaccessible. Cognitive apprenticeship teaching
methods are designed to bring these tacit processes into the open,
where students can observe, enact, and practice them with help from
the teacher and from other students.

In addition to the emphasis on cognitive skills, there are two
major differences between cognitive apprenticeship and traditional
apprenticeship. First, because traditional apprenticeship is set in
the workplace, the problems and tasks that are given to learners
arise not from pedagogical concerns but from the demands of the
workplace. Cognitive apprenticeship, as we envision it, differs from
traditional apprenticeship in that the tasks and problems are chosen
to illustrate the power of certain techniques and methods, to give
students practice in applying these methods in diverse settings, and
to increase the complexity of tasks slowly, so that component skills
and models can be integrated. In short, tasks are sequenced to reflect
the changing demands of learning. Letting the job demands select
the tasks for students to practice is one of the great inefficiencies of
traditional apprenticeship.

A second difference between cognitive apprenticeship and
traditional apprenticeship is the emphasis in cognitive apprentice-

ship on generalizing knowledge so that it can be used in many different settings. Traditional apprenticeship emphasizes teaching skills in the context of their use. We propose that cognitive apprenticeship should extend practice to diverse settings so that students learn how to apply their skills in varied contexts. Moreover, the principles underlying the application of knowledge and skills in different settings should be articulated as fully as possible by the teacher, whenever they arise in different contexts.

## A Framework for Designing Learning Environments

Our introductory discussion of cognitive apprenticeship has raised numerous pedagogical and theoretical issues that we believe are important to the design of learning environments generally. To facilitate consideration of these issues, we have developed a framework consisting of four dimensions that constitute any learning environment: content, method, sequence, and sociology. Relevant to each of these dimensions is a set of characteristics that we believe should be considered in constructing or evaluating learning environments. These characteristics are described in detail below, with examples from reading, writing, and mathematics.

*Content.* Recent cognitive research has begun to differentiate the types of knowledge required for expertise. In particular, researchers have begun to distinguish between the concepts, facts, and procedures associated with expertise and various types of strategic knowledge. We use the term *strategic knowledge* to refer to the usually tacit knowledge that underlies an expert's ability to make use of concepts, facts, and procedures as necessary to solve problems and accomplish tasks. This sort of expert problem-solving knowledge involves problem-solving heuristics (or "rules of thumb") and the strategies that control the problem-solving process. Another type of strategic knowledge, often overlooked, includes the learning strategies that experts use to acquire new concepts, facts, and procedures in their own or another field.

*Domain knowledge* includes the concepts, facts, and procedures explicitly identified with a particular subject matter that are generally explicated in school textbooks, class lectures, and demonstrations. This kind of knowledge, although certainly important, provides insufficient clues for many students about how to solve problems and accomplish tasks in a domain. Examples of domain knowledge in reading are vocabulary, syntax, and phonics rules.

*Heuristic strategies* are generally effective techniques and approaches for accomplishing tasks that might be regarded as "tricks of the trade"; they do not always work, but when they do, they are quite helpful. Most heuristics are tacitly acquired by experts through the practice of solving problems; however, there have been noteworthy attempts to address heuristic learning explicitly (Schoenfeld, 1985). For example, standard heuristic for writing is to plan to rewrite the introduction and, therefore, to spend relatively little time crafting it. In mathematics, a heuristic for solving problems is to try to find a solution for simple cases and see whether the solution generalizes.

*Control strategies,* as the name suggests, control the process of carrying out a task. These are sometimes referred to as "metacognitive" strategies (Palincsar & Brown, 1984; Schoenfeld, 1985). As students acquire more and more heuristics for solving problems, they encounter a new management or control problem: how to select among the possible problem-solving strategies, how to decide when to change strategies, and so on. Control strategies have monitoring, diagnostic, and remedial components; decisions about how to proceed in a task generally depend on an assessment of one's current state relative to one's goals, on an analysis of current difficulties, and on the strategies available for dealing with difficulties. For example, a comprehension-monitoring strategy might be to try to state the main point of a section one has just read; if one cannot do so, then one has not understood the text, and it might be best to reread parts of it. In mathematics, a simple control strategy for solving a complex problem might be to switch to a new part of a problem if one is stuck.

*Learning strategies* are strategies for learning any of the other kinds of content described above. Knowledge about how to learn ranges from general strategies for exploring a new domain to more specific strategies for extending or reconfiguring knowledge in solving problems or carrying out complex tasks. For example, if students want to learn to solve problems better, they need to learn how to relate each step in the sample problems worked in textbooks to the principles discussed in the text (Chi, Bassok, Lewis, Reimann, & Glaser, 1989). If students want to write better, they need to find people to read their writing who can give helpful critiques and explain the reasoning underlying the critiques (most people cannot). They also need to learn to analyze others' texts for strengths and weaknesses.

*Method.* Teaching methods should be designed to give students the opportunity to observe, engage in, and invent or discover expert strategies in context. Such an approach enables students to see how these strategies combine with their factual and conceptual knowledge and how they use a variety of resources in the social and physical environments. The six teaching methods advocated here fall roughly into three groups. The first three (modeling, coaching, and scaffolding) are the core of cognitive apprenticeship, designed to help students acquire an integrated set of skills through processes of observation and guided practice. The next two (articulation and reflection) are methods designed to help students both to focus their observations of expert problem solving and to gain conscious access to (and control of) their own problem-solving strategies. The final method (exploration) is aimed at encouraging learner autonomy, not only in carrying out expert problem-solving processes but also in defining or formulating the problems to be solved.

*Modeling* involves an expert's performing a task so that the students can observe and build a conceptual model of the processes required to accomplish it. In cognitive domains, this requires the externalization of usually internal processes and activities—specifically, the heuristics and control processes by which experts apply their basic conceptual and procedural knowledge. For example, a teacher might model the reading process by reading aloud in one voice while verbalizing her thought processes in another voice (Collins & Smith, 1982). In mathematics, Schoenfeld (see Collins et al., 1989) models the process of solving problems by having students bring difficult new problems for him to solve in class.

*Coaching* consists of observing students while they carry out a task and offering hints, scaffolding, feedback, modeling, reminders, and new tasks aimed at bringing their performance closer to expert performance. Coaching may direct students' attention to a previously unnoticed aspect of the task or simply remind them of some aspect of the task that is known but has been temporarily overlooked. The content of the coaching interaction is immediately related to specific events or problems that arise as the students attempt to accomplish the target task. In Palincsar and Brown's (1984) reciprocal teaching of reading, the teacher coaches students while they ask questions, clarify their difficulties, generate summaries, and make predictions.

*Scaffolding* refers to the supports the teacher provides to help students carry out the task. These supports can take either the form of suggestions or help, as in Palincsar and Brown's (1984) reciprocal teaching, or the form of physical supports, as with the cue cards used by Scardamalia, Bereiter, and Steinbach (1984) to facilitate writing or the short skis used to teach downhill skiing (Burton, Brown, & Fisher, 1984). When a teacher provides scaffolding, she or he executes parts of the task that the student cannot yet manage. Fading involves the gradual removal of supports until students are on their own.

*Articulation* includes any method of getting students to articulate their knowledge, reasoning, or problem-solving processes in a domain. We have identified several different methods of articulation. First, inquiry teaching (Collins & Stevens, 1982, 1983) is a strategy of questioning students to lead them to articulate and refine their understanding of concepts and procedures in different domains. For example, an inquiry teacher in reading might systematically question students about why one summary of the text is good but another is poor, to get the students to formulate an explicit model of a good summary. Second, teachers might encourage students to articulate their thoughts as they carry out their problem solving, as do Scardamalia et al. (1984). Third, teachers might have students assume the critic or monitor role in cooperative activities and thereby lead students to formulate and articulate their ideas to other students.

*Reflection* involves enabling students to compare their own problem-solving processes with those of an expert, another student, and, ultimately, an internal cognitive model of expertise. Reflection is enhanced by the use of various techniques for reproducing or "replaying" the performances of both expert and novice for comparison. The level of detail for a replay may depend on the student's stage of learning, but usually some form of "abstracted replay," in which the critical features of expert and student performance are highlighted, is desirable (Collins & Brown, 1988). For reading or writing, one method to encourage reflection might consist of recording students as they think out loud and then replaying the tape for comparison with the thinking of experts and other students.

*Exploration* involves pushing students into a mode of problem solving on their own. Forcing them to do exploration is critical if they are to learn how to frame questions or problems that are interesting and that they can solve. Exploration as a method of teaching involves setting general goals for students and then encouraging them to focus on particular subgoals of interest to them, or even to revise the general goals as they come on something more interesting to pursue. For example, in reading, the teacher might send the students to the library to investigate theories about why the stock market crashed in 1929. In writing, students might be encouraged to write an essay defending the most outrageous thesis they can devise. In mathematics, students might be asked to generate and test hypotheses about teenage behavior given a database on teenagers detailing their backgrounds and how they spend their time and money.

**Sequencing.** Designers need to support both the integration and the generalization of knowledge and complex skills. We have identified some principles that should guide the sequencing of learning activities to facilitate the development of robust problem-solving skills.

*Increasing complexity* refers to the construction of a sequence of tasks such that more and more of the skills and concepts necessary for expert performance are required (Van Lehn & Brown, 1980; Burton et al., 1984; White, 1984). There are two mechanisms for helping students manage increasing complexity. The first mechanism is to sequence tasks in order to control task complexity. The second mechanism is the use of scaffolding, which enables students to handle at the outset the complex set of activities needed to accomplish any interesting task. In reading, for example, increasing task complexity might consist of progressing from relatively short texts using straightforward syntax and concrete description to texts in which complexly interrelated ideas and the use of abstractions make interpretation difficult.

*Increasing diversity* refers to the construction of a sequence of tasks in which an increasingly wider variety of strategies or skills is required. As a skill becomes well learned, it becomes increasingly important that tasks requiring a diversity of skills and strategies be introduced so that the student learns to distinguish the conditions under which they do (and do not) apply. Moreover, as students learn to apply skills to more diverse problems, their strategies acquire a richer net of contextual associations and thus are more readily available for use with unfamiliar or novel problems. For reading, task diversity might be attained by intermixing reading for pleasure, reading for memory (studying), and reading to find out some particular information in the context of some other task.

*Global before local skills* refers to a sequencing principle with the chief effect of allowing students to build a conceptual map, so to speak, before attending to the details of the terrain (Norman, 1973). For example, in tailoring (Lave, 1988), apprentices learn to put together a garment from precut pieces before learning to cut out the pieces themselves. In general, having students build a conceptual model of the target skill or process (which is also encouraged by expert modeling) accomplishes two things. First, even when the learner is able to accomplish only a portion of a task, having a clear conceptual model of the overall activity helps him make sense of the portion that he is carrying out. Second, the presence of a clear conceptual model of the target task acts as a guide for the learner's performance, thus improving his ability to monitor his own progress and to develop attendant self-correction skills. This principle requires some form of scaffolding. In algebra, for example, students may be relieved of having to carry out low-level computations in which they lack skill in order to concentrate on the higher-order reasoning and strategies required to solve an interesting problem (Brown, 1985).

*Sociology.* The final dimension in our framework concerns the sociology of the learning environment. For example, tailoring apprentices learn their craft not in a special, segregated learning environment but in a busy tailoring shop. They are surrounded by both masters and other apprentices, all engaged in the target skills at various levels of expertise. They are expected to engage from the beginning in activities that contribute directly to the production of actual garments, advancing quickly toward independent skilled production. As a result, apprentices learn skills in the context of their application to realistic problems, within a culture focused on and defined by expert practice. Furthermore, certain aspects of the social organization of apprenticeship encourage productive beliefs about the nature of learning and expertise that are significant to learners' motivation, confidence, and, most importantly, their orientation toward problems that they encounter as they learn. From our consideration of these general issues, we have abstracted critical characteristics affecting the sociology of learning.

*Situated learning* is a critical element in fostering learning by having students carry out tasks and solve problems in an environment that reflects the nature of such tasks in the world. Where tasks have become computer based in the world, it is important to make them computer based in school. For example, reading and writing instruction might be situated in the context of students putting together a book on what they learn about science. Dewey created a situated learning environment in his experimental school by having the students design and build a clubhouse (Cuban, 1984), a task that emphasizes arithmetic and planning skills.

*Community of practice* refers to the creation of a learning environment in which the participants actively communicate about and engage in the skills involved in expertise, where expertise is understood as the practice of solving problems and carrying out tasks in a domain. Such a community leads to a sense of ownership, characterized by personal investment and mutual dependence. It cannot be forced, but it can be fostered by common projects and shared experiences. Activities designed to engender a community of practice for reading might engage students and teacher in discussing how they interpret what they read and use those interpretations for a wide variety of purposes, including those that arise in other classes or domains.

*Intrinsic motivation* is related to the issue of situated learning and the creation of a community of practice. Lepper and Greene (1979) and Malone (1981) discuss the importance of creating learning environments in which students perform tasks because they are intrinsically related to an interesting or at least coherent goal rather than for some extrinsic reason, such as getting a good grade or pleasing the teacher. In reading and writing, for example, intrinsic motivation might be achieved by having students communicate with students in another part of the world by electronic mail (Collins, 1986; Levin, 1982).

*Exploiting cooperation* refers to having students work together in a way that fosters cooperative problem solving. Learning through cooperative problem solving is both a powerful motivator and a powerful mechanism for extending learning resources. In reading, activities to exploit cooperation might involve having students break up into pairs, where one student articulates his thinking process while reading and the other student questions the first student about why he made different inferences.

Exhibit 7.1 summarizes the characteristics of each of the four dimensions included in our framework for designing learning environments. The content and sequencing dimensions of learning environments provide a striking contrast to the focus on isolated mastery of discrete lower-level skills that is characteristic of compensatory education programs developed in response to Chapter 1 legislation (Means & Knapp, Chapter One). However, our framework is entirely consistent with the goals of compensatory education, particularly with respect to the high level of teacher-student interaction that both the methods and sociology dimensions advocate. Though the cognitive apprenticeship environment is important for all students, we argue that it is particularly effective for students who are considered disadvantaged or "at risk" because learning is embedded in a setting that is more like work, where the tasks have some "authentic" relationship to students' lives and a community of people is working together to accomplish real-world goals (Brown, Collins, & Duguid, 1989). We contend that disadvantaged students who learn in an apprenticeship environment will not only learn the basic reading, writing, and mathematics skills that they have had difficulty learning either in regular classrooms or in Chapter 1 programs but also develop the more advanced skills char-

**Exhibit 7.1. Design Principles for Cognitive Apprenticeship Environments.**

## Content

*Types of knowledge required for expertise*

- Domain knowledge: Subject-matter–specific concepts, facts, and procedures
- Heuristic strategies: Generally applicable techniques for accomplishing tasks
- Control strategies: General approaches for directing one's solution process
- Learning strategies: Knowledge about how to learn new concepts, facts, and procedures

## Method

*Ways to promote the development of expertise*

- Modeling: Teacher performs a task so students can observe
- Coaching: Teacher observes and facilitates while students perform a task
- Scaffolding: Teacher provides supports to help the student perform a task
- Articulation: Teacher encourages students to verbalize their knowledge and thinking
- Reflection: Teacher enables students to compare their performance with that of others
- Exploration: Teacher invites students to pose and solve their own problems

## Sequencing

*Keys to ordering learning activities*

- Increasing complexity: Meaningful tasks gradually increasing in difficulty
- Increasing diversity: Practice in a variety of situations to emphasize broad application
- Global to local skills: Focus on conceptualizing the whole task before executing the parts

## Sociology

*Social characteristics of learning environments*

- Situated learning: Students learn in the context of working on realistic tasks
- Community of practice: Communication about different ways to accomplish meaningful tasks
- Intrinsic motivation: Students set personal goals to seek skills and solutions
- Cooperation: Students work together to accomplish their goals

acteristic of expertise. The remainder of this chapter is devoted to introducing two apprenticeship learning environments currently being designed and evaluated.

## Two Examples of Cognitive Apprenticeship
## for Disadvantaged Students

We have been working at two schools during the last year where the majority of the students might be considered at risk. We will briefly describe how different forms of a cognitive apprenticeship have been implemented at the Charlotte Middle School in Rochester, New York, and the Central Park East Secondary School in Harlem to demonstrate alternative approaches to applying the principles of context, method, sequencing, and sociology outlined above.

*Discover Rochester.* Charlotte Middle School is an urban school located in a socioeconomically disadvantaged neighborhood. It has approximately 64 percent minority students and provides free or reduced-cost lunches for 56 percent of its students. Close to 30 percent of the students have been identified as moderate to high in terms of being "at risk," which means that they can be characterized by two or more of the following criteria: multiple suspensions, excessive absences, repetition of a grade, failure of two or more classes in one year, and California Achievement Test scores three or more years behind grade level.

A team consisting of two University of Rochester researchers and the eighth-grade math, science, history, English, and writing teachers conceptualized and implemented the Discover Rochester project. Generally speaking, the researchers provided theoretical background and computer training for the teachers, and the teachers contributed their expertise in curriculum design. All team members served as leaders and facilitators during actual classroom sessions, and all contributed to both formal and informal program evaluation and assessment of student progress.

The goal of this project is to raise the skill levels of urban middle school students beyond basic skills to develop sophisticated skills that will help them succeed at work and in everyday life (Resnick, 1987). It provides a model for redesigning middle school learning environments based on many of the principles advocated above, yet cast within the current constraints of an urban school system. The aim is to increase student motivation, effort, and learning by providing a learning environment sensitive to individual needs, interests, and abilities. To accomplish this, students are provided with computer tools that aid them in learning general thinking and problem-solving skills as they explore their community and experience ways of applying their school learning in the real world.

In a pilot of the Discover Rochester project at the Charlotte Middle School, "at-risk" eighth-graders spent one day each week exploring aspects of the Rochester environment from scientific, mathematical, historical, cultural, and literary perspectives. They worked in groups to conduct their own research about topics ranging from weather to industry to theater to employment, using a variety of strategies including library and archival research, telephone and face-to-face interviews, field observation, and experimentation. On the basis of their research, students developed a HyperCard exhibit for the Rochester Museum and Science Center, including text, audio, graphics, maps, and music.

The primary focus of the Discover Rochester curriculum is on explicitly teaching general strategies while students investigate multiple aspects of their own community in order to design an interactive learning exhibit. Thus, students' learning is situated in an exploration of real-world topics for a real-world purpose. The particular skills targeted by the Discover Rochester curriculum are both control and heuristic strategies for learning and communicating information. Students learned to coordinate five types of skills to complete their exhibit: question posing, data gathering, data interpretation and representation, presentation, and evaluation—an elaborated version of the Bransford, Sherwood, Vye, and Rieser (1986) IDEAL program.

In the context of the interdisciplinary work, students practiced a variety of heuristics for accomplishing each subtask. Specifically, explicit instruction was provided in the following heuristic strategies for research and communication:

• *Question posing:* (1) brainstorming techniques for generating interesting topics and deciding what students want to discover about those topics and (2) typical sequences of questions beyond the traditional "Who? What? Why? Where? When? How?" (for example, when asking about someone's job, generally ask for the job title, responsibilities and risks, necessary training, and so on)

- *Data gathering:* (1) reading and listening comprehension skills; (2) strategies for using indexes, headings, tables of contents, and so on for finding information in texts; (3) interviewing techniques; (4) strategies for using other nontraditional data sources, such as photographs and museum exhibits; and (5) various techniques for recording and storing information (for example, notes, tapes, photos, and photocopies)
- *Data interpretation and representation:* (1) strategies for viewing data in historical and social contexts, (2) strategies for organizing and analyzing data (for example, categorization), and (3) various techniques for representing information (for example, expository vs. narrative writing; paragraphs vs. lists vs. tables; and visual representations such as maps, time lines, and graphs)
- *Presentation:* (1) strategies for considering the interests and abilities of the audience; (2) strategies for clear organization, consistency, readability, and so on; (3) specific skills for designing computer presentations, such as designing modules, and creating options for interactivity; and (4) skills for verbally describing a nonverbal presentation
- *Evaluation:* (1) strategies for self-evaluation as well as peer evaluation, (2) techniques for surveying users to get their feedback about a presentation, and (3) strategies for considering and incorporating suggestions

In terms of sequence, instruction progressed from global to local focus and from less to more complex tasks by starting with an overview of all five skill areas, highlighting heuristics already possessed by students or easily within reach. For example, when asked about alternative representations for information, students readily suggest paragraphs, lists, and drawings. The lesson then would begin with showing how the same information can be presented in all three forms and proceed to discussion of which forms would be best in which situations. As students began to understand the overall goals, teachers introduced the more advanced heuristics. For example, once students started to generate and evaluate alternative representations using text and pictures, teachers introduced new types, such as time lines, graphs, and maps. Diversity increased as students worked on more and more aspects of the exhibit. For example, teachers and students began to discuss diverse types of graphs, such as line, bar, pie, and so on, as a wider variety of graphing situations arose. Also, the interdisciplinary aspect of the project incorporates domain knowledge from four subject areas to highlight the use of similar general strategies in all of them. For example, history concepts of city growth and science concepts of animal and plant distribution might both be represented using maps.

The teaching methods used in the Discover Rochester project exemplify all six of the principles described under "Method" above. The lesson sequences began with explicit descriptions of heuristics for each type of skill and teacher modeling to demonstrate alternative approaches. Next, students practiced on prepared materials designed to provide scaffolding in some of the five skill areas to allow students to focus their attention on particular areas. Finally, students spent most of their time in individual or small-group practice in the context of self-directed exploration. As students worked on their projects, teachers provided additional coaching and scaffolding as needed. Students also spent a significant amount of time articulating their understanding and reflecting on their progress as they designed and evaluated their exhibit.

The Discover Rochester learning environment was designed to embody a community of practice by resembling the natural work environment. Students worked primarily in one room for a two-period block of time in the morning and another in the afternoon, rather than switching rooms every forty minutes. Students had ready access to computer tools for facilitating their work (eight Macintosh computers for twenty students). They learned to use MacPaint, MacWrite, CricketGraph, and HyperCard to the extent that they found these software tools useful. Students also took an active role in directing their own learning. By selecting their own topics within Discover Rochester and choosing when to work independently and collaboratively, they could focus on their own interests, which increased their motivation for learning.

For example, at the beginning of the project, students and teachers worked as a group to brainstorm about possible topics for study. They used maps, phone books, information from the chamber of commerce, and other sources to help generate ideas. Students formed groups based on mutual interest. One group decided to study Rochester's environment. They chose weather as one subtopic and generated questions about the recent year's precipitation, temperature, and wind patterns; how those patterns compare with the thirty-year norms; how proximity to Lake Ontario affects the weather; and so on. With these questions in mind, they assigned each group member to research one subtopic and even planned strategies for finding information (for example, interview a meteorologist, gather weather reports from local papers, check the library for information on climate normals). Data gathering proceeded somewhat independently, but interpretation, presentation, and evaluation were done more collaboratively to encourage consistency in the final product. Throughout the process, students called on teacher or peer assistance when they needed it. In addition, explicit lessons in general techniques (for example, effective interviewing techniques) were interspersed with the ongoing activity of the group, and teachers sought opportunities to practice subject area skills (for example, interpreting graphs).

During the pilot project, we observed impressive improvement in the students' intrinsic motivation. Initially, students were sluggish, uncooperative, and unimaginative. Some refused to talk at all. The initial brainstorming session was more a lesson for the teachers in pulling teeth. As the students developed new skills (particularly computer skills), they began to participate more often, and many students took initiative beyond expectations. One student took two pages of notes from library work done during a free period. Another contacted administrators and legal counsel about the possibility of conducting a survey in the school. A third learned how to do animation in HyperCard. A fourth student made posters for the community showcase day, and about a third of the group started working voluntarily during their lunch periods. The students not only developed the five aspects of research and communication skills but also generated creative strategies for gathering and presenting information.

As the students became more engrossed in the project, behavior problems became almost nonexistent. During the first few days, there was a lot of off-task behavior in both large- and small-group work, and students were more interested in what happened in the hall between periods than in what happened in the classroom. Over time, students started ignoring the activity in the hall between periods as they pored over their work. Other teachers could not believe that we would take these "troublemakers" on field trips, but the students were polite and cooperative on all three trips we took.

On the first day of the project, students in the hall questioned why the "dummies" got to use the new computers and they did not. The participating students initially perceived themselves according to the labels of their peers. As they became proficient with the computers, they received a lot of positive attention from both peers and teachers who were curious, envious, and in awe of what the participants had accomplished. They began to perceive themselves as more competent than they had before, both in terms of their current skills and in terms of their future career plans. One girl, who won the award for being the hardest-working student, commented in a television interview that she believed that she could do more things than she had before. Another has decided to pursue a career that involves computers.

As the students explained their work to others, it was obvious that they felt a sense of pride in how much they had learned. At the same time, their standards for "good work" became stricter. Initially, students approached their work by looking for the quickest and easiest solutions. Before the students' first version of the Hyper-Card exhibit went into the museum, they talked about how good it was and were convinced that there was nothing they wanted to change. After interviewing students from other schools who actually used the exhibit and found it boring, participants started reflecting on ways to improve their work. They actually implemented many of their ideas and started paying more attention to detail and to audience as they added to the project; more significantly, as they explained their work to peers and adults on the showcase day, they discussed what they would like to improve in addition to bragging about what they had done.

Many of the students involved in the project qualified for Chapter 1 instruction. Some had been placed in pull-out programs for reading, and others received in-class help from the writing resources teacher. Despite the fact that these students missed their special instruction to participate in the project, their teachers reported that they improved more over the course of the project than did similar students who had received the regular Chapter 1 instruction.

Though the students and teachers who participated in the Discover Rochester pilot project spent only one semester working together, they began to develop new skills, pride in their work, and a sense of community. By sharing experiences, helping each other conquer difficult problems, and working toward a common goal, they began to show signs of the investment and mutual dependence that help shift distraction to focus, resistance to initiative, and a critical attitude to a constructive one.

These informal evaluations of student progress are positive, but more formal evaluation of the project is necessary to determine whether the program is achieving each of its specific goals, why it is working or not working, and how the effective parts of the project can be exported to other sites and other grade levels. Such formal evaluations will be initiated during the 1990–91 schoolyear. In the meantime, however, similarly positive results are emerging from other projects incorporating aspects of the framework we have provided. For example, Roy Pea (Institute for Research on Learning) and Richard Lehrer (University of Wisconsin, Madison) have implemented programs in middle school science, social studies, and problem-solving classes. Also, the Genesee River Valley Project is an example of an interdisciplinary curriculum, like Discover Rochester, that has been developed for third- to sixth-grade urban students. For large-scale implementations such as these, the formal evaluation must unfortunately be postponed until a stable implementation is achieved, which is often a multiyear process. The Central Park East program is such a case.

***Central Park East Secondary School.*** For the past twelve years, Central Park East Elementary and Secondary Schools have been creating and refining a learning environment that successfully challenges prevailing assumptions about the problems that urban minority students have in achieving higher-order learning goals. The secondary school has from three hundred to four hundred students and serves a primarily minority population (about 90 percent), many of whom are eligible for the free-lunch program (about 60 percent). The school's curriculum affirms the central importance of students' learning how to learn, how to reason, and how to investigate complex issues that require collaboration, personal responsibility, and a tolerance for uncertainty.

Central Park East Secondary School (CPESS) receives slightly over half its students from three elementary schools based on the Central Park East (CPE) model. In general, students are selected for the schools on a first-come, first-served basis, but preferences are given to siblings and, in the secondary school, to students who are likely to adapt to the culture of the school. Of the first class that entered CPESS five and a half years ago, approximately 75 percent are still in the school, 15 percent changed schools after the eighth grade, and 10 percent left because they moved or by mutual agreement. In later classes, fewer have left the school, and school officials know of only one actual school dropout. Attendance at the school averages over 90 percent, and there are very few suspensions or fights. The students do better than city or state averages on the Regency Competency Exams. In summary, the school is remarkably successful in educating its students by almost any measure.

In every class, students learn to ask and answer these kinds of reflective questions:

1. From what viewpoint are we seeing, reading, or hearing this?
2. How do we know what we know? What's the evidence, and how reliable is it?
3. How are things, events, or people connected? What are the cause and effect? How do they fit?
4. What if . . . ? Could things be otherwise? What are or were the alternatives?
5. So what? Why does it matter? What does it all mean? Who cares?

A core of curriculum is offered to all students, organized around two major fields: mathematics-science for two hours and humanities (art, history, social studies, literature) for two hours. Every effort is made to integrate academic disciplines, so that students recognize and understand the relationships among different subjects of study. The communication skills of writing and public speaking are taught in all subjects by all staff. The organization and scheduling of the curriculum allow for maximum flexibility. Each team of teachers offers a variety of styles of teaching, including group presentations, smaller seminars, one-on-one coaching, and independent work in the studios, science labs, and library.

At CPESS, the schoolyear is divided into trimesters, and student work in each interdisciplinary curriculum area (math-science and humanities) is organized around comprehensive student projects, called exhibitions. The team of teachers in two grades of math-science, for example, collaboratively generates the curriculum for the trimester and specifies the requirements for the exhibition. Staff development at the school consists almost entirely of teachers meeting together in small groups for half a day each week to plan curriculum, as do the math-science teachers. By the end of the trimester, each student has completed a product that fulfills the requirements for the exhibition. In addition, each has done an oral presentation for a teacher in which he or she explains the exhibition and demonstrates understanding of the fundamental ideas.

The exhibitions the teachers assigned were based on real problems of the world. For example, in the first trimester of the math-science classrooms where we have been working, ninth- and tenth-grade students designed amusement park rides and specified—through multiple representations—the physical motion principles exhibited by their designs. In the second trimester, they focused on the physics concepts for a projectile motion of their own choosing (for example, a foul shot in basketball, a curve ball in baseball). In the third trimester, the students worked on exhibitions involving two-body collisions. In the latter two trimesters, their work involved using a sophisticated simulation system for the Macintosh called Physics Explorer (there were four Macintosh computers in two of the four ninth–tenth-grade math-science classrooms). They created models reflecting the kinds of motion they were studying and developed graphs plotting vector components against time.

Much of their written work involved explaining changes in the vector components. Every student in the ninth and tenth grades at CPESS is working on serious physics problems, whereas, at most, 10 percent of students in the rest of the country study physics.

Three aspects of the way the school is organized reflect a cognitive apprenticeship approach to education. First, learning is situated by having students engage in projects that relate to the world about them and help them to make sense of that world. Because of their long-term nature, the projects reflect much more closely the nature of work. Students become invested in them over time and gain an ownership of the ideas they develop. For example, in the projectile motion project, one student calculated the speed and angle necessary for a stunt car driver he admired to jump over the Grand Canyon (which is not possible). When they work on projects, students use a variety of resources: the library, computers, and, importantly, the adults and other students around them, just as people do when they work. The teacher assumes the role of coach to help the students attack the problems that arise as they work on their projects, and so the student has a kind of autonomy not present in most schooling.

The second aspect of the school that we think critical is the emphasis on articulation, reflection, and exploration in learning. In presenting their exhibitions, students are required to make coherent presentations of their materials and to spontaneously answer difficult questions that probe students' understanding of what they have done. The effect of this training showed up in one tenth-grade girl, who on our first visit to the school was asked by her teacher to explain to us what she had done on a difficult math problem that she knew she had worked incorrectly (the problem: find the area above a right triangle inscribed in a circle, given an angle of 30 degrees and the length of the hypotenuse). As she articulately explained her work, our questions about why she had done each step helped her find the two errors she had made. The emphasis on reflection is embedded in the kinds of questions students are taught to ask and in the ways that they are forced to think about what they have done in order to explain and justify their work. The emphasis on exploration derives from the project-based nature of much of their work and the autonomy this fosters in students to control their own learning.

The third aspect we think is critical to the school's success is the learning culture that has arisen among the students and staff of the school. Developing this culture depends partly on starting in one of the three elementary schools that feed students to CPESS and that share the same philosophy of caring about students. Such caring is evident in the fact that there are only about five fights in the school each year, many fewer than in the other schools serving the same population. But it is most evident in the way the students bond to teachers, particularly their advisers (one staff to every twelve or thirteen students) and in the community sense that derives from the small size of the school and the trips they take together. This community feeling in the school fosters cooperation as students try to accomplish the difficult tasks they are given.

## Conclusion

By giving students long-term projects that deeply engage them and constructing an environment that embodies the principles described in our framework, these two schools have gone some way toward fostering cognitive apprenticeship. Many of the students at the two schools are the kinds of students who are labeled "at risk" in other environments. But working on difficult projects that make sense to them and challenge them leads to dramatic increases in their motivation to learn and think. Instead of treating these students as failures, the programs succeed by treating students as adult workers.

By centering education around projects, we do not rule out teaching particular disciplines. Central Park East Secondary School, for example, centers its projects in particular disciplines, such as history or physics. The projects are designed to teach the most essential knowledge in the different disciplines. But all the projects are interdisciplinary: for example, the project on projectile motion involved reading, writing, mathematics, and history as well as physics. What we are advocating, then, is quite compatible with practice in our best schools.

Most schooling emphasizes the teaching of abstract knowledge, such as arithmetic algorithms and grammar rules, that have little grounding in what students see as useful. Schools usually attempt to teach students to apply these abstractions with word problems and other artificial tasks. Our argument (Brown et al., 1989) is that this approach is backward. We need to engage students in authentic tasks and then show them how to generalize the knowledge they gain. Instead, educators have usually attempted to give students who do not master the abstractions more and more practice on simplified versions of the same kinds of tasks. This approach is a recipe for destroying anyone's motivation to learn or think.

Embedding education in authentic tasks makes what is taught both useful and usable. It is useful because it reflects the kinds of activities people encounter in the world. It becomes usable because students learn to apply the knowledge in accomplishing tasks. What are authentic tasks? Our argument is that they should reflect the changing nature of work and life. They include tasks such as (1) understanding complex systems (for example, computer systems, electronic systems), (2) finding information about different topics in a large database, (3) writing a report or making an argument about some topic, (4) analyzing trends in data, (5) investigating a particular topic to answer some open-ended question, (6) interpreting a difficult text, and (7) learning about some new domain. Accomplishing such tasks in the future will depend on using computers and electronic networks. We should not continue to educate students to communicate and calculate and learn and think with primitive tools such as card catalogues and arithmetic algorithms. It is like teaching people to drive a car by having them practice riding a bicycle.

The place to encourage change in education toward a more rational system is in education for the so-called disadvantaged students, because these are the students who have not been able to acquire even the basic skills in regular classrooms and because the current compensatory programs are often "widening the gap in terms of achievement of the more advanced skills" (Means, Schlager, & Knapp, 1990). We see the beginnings of an apprenticeship approach at Charlotte and Central Park East, and we think it is worth a major investment in resources to evaluate these models carefully and try to replicate them elsewhere in our failing schools. We suggest that both the design and evaluation of subsequent apprenticeship environments be based on the four dimensions in the framework we proposed:

- *Content:* focus instruction and assessment on general strategies for accomplishing tasks, for directing one's own behavior, and for learning new material as well as on domain-specific concepts, facts, and procedures
- *Method:* use teaching methods in which students learn by observation and guided practice in the context of defining and solving problems and in which discussing and evaluating developing skills are as important as practicing them
- *Sequence:* sequence lessons so that students begin with a clear sense of the high-level skills they are seeking and then acquire the component skills as they work on authentic problems of increasing complexity and diversity
- *Sociology:* offer students an environment that reflects the changing nature of work in society by initiating realistic activities, promoting communication and collaboration among students and teachers, and providing appropriate tools for learning

## References

Bransford, J. D., Sherwood, R., Vye, N., & Rieser, J. (1986). Teaching thinking and problem solving: Research foundations. *American Psychologist, 14* (10), 1078-1089.

Brown, J. S. (1985). Idea-amplifiers: New kinds of electronic learning. *Educational Horizons, 63*, 108-112.

Brown, J. S., Collins, A., & Duguid, P. (1989). Situated cognition and the culture of learning. *Educational Researcher, 18* (1), 32-42.

Burton, R., Brown, J. S., & Fisher, G. (1984). Skiing as a model of instruction. In B. Rogoff and J. Lave (Eds.), *Everyday cognition: Its developmental and social context.* Cambridge, MA: Harvard University Press.

Chi, M.T.H., Bassok, M., Lewis, M. W., Reimann, P., & Glaser, R. (1989). Self-explanations: How students study and use examples in learning to solve problems. *Cognitive Science, 13*, 145-182.

Collins, A. (1986). Teaching reading and writing with personal computers. In J. Orasanu (Ed.), *A decade of reading research: Implications for practice.* Hillsdale, NJ: Erlbaum.

Collins, A., & Brown, J. S. (1988). The computer as a tool for learning through reflection. In H. Mandl and A. Lesgold (Eds.), *Learning issues for intelligent tutoring systems.* New York: Springer.

Collins, A., Brown, J. S., & Newman, S. E. (1989). Cognitive apprenticeship: Teaching the craft of reading, writing, and mathematics. In L. B. Resnick (Ed.), *Knowing, learning, and instruction: Essays in honor of Robert Glaser* (pp. 453–494). Hillsdale, NJ: Erlbaum.

Collins, A., & Smith, E. E. (1982). Teaching the process of reading comprehension. In D. K. Detterman and R. J. Sternberg (Eds.), *How much and how can intelligence be increased?* Norwood, NJ: Ablex.

Collins, A., & Stevens, A. L. (1982). Goals and strategies of inquiry teachers. In R. Glaser (Ed.), *Advances in instructional psychology* (Vol. 2). Hillsdale, NJ: Erlbaum.

Collins, A., & Stevens, A. L. (1983). A cognitive theory of interactive teaching. In C. M. Reigeluth (Ed.), *Instructional design theories and models: An overview.* Hillsdale, NJ: Erlbaum.

Cuban, L. (1984). *How teachers taught.* New York: Longman.

Lave, J. (1988). *The culture of acquisition and the practice of understanding* (Report No. IRL88-0007). Palo Alto, CA: Institute for Research on Learning.

Lepper, M. R., & Greene, D. (1979). *The hidden costs of reward.* Hillsdale, NJ: Erlbaum.

Levin, J. A. (1982). Microcomputer communication networks for education. *The Quarterly Newsletter of the Laboratory of Comparative Human Cognition, 4* (2), 34–36.

Malone, R. (1981). Toward a theory of intrinsically motivating instruction. *Cognitive Science, 4,* 333–369.

Means, B., Schlager, M., & Knapp, M. (1990). *Compensatory education in literacy and mathematics: Current practices and prospects for change.* Menlo Park, CA: SRI International.

Norman, D. A. (1973). Memory, knowledge, and the answering of questions. In R. L. Solso (Ed.), *Contemporary issues in cognitive psychology: The Loyola symposium.* Washington, DC: Winston.

Palincsar, A. S., & Brown, A. L. (1984). Reciprocal teaching of comprehension-fostering and monitoring activities. *Cognition and Instruction, 1,* 117-175.

Resnick, L. B. (1987). Learning in school and out. *Educational Researcher, 16* (9), 13-20.

Scardamalia, M., Bereiter, C., & Steinbach, R. (1984). Teachability of reflective processes in written composition. *Cognitive Science, 8,* 173-190.

Schoenfeld, A. H. (1985). *Mathematical problem solving.* Orlando, Fl: Academic Press.

Van Lehn, K., & Brown, J. S. (1980). Planning nets: A representation for formalizing analogies and semantic models for procedural skills. In R. E. Snow, P. A. Federico, & W. E. Montague (Eds.), *Aptitude learning and instruction: Vol. 2. Cognitive process analyses of learning and problem-solving.* Hillsdale, NJ: Erlbaum.

White, B. Y. (1984). Designing computer games to help physics students understand Newton's laws of motion. *Cognition and Instruction, 1,* 69-108.

Zuboff, S. (1988). *In the age of the smart machine: The future of work and power.* New York: Basic Books.

# COMMENTARY

## Herb Rosenfeld

For the last thirty years I have been a teacher, curriculum developer, school administrator, and staff developer in the New York City Public School System. This career has included working at Walton High School, the Bronx High School of Science, Manhattan Center for Math and Science, and, most recently, the Central Park East Secondary School (CPESS), one of the schools described by Collins, Hawkins, and Carver in their chapter on cognitive apprenticeships for disadvantaged students.

Early in my career, I became interested in the mathematics curriculum and the difficulties generated by the seemingly random selection of ideas that are studied. One startling realization was that the congruence proofs students did in their study of plane geometry did not give them an insight into the nature of a deductive system or into the significance of Euclidean geometry in the development of mathematics and science. My concern with what was not working in math classes ultimately led me to look more closely at problems of classroom management, teacher-student and teacher-teacher relationships, staff development, school leadership, and the basic tenets of pedagogy and school organization.

### The Roots of Central Park East

In the fall of 1984 Deborah Meier asked me to join her in establishing a grade 7–12 public secondary school in East Harlem. Students would be accepted into CPESS on a first-come, first-served basis. As assistant director, my responsibilities included not only the role of vice principal but also leadership in the development of the math-science program. The vision that Deborah and I developed was

244

generated from a small number of axiomatic beliefs about the way children learn and was greatly informed by the work of Ted Sizer. In fact, our school became a charter member of Sizer's Coalition of Essential Schools.

Classroom experience dictated to both of us that students have unique ways of making sense of the world and that teachers must be able to observe and talk to students while they are on task. The Coalition of Essential Schools reflects this same belief in its position that students must be workers and teachers must be their "coaches." To create an arrangement where this could happen without affecting our budget, we felt that we had to rethink our daily schedule so that class size could be reduced to a maximum of twenty students.

In addition to the belief that people learn best by doing, we believed that ideas are more deeply understood and appreciated when they are embedded in a context (mathematics embedded in science, literature embedded in history, and the like). Further, we agreed with Sizer's argument that high schools take on so many tasks that they rarely do any one of them very well. Accordingly, we selected two main academic focuses—math-science and humanities (a single curriculum for literature, history, and fine art). We chose to offer only a single foreign language (Spanish). Finally, our conviction that people function best in a personalized atmosphere led us to assign each member of the faculty (including Deborah and myself) the responsibility for a daily advisory with between ten and fifteen students. The result is an academic school day consisting of two two-hour-long blocks (math-science and humanities) and two one-hour classes (Spanish and advisory). An additional hour at midday allows for lunch, physical education, student-teacher conferences, and access to the library and computers. This schedule made it possible to reduce maximum class size to twenty. Since students work with only three different teachers each day (their adviser is almost always one of their academic teachers as well), the teachers and students develop strong personal relationships.

### Components of Cognitive Apprenticeship at CPESS

Collins et al. describe their concept of a cognitive apprenticeship in terms of the way it deals with four key aspects of pedagogy: content, sequencing, methods, and sociology. These aspects of the program at CPESS and the ways in which they embody principles of cognitive apprenticeship are described below.

*Content.* The development of the CPESS curriculum started with the question that Ted Sizer poses, "How can we help students to use their minds well?" Our answer is that the curriculum must concentrate on students developing habits of mind that will make it possible for them to be lifelong independent learners. Thus, in designing our curriculum we put emphasis on content that will help students acquire learning strategies, heuristics, and control strategies that will serve them not only in future schooling but also throughout their lives as critical, informed citizens. We call upon students to construct arguments to grapple with questions such as "Can we be sure that our economy will rebound, or are we headed for a real depression?" In doing so, we force them to focus on the validity of their evidence and appreciate the complexity of the possible conclusions. They learn to be conscious of the context of a discussion (Where did it come from? Where is it going?). They learn to ask the question "What if it were otherwise?" and to be comfortable making predictions and expressing opinions.

In terms of the domain knowledge in our curriculum, an important goal for us was to integrate the ideas of two or more disciplines (history and literature, or mathematics and science). We decided to organize our ideas around a theme, such as "the peopling of America." Given a theme, we were able to generate the course by posing a series of questions such as "Were the Native Americans the first Americans?" or "Were each of the incoming groups welcomed in a similar fashion?"

As we continue to develop curriculum content, we are guided by the following questions:

- Will it make "sense" to our students and their families?
- Can it be connected to, or drawn from, students' everyday lives?
- Will students have to use their minds?
- Is there an opportunity to find unique ways of doing it?
- To what extent does it integrate the disciplines?
- Will there be opportunities for sutdents to reflect on the way

that their understanding of the world is at variance with another model?

• Does it grapple with "big ideas"?

While we are mindful of students' needs to master skills and procedures that are often unrelated to a recognizable context, we work as much as possible to present these competencies as offshoots of meaningful projects. For example, in designing a building, one might need to find the height of the neighboring structures. In that context, proportional reasoning, symmetry, and size and scale take on a real and vital meaning.

*Examples from the Mathematics Curriculum.* Although we did not use the term *situated learning* as we began the design of our mathematics curriculum, our concerns were certainly very much like those expressed by Collins et al. The traditional mathematics curriculum has a number of formidable obstacles one must overcome if one aspires to making mathematics accessible to all students (including those who are not college bound). The first, and perhaps foremost, barrier is the sequential, cumulative buildup of abstract concepts in the traditional curriculum. It is in the nature of mathematics that information is built upon already established or accepted truths. For example, if I know that the product of a positive number and a negative number is a negative number, then I can use this information to prove that the product of two negative numbers is a positive number. This "deductive proof" concept is the basis of abstract mathematical thinking and is a very difficult idea for high school students to grasp. Consequently, a watered-down, less formal version of accumulating mathematical knowledge (that is equally as puzzling) has become the conventional curriculum in most high schools. This conventional curriculum requires the student to be adept at factoring trinomials before learning to solve a quadratic equation. What is more, the student is required first to learn to complete the square in order to understand the derivation of the quadratic formula before getting practice in using it. Factoring and completing the square are skills that atrophy at a rapid rate. (How many of your educated colleagues can complete the square?) An alternative approach is to have students grapple with situations that require the use of a quadratic equation and then find the simplest way to solve it. I would be proud of a student who, faced with an event that could be better understood by solving a quadratic equation, goes to a text to find the formula and then applies it.

It was our conviction that the practice of teaching skills and concepts unconnected to practical applications was the major factor in leaving students confused and turning them away from mathematics (and often from school itself). Hence, we were determined to make the heart of our curriculum a collection of ideas and skills linked to and embedded in a problem context meaningful to students.

There is much mathematics embedded in the questions that normally turn up in science classes, and students can use it to generate more mathematical ideas and a deeper understanding of the science concepts. For example, the study of the human body as a system fosters the need to collect, organize, and graph data, in addition to measuring the many rates of change that keep the system going. We challenge students with questions such as: How could I calculate the average diameter of my body cells? What is the distance between my ears? How could one actually make these measurements accurately? A student will know how to measure the length of his or her index finger but will have trouble with measures of body parts that cannot be done directly. Simple counting and measurement are familiar concepts to most students. The mathematical investigation of the more complex questions about the human body extends and uses that familiarity, while giving rise to even more complex questions and a deeper understanding of the ideas behind the questions.

Another curriculum theme used at CPESS—the exploration of motion, energy, and astronomy—strongly requires that one can uniquely determine the position (location) of an object at any given time. This involves graphing and mapping skills in addition to the measurement of rates, distances, and sizes. Some of the same skills used to analyze data and make predictions in studying the human body are also part of this work. Moreover, throughout science, the same geometric shapes show up repeatedly in contexts ranging from the path of a heavenly body to the shape of the human skull. The mathematical and scientific ideas reinforce each other and eventually become one.

In the grades 9-10 math-science class studying motion, students were asked to design an amusement park ride as an exhibition. This project lasted for an entire trimester and included a scientific analysis and model (or computer simulation). These tasks led to the study of equations, trigonometric functions, and plane vectors. Much of our time was spent on the graphs of functions and "what they tell us." We decided to supplement this work with some of the ideas of geometry that did not turn up in designing amusement park rides (for example, parallelograms, mathematical transformations, and matrixes) and with the study of probability. In addition, we spent time considering purely scientific questions (that did not include location or counting) such as "How much of the moon do we get to see?"

*Sequencing.* Our curriculum content starts with a "big idea," for example, motion. We then immediately present the students with a motivating global situation (for example, designing an amusement park ride). Students invariably create a design that is too complicated for them to analyze. We are then propelled to the simplest motion that we can imagine, free fall. Then we might move on to projectile motion and combine the two motions, and so on. This is clearly an example of increasing complexity and diversity as described by Collins et al. It should be kept in mind, however, that although the sequence of student work moves from simple to complex problems, the entire unit is introduced with a complex question that serves as a context and motivator for working on both the simple and the more complex problems. This is typical of the way that the sequence for curriculum content at CPESS develops.

*Methods.* CPESS students learn and demonstrate their mastery by doing short- and long-term projects. Projects consist of research papers, oral presentations (defenses), physical models, and/or computer simulations. Any or all of this work may be supported by technology. These projects often speak to open-ended situations that allow for much speculation and can be thought of in several different ways.

The classroom is run like a workplace. Everyone has a job to do. Students work in groups, and the teacher acts as a mentor/ coach to each of the groups and to each student in the group. In the course of this activity teachers model heuristics and control processes for problem solving, critical mathematical and scientific thinking, and formulating questions (inquiry).

The kind of project work assigned to students at CPESS is designed to foster exploration and reflection. During a typical two-hour class, students confer with their cohort groups, search out references in the school library (the classroom library could not possibly contain all the research materials necessary to support all of the activity going on in the class), speak with the teacher about their projects, find materials and advice for their models in the art studio, use the computer for simulations and word processing, and reflect on their progress thus far and their design for the project. Their activities mirror those of researchers and designers in the real world. We believe that in this way they experience a real cognitive apprenticeship.

As students work on their projects, teachers provide coaching to help them see additional aspects of a problem, connect their current work to things they already know, execute a procedure more skillfully, and so on. Skillful implementation of the technique Collins et al. call scaffolding is a major issue for our teachers. There is a tendency for teachers to "give away the game" and deprive students of the opportunity to struggle through a creative moment. However, it is often difficult to get students started on the kind of "thinking" problems used in our curriculum without an intellectual push. Finding the right balance—and selecting appropriate amounts and kinds of scaffolding—is a tough problem, mostly because teachers need more experience working with students in this way.

Articulation is a major goal in our school. The exhibitions give students an ample opportunity to work on writing, oral presentation, and model/simulation making. Exhibitions often give rise to the use of technology as a medium of articulation. During the presentations, students have an opportunity to critique each other, and some teachers have them make formal evaluations of presentations. Often alternative approaches are considered in these sessions.

Part of what makes the methods used at CPESS unusual is the way in which student work is evaluated. For each project, the teacher prepares a narrative report, designed so that it can be understood by the student and his family. This report assesses the students' strengths and weaknesses and suggests a plan for working toward growth. Students' work is evaluated in terms of the following categories:

- Organization of the work as a whole
    Does it make its point?
    Is it easily understood?
    Does it hang together?

- Understanding of the math-science ideas
    Does it probe ideas deeply?
    Does it use examples and/or applications to illustrate ideas?
    Does it make connections between ideas?
    Does it properly cite evidence?
    Does it explain observations?
    Does it conjecture?
    Does it hypothesize and then test for validity?

- Process skills
    Are the data correct?
    Are appropriate formulas correctly used?
    Does it pay attention to details (labels, units, and the like)?
    Are skills appropriately applied with competence?
    Are incidental interesting facts introduced?

*Sociology.* Experience demonstrates that when students are interested in their work, learning flows naturally. Students also function best in an environment of mutual respect. So, for starters, the curriculum must be demystified, a process that creates the kind of situated learning described by Collins et al. Consider the following typical classroom conversation:

"Where are we going in this year's work?"

"We are going to study motion."

"Why?"

"Well, all things are in motion."

"You mean, I am in motion . . ."

This is a dialogue of mutual respect with more complex questions developing as we up the intellectual ante. The teacher (coach) carries on this dialogue with small (three to four) groups of students, the entire class, or individual students (for example, when a student presents her or his project). Students carry on the same kind of dialogue within their cohort teams and as they present their work to each other. CPESS is a task-driven environment in which students work in groups and develop both group products and singular ones. This environment allows for knowledge sharing, strategy building, and the analysis of each other's work. It seeks to develop intrinsic motivation by stimulating students to pose and investigate questions that are interesting and meaningful to them.

It is an atmosphere that encourages intellectual challenge, that poses open-ended questions like "What if gravity was a horizontal force?" and requires rigorous defense of arguments made in the ensuing discussion. Encouraging this kind of imagining in students demonstrates mutual respect and encourages the development of what Collins et al. call a community of practice as students work with teachers and with each other on authentic, serious problems.

### Staff: Teaching, Learning, and Leadership

The cognitive apprenticeship, as described by Collins et al. and embodied in the program at CPESS, requires teachers to play a very different role from that of dispenser of knowledge (the role seen in most conventional classrooms). Teachers need support in assuming this role, and our experiences at CPESS may be helpful to other schools considering such innovations.

The integrated, two-hour-long classes are led by a teacher in one of the disciplines (for example, either a math or a science teacher), but each teacher works toward becoming a generalist (that is, a math-science teacher) who is equally able in both areas.

Teachers have a great deal of responsibility and decision-making power in our school. The teachers in a particular curriculum thread work in teams (in the same mode as the students who are working in groups) to build a course of study, research and create learning materials, schedule trips, bring in outside resources, create modes of student assessment, and generally support each other. A significant aspect of this collaborative effort is the sharing of each other's specialties (most high school teachers have taught courses outside of their area of specialty but have had to learn the course content on their own). This sharing often leads to brainstorming about classroom management, ways of constructively relating to particular students, and strategies for solving pedagogical problems in general. The process is, in fact, a built-in peer staff development structure. The team members are scheduled so that their in-school planning hours coincide. They have a single block of three hours for planning one morning each week as well as lunch hours (which they often spend together).

Because curriculum teams need leadership, a team leader is designated for each curriculum. The leader coordinates the team's activities, sets deadlines, looks ahead to what is down the road, finds new teaching materials, brings in outside experts, keeps up with national and local research on classroom practices, confers regularly with both the administration and with other team leaders, arranges for team representation at significant events in and out of the school, helps out in classes, holds the team to its mission, and generally becomes an expert on our way of working with students. In short, the leader's role is to be the foremost advocate of the collaborative effort.

In our community of learners, the teachers as well as the students are growing. The team leader does not evaluate the team members (the team does that); rather, he or she works with the team to facilitate a better understanding of their roles as teachers and helps them to use their strengths to perform these roles optimally. In this way, staff development is built into our collaborative team design.

In addition to the teacher team activities described above, our ongoing development as a school requires regular full staff meetings and retreats to grapple with and reflect on schoolwide issues. These issues include governance, curriculum sharing, world events and our school, staff relations, national trends in our work, the school's mission, and an ever-growing common vision.

## How Well Do These Concepts Work at CPESS?

I believe that CPESS provides a wonderful growing experience for students. The evidence is manifest in the way the students behave in school. They are nonviolent and respectful to each other as well as to staff members. They are intellectual risk takers: They will tackle complex questions. They study math and science throughout their secondary school career. They are almost all going on to further education after graduation. Their families enthusiastically work with the staff on educational issues concerning their children. The staff works hard on all of the issues surrounding our students' education, and the school as a whole profits from the staff's mandate to make curriculum and governance decisions.

Everyone agrees that there is still room for much growth. There is much work to be done on stoking student curiosity to further increase intrinsic motivation. We are still working out a concept of homework that makes sense for students in our kind of program. We are seeking better ways to obtain diagnostic information from student behavior in class by taking anecdotal notes that will help us identify the way that each student takes in and processes ideas and what he or she really understands about the concepts we are studying. There is much more thinking to be done about the entire student assessment issue. We continue to search for connections among disciplines—to look for math content within science and literature and art within history. In other words, we are still seeking to integrate ideas better and are considering exploring different combinations of subjects (such as math with art or math with social studies). We are also still working on issues concerning the use of software and the further infusion of technology into our curriculum. But this search for continued improvement in no way detracts from the value of what has been achieved already. After all, the capacity for reflection and the disposition to strive toward continued improvement in one's design are two of the basic goals of the cognitive apprenticeship.

# 8

# Conclusion: Implementing New Models for Teaching Advanced Skills

*Michael S. Knapp, Barbara Means,*
*and Carol Chelemer*

AMERICAN EDUCATION IS AT A CRITICAL JUNCTURE, AND SCHOOLS, DIS-
tricts, and states are undertaking reform efforts at an unprecedented
level. This is true both for education aimed specifically at the educationally disadvantaged and for education in general. Concerned
about the poor showing of American students in international comparisons of science and mathematics achievement, advocates have
warned that the erosion of American educational standards "threat-
ens our very future as a Nation and a people" (National Commission on Excellence in Education, 1983) and that our choice for the
future is "high skills or low wages" (Commission on the Skills of
the American Workforce, 1990). Cast in this light, education is seen
as the cornerstone for American economic competitiveness, and as
a result, politicians are giving education an unparalleled degree of
attention, as attested to by the National Education Goals. Not coin-
cidentally, educators are seriously debating the kind of structural
reform that would have been considered wildly idealistic just a decade ago.

The instructional models described in this book are specifically concerned with the teaching of those skills generally described
as "advanced" and with students considered "at risk" in conventional classrooms. This focus is thoroughly compatible with—and,
in fact, a central part of—the current broad movement for educa-

tional reform. The crux of the problem is that students leave our nation's secondary schools without the kinds of skills we are concerned with in this book—the ability to understand what they read, to realize when they do not know enough, to apply mathematics to novel situations, and to compose effective documents. Moreover, as the proportion of students from poor and linguistic minority backgrounds in our schools continues to increase, American education cannot succeed unless it succeeds with them. This is not to say that other students will be shortchanged—quite the opposite, because the principles of instruction advocated here for disadvantaged students are precisely the same principles recommended elsewhere for *all* students. Doing a better job of serving those students considered at risk can be part of doing a better job for everyone.

The models presented in this book for teaching advanced skills to at-risk students share a common grounding in cognitive research and theory. This basis in principles derived from the psychology of learning is one of their major strengths. In addition, these instructional models have been applied successfully in specific real-world classrooms with educationally disadvantaged students. Thus, there is both theoretical and empirical support for their use.

Convincing demonstrations are a first, and necessary, step in the spread of powerful educational ideas. But much work remains before large-scale implementation of the ideas presented in this book occurs. For one thing, educators should consider how much is known about the instructional models—how widely they have been applied and how extensively they have addressed important issues faced by practitioners. For another, educators should understand how extensively these models change the teacher's role and, consequently, what this fact implies for teacher preparation and support. Even when these matters are better understood, questions still remain regarding the incorporation of these models into programs specifically designed for the educationally disadvantaged—in particular, compensatory education services funded by the federal and state governments. Finally, questions of overall implementation strategy must be considered. In this concluding chapter, we examine these questions in turn.

## Do We Know Enough to Implement?

Educators wondering whether, and how, to implement the instructional models described in this volume need to be convinced that the models work in their kind of school or program with the kind of student population they face every day. There are clearly some gaps in the research base to date as well as some issues not fully addressed by the models' originators. Understanding what is and is not known about the instructional models and their effectiveness will help practitioners to make informed decisions about the models' future use.

In considering these instructional models, practitioners will need to understand that the empirical research base for their application is limited by the recency of the models and that the models themselves are neither full-blown curriculum packages nor comprehensive guides to implementation. Rather, the authors in this book offer a series of instructional principles and strategies to be applied flexibly and pervasively within academic programs of various kinds.

### Strength of the Evidence

Most of the individual models described in this volume have not been implemented and evaluated on a wide scale. The reciprocal teaching techniques described by Palincsar and Klenk in Chapter Four have received the most widespread implementation and garnered the greatest body of evidence for effectiveness, but even this model has not been subject to the kind of national implementation and third-party evaluation used in federally mandated studies such as those for Follow Through models, conducted in the 1970s (Stallings & Kaskowitz, 1974). The other models have been implemented with a limited age range (for example, the CGI program described by Peterson, Fennema, and Carpenter in Chapter Three), a limited set of schools (for example, those described by Collins, Hawkins, and Carver in Chapter Seven), or even with just a single teacher (the program developed and studied by Resnick, Bill, Lesgold, and Leer and described in Chapter Two). Thus, we do not have empirical evidence that the individual models are effective with other curricula, students of different ages, or other teachers. Most importantly, the majority of implementations to date have been joint efforts between a committed teacher, school, or district and a team of university-based researchers. The commitment to the instructional model and level of understanding among these self-selected groups is likely to be higher than among teachers or schools in general.

Thus, questions remain about the effectiveness of these models, if implemented on a wider scale in schools where teachers need to learn about the models' basic principles and must do so without the ongoing participation of researchers. Clearly, we need to gather information over a period of time and from different instances to learn about the specific conditions under which each instructional method takes hold and flourishes.

Notwithstanding the caveats discussed above, the programs described here provide an "existence proof" for models of teaching advanced skills to educationally disadvantaged students. The principles on which they are based have strong support in basic research on the psychology of learning. In addition, as a group, the programs in this volume have been implemented with children of a wide range of ages (from first grade through senior high school) and settings (from San Jose, California, to Harlem). Those commenting on the models describe similar success stories with students from an even wider range of language and cultural backgrounds in schools serving poor children in cities as diverse as Chicago, San Diego, and Cambridge (Massachusetts) and states including Texas, Tennessee, and Arkansas.

### Nature of the Models

While the work described in this volume demonstrates that advanced skills can be taught to at-risk students throughout their education, educators will need to adapt the principles and strategies presented in this volume when applying them to a particular group of students and a particular curriculum unit. In making the instructional model fit the situation and needs of the individual classroom or school, educators will need to rely on much more than research evidence demonstrating that the principles and strategies are sound. By their very nature, these models will never lend themselves to the writing of recipes for implementation. The teacher's actions will be different depending not only on the particular content being used but also on the background knowledge and strengths and weaknesses of the particular set of students. While this requirement places heavy demands on would-be implementers, it also means that educators in a particular site will need to internalize the ideas behind a particular model before they can apply it in their setting. This kind of internalization and customization is very labor intensive but, on the positive side, has been found to be an important element in successful school reform.

As the models are implemented more widely, we expect to see the creation of more preservice and in-service staff development materials that will assist teachers in the process of incorporating these principles and strategies into their practice. These will not eliminate the need to recreate the instructional model to fit the particular content and set of students but will provide a framework for the process and supports for training teachers to carry it out.

### Issues Requiring Further Study

Besides the need to broaden the base of evidence regarding the efficacy of these models, there are some important unanswered questions about the instructional models themselves. Although overwhelmingly enthusiastic about the basic premises underlying these models, the commentaries by practitioners in this volume point out several areas in which the approaches are not fully developed. Failing to attend to them will limit the models' applicability to the wide range of settings in which they might otherwise be implemented.

*Motivation Issues.* Although all of the chapter authors would agree that students' social-emotional development and self-concept are essential to learning, the model descriptions give limited attention to this issue. In part, this omission reflects the models' theory base in cognitive psychology, with its overwhelming emphasis on *intellectual* development. In part, however, this reflects a belief on the part of model developers that by giving students challenging, authentic tasks and the experience of succeeding on those tasks, we will enhance their self-concept. A vivid illustration of this belief is the low-achieving student, described by Peterson et al. in Chapter Three, who learned to solve and pose math problems in the CGI classroom even though he sometimes still needed a number line to remind him of the order of the numerals. With the experience of success in the classroom, the boy came to see himself as someone who was capable and "loved" mathematics. The data for all the students in CGI classes support this idea that although self-concept is not addressed directly by the program, students' motivation and self-concept about mathematics are enhanced. Similarly, Palincsar and Klenk (in Chapter Four) and Collins et al. (in Chapter Seven) both report anecdotal evidence of classes of students regarded as unmotivated who blossom after exposure to one of these innovative programs.

Nevertheless, in Chapter Four, Padron suggests that this will not necessarily happen for all students and that, for some, issues of social development and self-concept need to be addressed directly if the students are to profit from a cognitively oriented program. This issue needs to be considered in implementing these programs with at-risk students. Further research is needed to provide guidance as to the value added by explicitly addressing motivation and self-concept issues. Certainly such noncognitive outcomes should be measured in implementation programs, as indeed they have been for most of the models described here.

***Dealing with Diverse Cultural and Linguistic Backgrounds.*** Although these models have been implemented successfully with students from a range of socioeconomic, ethnic, and language backgrounds, several of the commentaries suggested that more attention needs to be directed to this issue. In designing these instructional models, these researchers sought ways to build on students' prior knowledge and to link up with their experiences outside the classroom. Careful consideration needs to be given to the match between that out-of-school experience and the material that is used in the classroom. This requires familiarity with that background on the part of the teacher and can be difficult in cases where the class contains students from many different cultural and linguistic backgrounds.

Padron suggests in Chapter Four the strategies of using

material and problems common to all cultures and of building up familiarity to the material used within class, as done in the latest reciprocal teaching research using a series of related texts on the topic of animal survival. Richards suggests in Chapter Three using a variety of materials, some specifically geared to each cultural group, as in the case of the math problem couched in terms of a Haitian folk tale. This latter technique can also be useful in addressing a related problem—the tendency for certain children, and sometimes children from certain language or cultural groups, to dominate small-group discussion. By manipulating the materials used in class to include problems that are most familiar to the children who usually participate less, the teacher can increase the likelihood that these students will play a leadership role in solving the problem.

Another student diversity issue, raised in Chapter Two by Vye, Sharp, McCabe, and Bransford, is the applicability of these models to students with language differences or deficiencies. Many of the techniques call for a great deal of verbal participation on the part of students, and questions remain concerning how these models will work for students who have language difficulties or those whose first language or dialect is not that dominant in the classroom. Vye et al. encourage the use of video presentation of problem situations. This can do much on the reception side of communication to help students get into the problem, but we have not yet seen approaches that those with limited English or low verbal skills can use on the production side to participate in the dialogue used in these instructional models.

*Effects on Basic Skill Acquisition.* An issue for further research is the effect that these programs have on the learning of basic skills. Many educators who are attracted to these models for teaching advanced skills may be reluctant to make the investment in implementing them for fear of a negative impact on basic skills learning. As discussed in the introduction to this volume, most district and state evaluation programs use school achievement measures that are heavily oriented to basic skills. Funding, programs, reputation, and jobs are often riding on the outcome of these tests.

Few would want to implement a program that would result in declining basic skills scores.

The assumption underlying these models is that basic skills are best taught in the context of more complex problems. The model developers vary in how much attention they would give to basic skills learning outside the problem context (although all would give less emphasis than in the average classroom today). In terms of empirical findings, however, the database is still relatively thin. Results reported by both Resnick et al. (in Chapter Two) and Peterson et al. (in Chapter Three) suggest that basic math skills and number facts are learned *better* within their cognitively oriented programs, but we need to be cautious about assuming that this finding will hold under all conditions. Studies on other programs aimed at teaching problem solving have reported no effect on the acquisition of lower-level skills or even poorer performance compared to those whose instruction was aimed at basic, rather than advanced, skills. We need to provide instruction that induces students to acquire both basic and advanced skills. Additional empirical data are needed to clarify the most effective balance of instructional approaches for achieving both goals.

***Limits to What Can Be Taught Directly.*** In his review in Chapter Five of the model of writing offered by Bryson and Scardamalia, Daniels questions whether the skilled writers' processes of composing can really be taught directly. His question is an important one, which has implications far beyond the teaching of writing. An ongoing, lively debate within the research community questions whether the abstract skills of problem solving *can* be taught—certainly there have been many failed attempts to teach problem-solving skills in a way that will lead to their application to a wide range of content, and there have been few success stories (Perkins & Salomon, 1989; Pressley, Snyder, & Cariglia-Bull, 1987). This debate should serve to remind us that many of the skills of reasoning, composing, and judging that we value most will not be easily learned by any students, disadvantaged or not. Nevertheless, the models described in this volume provide the context and the experience within which such skills can, over time, be acquired. Certainly they are more likely to be learned in classrooms where they are modeled and practiced than in classes that ignore them.

## What Do These Models Imply for Teacher Preparation and Support?

Stronger evidence about efficacy and increased attention to the design issues discussed above will not change a central fact about these instructional models that has profound implications for implementation. The required changes in attitude toward the at-risk student, reshaping of the curriculum, and new instructional strategies, discussed in the introduction to this volume, bring with them a transformation of the role of the teacher. The instructional models described here require both a letting go and an assumption of power on the teacher's part, and both pose new challenges to teachers, administrators, and teacher preparation programs.

*A New Role for Teachers.* The chapter authors are unanimous in calling for the teacher to become a "coach" rather than a dispenser of knowledge. This means that the teacher's part of instruction cannot be fully scripted in advance, in the way that many teachers' guides lay out what they will present, what exercises will be given, and how student performance on these exercises will be graded. Rather, teachers are called upon to give students more say in defining what they work on (as in the Rochester and Central Park East programs described by Collins et al. in Chapter Seven) and in how they approach problems (as in the CGI classrooms described by Peterson et al. in Chapter Three). At the same time, the teacher plays an active role in monitoring not just the product of the student's activity but also the *process* whereby the student achieves that product. The teacher offers support (scaffolding) when necessary and asks questions that help the student reflect on what has been done thus far, discover alternative strategies, and understand concepts. This intellectual coaching requires on-the-spot decision making. The teacher's actions will depend on what the students have done. The teacher must be a good diagnostician, sensing the source of a student's confusion from a few actions or words, and must be dynamic and flexible in applying teaching strategies.

These models also pose additional challenges to teachers in terms of knowledge requirements. Advanced skills deal with parts of the curriculum that are the most challenging. It is more difficult for teachers to direct and provide feedback for composing extended pieces of writing than it is for them to correct spelling or grammar exercises. Moreover, the models described here tend to transcend traditional subject matter barriers. Reciprocal teaching techniques are used as students work with science or social studies textbooks. Composition, social studies, and computer skills are combined as students prepare projects describing their city. For the elementary school teacher, these models require a depth of subject matter preparation that exceeds the norm in many schools; for the junior and senior high school teacher, they require not only depth but also an unusual degree of breadth across subject areas. Some of the programs described in this volume require teachers with knowledge in multiple areas, such as math and science or computers and literature and economics, to coach students through a genuinely interdisciplinary project.

Finally, these models pose challenges to teachers in terms of classroom management. For those who equate the well-controlled class with neat rows of desks and teacher control of who has the floor, a visit to one of the classrooms described in this volume would seem like stepping into chaos. With multiple small groups of students working in different parts of the room, perhaps on different content, with students talking not so much to the teacher as to each other, with heated debates over how to solve a problem, these classes can seem noisy and unstructured. Upon closer study, however, the observer should see that the students are talking about academic content, that they are really engaged in what they are doing. The teacher must be skilled enough to provide interesting content that engages students and at the same time serve as a facilitator to keep the groups on task, to provide assistance at key points, and to make sure that all students participate.

The skills and knowledge required of teachers to implement the kind of models described here are considerable indeed. The teacher loses the obvious leadership role as the director who dispenses knowledge in front of a class of docile students but takes on the much more subtle but extremely powerful role of the person who selects and develops meaningful learning activities and coaches students through them. In this new role, the teacher has an important part in selecting curricular topics or problems, in diagnosing student understanding or misunderstanding, in spontaneously adapting instructional content and techniques, in response to students' actions, and in exerting subtle rather than regimented control. Clearly, these models call for a high degree of skill and professionalism on the part of classroom teachers—they cannot be implemented by blindly following a concrete list of steps in a teacher's guide.

It is popular today to talk about "empowering" teachers. We are not sure that this is the right term, with its connotation that power is something "given" to teachers from an external source. The metaphor seems only half right. Certainly, the instructional models described in this volume require that teachers be given the power to make curricular and instructional decisions for their classrooms, a condition that implies a less directive role on the part of program designers and administrators. But equally important to implementing these models is the power that teachers must give themselves—the power that comes from possessing a high level of skill. Program administrators cannot bestow this power, but they can support its development by providing resources for in-service training, teacher networking, and professional development.

*Teacher Preparation, Selection, and Training Requirements.* The change in the teacher's role associated with these models of teaching advanced skills poses a major challenge to those responsible for preservice and in-service development of teachers. The high level of skill needed on the part of teachers and the discrepancy between the skills needed for these programs and the methods conventionally taught in teacher training suggest that these programs will be costly in terms of requirements for teacher in-service training and support. In times of tight budgets, some will question the realism of providing released time for teachers to acquire new skills and for supporting the kind of joint teaching, observation, and feedback that encourages teachers to learn from each other. Most of the implementations described in this volume used far more preparation of teachers (for example, eighty hours of training for CGI) than we see in the typical in-service training program. There is simply not enough experience with implementing the models to know how much this preparation time could be pared back without jeopardizing the effectiveness of the approach.

The issue of time and resources for teacher preparation will have to be addressed if these models are ever to enjoy widespread implementation. On the one hand, colleges of education, state agency staff, school district supervisors, and school administration and faculty will need to commit their intellectual and time resources. On the other hand, cost-effective ways for providing training and planning time need to be developed. The strategies and experiences of schools that are successful in providing this kind of support, such as that described by Rosenfeld in Chapter Seven, need to be documented and provided as models for other schools.

At the same time, it should be noted that the teacher skill requirements of these instructional models are highly compatible with the larger movement toward professionalization of teachers and teaching. Some of the best schools of education are turning to the kinds of instructional techniques described here, and we hope to see new teachers who have been trained in techniques of small-group instruction, problem solving–based curricular units, and diagnostic coaching. Given the amount of time and practice involved to acquire these skills, we believe that addressing them during preservice education is important. Given this background, the instructional models presented in this volume provide a framework for understanding how these pieces fit together.

## How Well Do These Models Apply to Compensatory Education?

Although they have been used with students eligible for federal or state compensatory education programs, the instructional models described here have yet to be applied within these programs. Thus, there is much to learn concerning how best to implement them within that framework. At the same time, the compensatory education community has what may be a unique opportunity to facilitate experimentation with these kinds of instruction. Taking advantage of this opportunity, however, means rethinking traditions that have become firmly established in many compensatory education programs.

### The Opportunity for Compensatory Educators

Compensatory education interventions such as the federal Chapter 1 program and its state-supported counterparts enjoy continued strong support from their respective funding sources and from the local educators who incorporate compensatory services into school district academic programs. This fact, coupled with new developments in the federal and state context surrounding these programs, makes them more able to incorporate the instructional models presented in this volume.

The teaching of "advanced skills" is now a legislated emphasis of the nation's largest compensatory education intervention, the federal Chapter 1 program. After several decades in which the law and program regulations placed explicit and sole emphasis on the teaching of basic skills, the most recent version of the law governing this program has called for instruction that promotes "advanced as well as basic skills." The framers of this legislation did not have a specific idea of what this meant for the day-to-day operation of the program in thousands of schools across the nation; nonetheless, at the level of programmatic rhetoric and intent, they announced that the teaching of advanced skills was an equally important goal toward which compensatory programs must strive.

Alongside the focus on advanced skills, compensatory educators and others concerned about the educationally disadvantaged have paid more attention to schoolwide solutions to what had been viewed heretofore as an individual or a small-group remedial problem. Experiments with "accelerated" schools and other schoolwide approaches have been initiated (see Quellmalz, Chapter Six, for a review of schoolwide approaches). Even established remedial programs have begun to pick up a schoolwide emphasis. The Chapter 1 program, for example, now requires reporting of student achievement for the entire school. In schools with student populations 75 percent or more of whom come from low-income families, recent rule changes facilitate setting up Chapter 1 programs as "schoolwide projects," and it appears that large numbers of such schools are currently organizing their Chapter 1 programs this way. Complementing this trend are numerous state "school improvement" programs and initiatives, not to mention widespread attempts at instituting site-based management, that encourage schoolwide solutions and provide authority and resources to do so.

In this context, the compensatory education community faces some key opportunities regarding the curriculum it teaches, the design of programs, and the nature of professional development for compensatory program staff.

With regard to curriculum, compensatory programs in language arts could expand their repertoire to include writing more often than is currently the case. As several of the instructional models described in this book make clear, writing instruction is easily integrated with the teaching of reading and may, in fact, enhance the process of learning to read. Assuming that writing instruction emphasizes meaningful communication rather than the mechanics of writing, compensatory program students could be given a big boost toward acquiring composition and comprehension skills from early grades.

Emphasizing writing in compensatory education programs implies deemphasizing other things, and the instructional models described in this volume offer some clear candidates: The repetitive teaching of decoding (or language mechanics), for example, may impart these skills to program participants, but in the view of the authors presented in this volume, it does relatively little to enhance comprehension skills. A comparable argument can be made about compensatory mathematics instruction, which has tended to emphasize arithmetic computation skills.

Changes in curriculum of the sort just described create a second opportunity: to provide extensive and ongoing professional development support for the program staff, who would be expected to implement instructional models with which they are unfamiliar. Compensatory education programs like Chapter 1 typically have resources that can be used for in-service teacher education and, to the extent possible, will need to maximize the amount of resources devoted to this purpose. In an era of tight local and state budgets, compensatory programs that are funded from the federal level may have the lion's share of in-service dollars that could be used to promote these kinds of instructional models.

Program managers have an equally good opportunity to experiment with program design. Design options that enable greater coordination between the regular program and compensatory programs or that encourage schoolwide solutions to the problem of orchestrating special program resources are likely to create conditions that encourage the spread of the instructional models that have been discussed in this volume. Given the current federal and state context, planners and managers of compensatory programs have an unprecedented chance to experiment with these kinds of design features.

### Traditions That Stand in the Way

To take advantage of these opportunities, the compensatory education community will need to reconsider some of its most established traditions. The clearest example of this has been discussed throughout the volume: Curricula for compensatory programs that focus on the mastery of discrete basic skills are antithetical to the direction of these instructional models. Three more traditions, concerned with operational features and program design, also deserve reexamination: the separateness of the compensatory programs, the widespread use of paraprofessional aides as instructional program staff, and the organization of compensatory services into short daily time blocks. Each of these traditions has developed for a variety of reasons, and each performs useful functions in compensatory programs as they typically have been conceived over the past few decades. But in light of the new instructional goals and possibilities implied by the models discussed in this volume, the trade-offs involved with each tradition need to be reconsidered.

*Separateness.* Over the years, compensatory programs have typically been established as an instructional service separate, even segregated, from the regular instructional program. In several ways this may have seemed to make sense: In many schools the regular program was either in disarray or clearly dysfunctional for the students assigned to compensatory programs; in such instances little was to be gained by connecting the two more closely together. Separated services also made it easier to demonstrate that targeted students were getting something that was different from what was happening in their regular assigned classrooms.

To be sure, over the past few decades, there has been a considerable movement to reduce the distance between compensatory and regular programs through the increased use of in-class delivery models, greater incentives for coordination, and other similar measures.

But the instructional models we have presented in this volume imply a more integrated learning experience for students, which means greater connection between compensatory and regular instruction and exposure to advanced skills in both aspects of the students' day. The issue is not one of "pull-out" services versus in-class instruction—an old and tired debate in the compensatory education world. Rather, the question is whether students will encounter the need for, and opportunity to use, advanced skills in all aspects of their instructional school day.

*Paraprofessional Aides.* Paraprofessional aides are in widespread use in compensatory education programs, and their presence accomplishes a number of things, among them the chance for targeted students to receive additional adult attention, a second adult in the classroom (for example, to work with one group while the teacher takes another), and greater cultural diversity among the instructional staff, as many paraprofessional aides are drawn from the communities from which students come. As a design feature, the use of aides is also considered by many program planners to be cost-effective (aides can be hired at a fraction of the cost of a trained specialist) and conducive to integration of the compensatory and regular programs (most aides are used within the regular classroom).

From the point of view of introducing the instructional models described in this book, the use of paraprofessional aides is problematic. The chief issue is one of training and background for the new instructional roles the aides will be carrying out. While many aides have become instructionally adept through their association with compensatory programs (and some come with excellent credentials to begin with), most lack the preparation for teaching composition, comprehension, and mathematical reasoning in the manner described in this volume. The need for in-service training and support for learning new instructional roles is the same as that described above for teachers but is generally more acute, since aides have had less training and experience. Many aides currently employed by compensatory programs are likely to feel uncomfortable teaching in the ways advocated in this volume. To supply the needed background is a tall order and may exceed the resources available for in-service training and support.

To the extent that program planners wish to use aides in significant instructional roles following the instructional models we have been describing, they will need to consider carefully what it will take to train instructional aides in the appropriate manner. But just as important, programs and schools that seek to adopt the approaches described in this volume should consider the possibility that various adult roles can be useful for carrying out cognitively powerful instruction. Paraprofessional aides, for example, may be especially good at connecting discussions or problem solving to the situations with which students are familiar. The new demands on the teacher's role discussed earlier need not imply that a *single* individual must do it all.

*Short Time Blocks.* Another deep-seated tradition is the decision by local program managers to provide compensatory services in short daily "doses" averaging between twenty and thirty minutes. This arrangement reflects a variety of factors: the logistical realities of many elementary schools, the belief that brief regular reinforcement of key skills will help low-achieving children, and the desire to spread services to a large number of students. The briefness of the time block may be compounded when compensatory programs are offered on a pull-out basis. Depending on the physical placement of the pull-out room and the school's ability to facilitate transition, the loss of time to the child may be small or great, but inescapably some time is lost.

The instructional models we have presented are not necessarily conducive to short time blocks. Their emphasis on discussion, for example, implies that children are given the time to wrestle with ideas or problems, present solutions to each other and to the teacher, and consider each other's contributions. That kind of activity is hard to fit into a small "slot" in the school day. Accordingly, compensatory program planners, in collaboration with classroom teachers and others involved in scheduling the academic program, will need to find ways to expand the length of time allocated to each compensatory instructional session, which may mean fewer meetings per week or even fewer students served. In the face of high demand for services, these will not be easy decisions to make.

## Where Should Educators Start?

Assuming both the will to change instruction for educationally disadvantaged children and awareness of the potential limitations of the instructional models discussed in this chapter, there remain questions of implementation strategy. Where should regular and compensatory educators put their energy to bring about the changes discussed here?

It is possible to answer, "Everywhere," but that begs the question of the most appropriate points of leverage and ignores the numerous and varied constraints facing staff in particular schools, programs, districts, and states. We discuss several issues that must be confronted by all who attempt to adopt or adapt the models we have been describing. Specifically, educators will need to decide whether to

- Focus on individual classrooms or the school as a whole
- Target "disadvantaged" students or all students
- Change what is taught or what is tested
- Mandate new approaches or offer support and assistance to teachers who choose to adopt them

In reality, educators need never face an either-or choice with respect to any of these issues. Nonetheless, in most situations, it is unrealistic to pursue everything at once, and so it is well to consider the strategic trade-offs regarding each issue.

*Focusing on Individual Classrooms or the School as a Whole.* While we have argued in the introduction to this book, as have several of the chapter authors, that the most enduring and powerful solutions are likely to imply schoolwide changes, this is not easily achieved and may not be the most appropriate starting point in some instances. More fundamentally, individual teachers, in compensatory programs and in the regular classroom, must become enthused, intrigued, or at least curious about the possibilities for teaching advanced skills to the students they face. At a minimum, a few teachers within a given school need to "catch the bug" and seek instructional ideas that they can try in their classrooms. That can occur with or without a schoolwide movement to address these issues. Other teachers are likely to pay attention when something starts to work in somebody's classroom down the hall.

*Targeting "Disadvantaged" Students or All Students.* The authors presented in this book imply or state that instruction must change in both the regular and compensatory programs if the educationally disadvantaged are to acquire advanced skills to a significant degree. By this line of argument, exposure to comprehension strategies in a pull-out room followed by discrete skill worksheets in the regular classroom is unlikely to teach students to read for meaning. This implies that, to the extent possible, attempts at implementing the models of instruction described in this book should aim at all students, rather than the smaller number who are the target of compensatory programs.

But attractive as this approach may be, there are circumstances under which schools would do well to address themselves primarily to a designated group of educationally disadvantaged youngsters. For example, if the regular classroom teachers have begun to build the ideas we have been describing into their routines but compensatory staff have not, then it might make sense to invest more time and energy in the programs specifically designed for a targeted clientele. In other instances, where program regulations require that compensatory staff limit their attention to identified children, the question is moot.

*Changing What Is Taught or What Is Tested.* In one sense, the most appropriate strategic choice seems obvious: The instructional models we have described must become a part of classroom practice, if only temporarily, before questions of testing are invoked. However, given the time and effort required to develop and implement a new testing program, planning for instruction and assessment really need to go on together.

As we argued earlier in the book, testing and assessment pose a special obstacle to the introduction of the instructional models that have been described in this volume. Unless educators are careful, they risk subverting their own attempts to introduce these instructional models by their choice of tests and the emphasis they place on test results. From a strategic point of view, we would argue that it is advisable to change the testing regimen at the earliest possible moment to reflect the new instructional emphases—if only by augmenting the test batteries to include measures of advanced skills (such as writing samples). This action is especially important in places where test results are taken seriously.

We recognize that tests made by teachers or included within textbooks can be more easily changed or supplemented than the testing and accountability systems designed by district offices or state educational agencies. The latter are politically and technically complicated to change, and doing so may well lie outside most educators' sphere of influence.

*Mandating New Approaches or Offering Support and Assistance.* Assuming a state, district, or school wishes to encourage the introduction of the instructional models we have described, it is tempting to mandate their introduction—for example, by changing a district's curriculum scope and sequence or by adopting a new set of materials that embody the kind of instructional model we have discussed.

We suspect that mandates and requirements have limited influence on those aspects of instructional practice most implicated in the models presented here, however. As we noted above, the instructional models in this volume require a great deal of new learning—or relearning—on teachers' part before becoming fully integrated into classroom practice. No kind of external mandate can make that learning take place. Rather, various forms of teacher assistance, from formal in-service sessions to informal peer networks or the approval of school principals, are probably necessary in most cases to help teachers through the period of struggle and discovery that accompanies the learning of substantially new approaches to teaching.

Even though formal and informal professional development may be the most important prerequisite for the kinds of instructional changes we have been describing, mandates may still play a useful role. They provide a kind of high-level legitimation for a new way of doing things and probably stimulate a lot of staff to pay attention to methods they formerly thought were out of favor. Conversely, mandates emphasizing basic skills instruction, testing programs that assess basic skills disproportionately, and related policies can do much to inhibit experimentation with instructional models aimed at advanced skills.

### A Calculated Risk

The attempt to implement the instructional models discussed in this volume implies major instructional and operational changes for regular and compensatory educators alike. In closing, it is well to acknowledge the risks involved in making these changes.

Perhaps the biggest risk of all is that teachers will internalize only part of what the authors in this volume are advocating, yet assume that they "have it all." Without extensive professional development, many teachers may "get the words but not the tune." Program planners can minimize the risk in implementing these programs by providing resources for the kind of ongoing feedback and help teachers will need to understand these instructional concepts and develop the skills needed to apply them.

The risk in adopting innovative forms of instruction is real, but in our view still worth it. Educators who are attracted to the models presented in this volume will need to weigh the relative certainty of compensatory and regular instruction that does a reasonably good job of imparting basic skills against the uncertainties of adopting new instructional approaches that promise to offer much more. We hope that in their thinking, educators consider seriously the world into which their students will emerge—a world that increasingly requires the kinds of advanced skills we have been discussing—and also the mounting evidence of the unrealized intellectual potential their students possess. To ignore these matters is to reinforce, not minimize, the educational disadvantage many students face.

In summary, while acknowledging that there is much that is not known concerning the models' implementation, we argue that the central *principles* are well known and well tested. We call on educators to move forward and begin applying these principles to the development of similar models adapted for their particular students, goals, and circumstances. Only through their efforts will we acquire the additional wisdom concerning when, where, and how these models work best.

## References

Commission on the Skills of the American Workforce. (1990). *America's choice: High skills or low wages!* New York: National Center on Education and the Economy.

National Commission on Excellence in Education. (1983). *A nation at risk: The imperative of educational reform.* Washington, DC: U.S. Government Printing Office.

Perkins, D. N., & Salomon, G. (1989, January–February). Are cognitive skills context bound? *Educational Researcher,* 16–25.

Pressley, M., Snyder, B. L., & Cariglia-Bull, T. (1987). How can good strategy use be taught to children? In S. M. Cormier & J. D. Hagman (Eds.), *Transfer of learning* (pp. 81–120). New York: Academic Press.

Stallings, J. A., & Kaskowitz, D. H. (1974). *Follow through classroom observation evaluation 1972–1973.* Final Report, U.S. Department of Education Contract No. OEC-0-8522480-4633(100). Menlo Park, CA: Stanford Research Institute.

# INDEX

## A

Accelerated Schools, 206
Administrators: academic policy review, 22–23; supportive role, 21–23
Advanced skills: and basic skills, 1; and disadvantaged students, 3; and mastery learning, 5–6. *See also* Comprehension skills
*Adventures of Jasper Woodbury, The,* 63–64
Algebra Project, 103–104, 105
Algozzine, B., 154, 167
Allington, R. L., 3, 7, 25, 156, 164
Anderson, C. W., 57, 66
Anderson, R., 134, 138, 140
Anson, R. J., 25
Anyon, J., 3, 25
Applebee, A. N., 142, 164, 187, 199
Apprenticeship: and formal schooling, 217; traditional vs. cognitive, 218–220. *See also* Cognitive apprenticeship
Archambault, F. X., 136, 138
Arkansas Department of Education, 206
Armbruster, B., 134, 138
Articulation, 223
Ashton-Warner, S., 181, 199

At-risk students: and Computer-Supported Intentional Learning Environments (CSILE) program, 143, 160–163; and cultural background knowledge, 7; and culturally relevant texts, 135–136; and decoding-based curricula, 125–126; and Discover Rochester project, 230–235; empowering, 158–159; and inequitable reading instruction, 156, 171; and intellectual potential concept, 187–188; and instructional cultural sensitivity, 134–136; and learner models, 8; and learning disabled, 154–155; literate culture exposure of, 160–163; and literate language use, 157; modeling of expert thinking skills, 158; needs, 134–137; percentage in U.S., 54; reciprocal teaching of, 116–128; and skills hierarchy assumption, 1; special writing needs, 155–159. *See also* Disadvantaged students; Mathematics instruction; Reading instruction; Writing instruction
Atwell, N., 173, 174, 175
Avelar La Salle, R., 910, 201

**277**

**B**

Back-to-basics movement, 113
Ball, D. L., 93, 94, 100, 104, 110
Balmuth, M., 189, 199
Barnes, D., 108, 111
Barton, J., 190, 199
Basic skills: and children's achieve-
    ment, 6; compensatory educa-
    tion emphasis on, 4–5; vs.
    critical literacy, 113–114; decon-
    textualization, 6, 11–12; drill
    and practice, 54, 137; embedded
    instruction, 11–12; and problem
    solving, 27–28
Bassok, M., 222, 241
Bean, R., 195, 199
Bereiter, C., 143, 144, 145, 147, 150,
    151, 152, 153, 155, 158, 159, 160,
    164, 165, 166, 223, 243
*Berenstein Bears and Too Much
    Junk Food, The*, 85
Bickell, W., 134, 140
Birman, B. F., 2, 25
Booth, W. C., 181, 199
Bourdieu, P., 157, 164
Brainstorming, 197
Bransford, J. D., 10, 26, 57, 66, 230,
    241
Brookover, W., 192, 199
Brophy, J. E., 7, 26
Brown, A. L., 114, 124, 129, 139,
    184, 202, 221, 223, 243
Brown, J. S., 51, 52, 55, 58, 66, 157,
    158, 165, 217, 218, 223, 224, 225,
    227, 241, 242, 243
Bryson, M., 143, 150, 151, 159, 164,
    165, 166
Burton, R., 223, 224, 241

**C**

Calfee, R. C., 126, 129, 185, 187,
    188, 189, 190, 191, 195, 199, 200
California Achievement Test
    (CAT), 46, 106–107, 229
Calkins, L., 173, 175
Campione, J., 134, 138
Cancino, H., 190, 199

Cardinality, 33
Carey, D., 57, 66, 76, 100
Cariflia-Bull, T., 262, 276
Carpenter, T. P., 70, 71, 75, 76, 77,
    78, 99, 100
Cazden, C. B., 129
Central Park East (CPE) model:
    content, 246–247; evaluation,
    254; mathematics curriculum ex-
    amples, 247–249; methods, 249–
    251; sequencing, 249; sociology,
    251–252; and student selection,
    236; staff development, 252–254
Central Park East Secondary
    School (CPESS) (New York):
    cognitive apprenticeship princi-
    ples, 246–252; cognitive appren-
    ticeship program, 138–239; and
    CPE model, 236; origins, 244–
    245
Chall, J. S., 180, 200
Chambers, D. L., 69, 100
Chapter 1 Technical Assistance
    Center, 204
Charlotte Middle School, Roches-
    ter, N.Y., 229–235
Chi, M.T.H., 222, 241
Chiang, C., 77, 100
Children's learning. *See* Learning
Children: academic achievement, 6;
    mathematical knowledge, 30–34,
    55–57, 68–74, 103–106; problem-
    solving ability, 34; thinking/
    learning research, 1, 70–74; trust
    in own mathematical ability,
    35–36. *See also* At-risk students;
    Disadvantaged students;
    Students
Chun, E., 106
Chunking, 189, 209
Clark, C. M., 75, 100, 185, 202
Coaching, 222–223
Cochran-Smith, M., 197, 200
Cognition and Technology Group
    at Vanderbilt, The, 55, 58, 63, 66
Cognitive apprenticeship: at Cen-
    tral Park East Secondary School,
    235–239; at Charlotte Middle
    School, 229–235; defined, 218;

and disadvantaged students, 229–239; and Discover Rochester project, 229; key characteristics, 218–219; and mathematics instruction, 51–52, 57–59; program design, 240–241; vs. traditional apprenticeship, 218–220

Cognitive research: and chunking, 209; and counting, 33; on comprehension processes, 5–6; and critical thinking disposition, 28; on early mathematical skills, 70–74; and expertise, 219; and learner involvement, 17–18; and mathematical abilities, 29, 56; and orchestration, 11; and reciprocal teaching, 124, 138; and skills transfer, 62–63

Cognitively Guided Instruction (CGI) Project: assumptions/characteristics, 74, 98–99, 102–103; classroom elements, 84–91; classroom example, 80–84; and compensatory education, 91–98; and disadvantaged students, 77–78; effectiveness, 76–78; and expansive vs. limited view of children's knowledge, 86–88, 89–91, 103–105; problem-solving focus, 84–86; teacher education, 74–75, 88–89; vs. traditional classroom, 79–80. *See also* Mathematics instruction

Cohen, D. K., 93, 100

Cole, M., 3, 13, 26, 155, 159, 165

Coley, J. D., 135, 139

Collins, A., 51, 52, 55, 58, 66, 157, 158, 165, 217, 218, 222, 223, 224, 227, 241, 242

Comer, J. P., 206, 215

Commission on the Skills of the American Workforce, 255, 276

Compare-contrast matrix, 182–184

Compensatory education: and administrators, 21–23; alternative models, 7–16; antithetical traditions, 269–272; changing, 272–275; and Cognitively Guided Instruction (CGI) approach, 91–

98; curriculum design opportunities, 267–269; description, 2; emphasis on basic skills, 4–5, 51; global skills approach, 10–12, 51; hierarchical skills assumption, 4–5; and instructional models, 266–272; and national test results, 2–3; and paraprofessional aides, 270–271; program design considerations, 20–21; and program planners/managers, 19–21; reform, 17–25, 255–256; remediation focus, 99; reshaping curriculum 9–10; and staff developers, 17–19; and student diversity, 12, 132; and teachers, 17; whole-school perspective, 23–25. *See also* Teaching

Comprehension skills: reading, 4, 7; research, 5–6. *See also* Advanced skills

Computer-Supported Intentional Learning Environments (CSILE) program, 143, 160–163

Content: control strategies, 221; domain knowledge, 220–221; heuristic strategies, 221; learning strategies, 221–222

Control strategies, 221

Coulson, R. L., 57, 67

Counting, 33, 37

Covey, S. R., 197, 200

Critical literacy: vs. basic skills, 113–114; curriculum, 189; defined, 177; principles, 185–191

Cuban, L., 197, 200, 226, 242

Curriculum design: and chunks concept, 189; and children's mathematical thinking, 71; cognitive apprenticeship, 240–241; and computer-based environment, 217; compensatory, 9–10, 13–16, 267–269; and constancy, 187; and critical literacy principles, 186–187; decoding-based, 125; and explicitness, 191; and lesson design, 190; for math thinking/problem solving, 95–

96; for mental model construction, 60–65; and organization, 189; and protoquantitative research, 56; problem-solving focus, 69–70, 106–108; reading-writing, 186; and rhetoric, 187; and schoolwide projects, 209–210; and students' prior knowledge, 57; and videodisc environments, 63–65. *See also* Instructional models; Reasoning-based mathematics program

**D**

Daniels, H., 169, 174, 175
Davidson, P., 108
De Castell, S., 141, 165
Decoding-based curricula, 125–126
De Corte, E., 34, 52
Delpit, L. D., 115, 129, 159, 165
Derver, S., 127, 130
Dewey, J., 158, 165
Dialogue: as central instructional mode, 15–16; and reciprocal teaching, 120
Dickson, W. P., 185, 202
Disadvantaged students: blame for low test scores, 3; and cognitive apprenticeship, 229–239; and compensatory programs, 3–4; and higher-level communication skills, 6–7; and higher-order skills instruction, 2–3; mathematics program, 29–50; positive view of, 8–9; problem-solving abilities, 28; and small-group work, 59–60; and whole-school perspective, 23–25. *See also* At-risk students
Discover Rochester project, 229–235
Domain knowledge, 220–221
Dossey, J. A., 69, 100
Drill and practice, 54, 137
Drum, P. A., 187, 189, 200
Duckworth, E., 75, 100, 197, 200
Duguid, P., 55, 58, 66, 227, 241
Dunn, K., 108, 111

Dunn, R., 108, 111
Duran, R. P., 129
Dweck, C. S., 196, 200

**E**

Education: crisis, 255; minimum-competency movement, 5; reform, 255–256. *See also* Compensatory education
Eubanks, E., 103, 111
Exploration, 224

**F**

Farr, M., 169, 175
Feltovich, P. J., 57, 67
Fennema, E., 70, 71, 75, 76, 77, 100
Fisher, G., 223, 224, 241
Flower, L., 143, 165
Foster, G. E., 133, 139
Franzen, A. M., 156, 164
Freudenthal, H., 105, 111
Fulghum, R., 185, 200
Funderburg, J. A., 191, 200
Funkhouser, J. T., 25
Furson, K., 70, 101

**G**

Gallistel, C. R., 33, 53, 56, 67
Garcia, G. N., 25
Garner, R., 184, 200
Gelman, R., 32, 33, 52, 56, 67
Genesee River Valley Project, 235
Ginsburg, H. A., 70, 101
Glaser, R., 222, 241
Glazier Elementary School (Los Angeles), 193–195
Glenberg, A. M., 62, 67
Good, T., 7, 26
Goodman, K. S., 186, 201
Goodman, Y., 186, 201
Graham, P. A., 187, 201
Graves, D., 168, 173, 174, 175
Graystone Elementary School (San Jose, Calif.), 179–191
Greene, D., 227, 242
Greeno, J. G., 29, 34, 53

Griffin, M. P., 129
Griffin, P., 3, 13, 26, 155, 159, 165
*Gulliver's Travels*, 107

**H**

Hamilton, V., 188, 201
Hamilton-Lee, M., 206, 215
Harris, H. W., 137, 139
Hasselbring, T., 10, 26
Hayes, J. R., 143, 165
Haynes, N. M., 206, 215
Heath, S. B., 157, 165, 168, 175, 201
Heisinger, C., 195, 201
Heller, L., 134, 139
Henry, M. K., 185, 190, 191, 200
Heuristic strategies, 221
Higher-level skills. *See* Advanced
  skills
Hilliard, 106, 108, 111, 113, 129
Hoffman, D. M., 135, 139
Holtzman, W., 134, 139
Horowitz, R., 182, 201
Hoskyn, J., 206, 215
Hull, G., 156, 157, 165
Hypothesis Experiment Instruction
  (HEI), 110

**I**

Illinois Writing Project, 168
Inquiring School: anecdote, 178–
  179; characteristics, 195–196;
  critical components, 196; defined, 177–178; development,
  195–198; and Glazier Elementary
  School, Los Angeles, 193–195;
  individual efficacy and leadership, 197; internal program evaluation, 197
Institute for Research on Learning,
  235
Instructional chaining, 127
Instructional models: and educational reform, 255–256; and
  compensatory education, 266–
  272; evaluation, 257–258; future
  research, 259–263; implementation, 257–263; nature, 258–259;

and staff development, 263–266.
  *See also* Language/communica-
  tion arts instruction; Literary instruction; Mathematics
  instruction; Reading instruction; Writing instruction
International Reading Association,
  194
Iowa Test of Basic Skills, 76
Itakura, K., 110

**J**

Joag-Dev, 134, 140
Johnson-Laird, P. N., 62, 67
Joram, E., 143, 150, 165
Jung, R. K., 25
Jungeblut, A., 142, 165

**K**

Kamehameha Early Education pro-
  gram (Hawaii), 126
Kamii, C., 105, 109, 110, 111
Karweit, N. I., 206, 215
Kaskowitz, D. H., 257, 276
King, C., 195, 199
Kinzer, C., 10, 26
Kirsch, I. S., 142, 165
KISS ("keep it simple, sweetheart")
  principle, 188, 196
Kliman, G., 107, 111
Kliman, M., 106, 107, 111
Klopfer, L., 55, 67
Knapp, M. S., 3, 26, 137, 139, 176,
  188, 201, 240, 242
Knight, S. L., 134, 140
Knowledge: and constancy in hu-
  man thought, 187; domain, 220–
  221; expansive vs. limited view,
  86–88, 89–91; and organization
  in human thought, 188; out-of-
  school, 12–13, 34, 36–37, 57; and
  rhetoric principle, 187; strategic,
  220. *See also* Mathematical
  knowledge

**L**

Lampert, M., 58, 67, 75, 101, 104,
  105, 111, 197, 201

Language/communication arts instruction, 6–7
Lave, J., 51, 53, 58, 67, 70, 101, 217, 242
Learning: as active, 17–18; and cognitive research, 1; decontextualized model, 158; discovery, 181–184; mastery, 5; situated, 58, 226; strategies, 221–222; through writing, 154, 158. *See also* Apprenticeship learning; Cognitive research; Learning environments; Mastery learning
Learning environments: and content, 220–222; design, 220–229; and method, 222–224; and sequencing, 224–225; sociology of, 225–229
Lee, C., 159, 165
Leggett, E. L., 196, 200
Lehr, J. B., 137, 139
Lehrer, R., 235
Leinhardt, G., 134, 140
Lepper, M. R., 227, 242
Levin, H. M., 137, 139, 206, 215, 227, 242
Levine, D., 103, 111
Levine, R., 103, 111
Lewis, M. W., 222, 241
Lindem, K., 62, 67
Lindquist, M. M., 69, 100
Lionni, L., 182, 201
Liston, D. P., 197, 203
Literacy: critical, 113–114, 177; language, 157; natural vs. taught, 114–115; writing as new, 141
Literacy instruction, for at-risk students, 198–199, 204. *See also* Reading instruction
Littlefield, J., 61, 67
Livermon, B. J., 206, 215
Loef, M., 76, 77, 101
Lower-level skills. *See* Basic skills
Luke, A., 141, 165
Lysynchuk, L., 134, 139
Lytle, S. L., 197, 200

**M**

McGill-Franzen, A., 3, 25
McGue, M., 154, 167

McLean, R. S., 160, 166
McNamara, T. P., 62, 67
Madden, N. A., 206, 215
Malone, R., 227, 242
Markman, M. E., 32, 53
Martus, M., 129
Mason, B. J., 176, 203
Mastery learning, 5–6
Mathematical knowledge: and apprenticeship environment, 51; assessing, 93–94, 105–106; and cardinality, 33; children's trust in own, 35–36; and counting, 33, 37; expansive view, 86; and integrating counting and proquantitative schemas, 33–34; and left-/right-brain theory, 108; and problem types, 71–72; and protoquantitative schemas, 30–32, 56; and solution strategies, 74, 108–110; students' formal/informal, 94–95; undervalue of at-risk students, 69
Mathematical Sciences Education Board, 69
Mathematics Curriculum Teaching Project (Australia), 104
Mathematics instruction: and basic math concepts, 57; and cognitive research, 29–30; as cognitive apprenticeship, 51–52, 57–59; compensatory, 2; and cultural folktales, 107; and discussion/argument, 43–46; in England/Australia, 104; and intuitive and formal linkage, 37; and key mathematical structures, 37–39; and literature, 107; and multiple problem-solving approaches, 14–15; and problem finding, 39–43; reasoning-based, 29–50; repackaging, 107; and textbook supplementation, 96–98; as undermining to children's own knowledge, 35; and videodiscs, 63–65. *See also* Cognitively Guided Instruction (CGI) Project; Reasoning-based mathematics program

Maximum-competency criteria, 113
Means, B., 240, 242
Mental models: defined, 61; skills,
    62–63; usefulness, 61; and video-
    disc environments, 63–65; and
    word problem types, 71–73; and
    writing skills, 158. *See also*
    Modeling
Meredith, R., 186, 201
Messick, S., 134, 139
Metacognition, 184
Metropolitan Reading Readiness
    Test, 47
Meyer, M., 62, 67
Modeling: and apprenticeship, 217;
    and at-risk student needs, 158;
    defined, 222; learner, 8; writing,
    174. *See also* Mental models
Moll, L., 12, 26
Monitoring Understanding and
    Strategic Execution (M.U.S.E.)
    program: modeling thought,
    153–155; procedural facilitation,
    153; strategy-focused instruction,
    151–152; theoretical principles,
    151–155
Moore, M. T., 25
Morrison, D. R., 25
Moses, R. P., 103, 105, 111
Mullis, I. V., 69, 100
Multicultural Reading and Think-
    ing (McRAT), 206
Murray, D. M., 147, 165

**N**

*Nation at Risk, A,* 113
National Assessment of Education
    Progress, 69
National Commission on Excel-
    lence in Education, 113, 255, 276
National Council of Teachers of
    Mathematics, 56, 65, 67, 69, 88,
    101, 103
National Education Goals, 255
National Research Council, 69, 101
Natural literacy, 114–115
*NEA Today,* 188, 201
Nelson-Barber, S., 187, 200

Newman, S. E., 51, 52, 157, 158,
    165, 214, 218, 242
Norman, D. A., 225, 242
Nufield Series (UK), 104

**O**

Oakes, J., 3, 26
Oka, E., 126, 130
Olson, D. R., 182, 201
Ontario Institute for Studies in Ed-
    ucation (OISE) Writing Re-
    search Group, 151
Orasanu, J., 187, 201
Orland, M. E., 25
Out-of-school experience/culture:
    and children's mathematical
    knowledge, 34, 36–37, 94–95;
    and curriculum design, 57; as
    instructional strength, 12–13;
    teachers' appreciation of, 99

**P**

Padron, Y. N., 132, 133, 134, 139
Palincsar, A. S., 124, 127, 129, 139,
    184, 202, 221, 223, 243
Paraprofessional aides, 270–271
Paris, P., 145, 148, 159, 166
Paris, S. G., 126, 130
Passeron, J., 157, 164
Pea, R., 235
*People Could Fly, The,* 188
Perkins, D. N., 184, 190, 202, 262,
    276
Perl, S., 156, 166
Peterson, P. L., 70, 75, 76, 77, 93,
    94, 100, 105, 185, 202
Phelps, L. W., 114, 130
*Polar Express, The,* 188
Poplin, M. S., 115, 130
Pressley, M., 139, 262, 276
Problem solving: and basic skills
    focus, 27–28; and Cognitively
    Guided Instruction (CGI) ap-
    proach, 84–85; and curriculum
    design, 95–96; as curricular fo-
    cus, 69–70, 106–108; and mental
    models, 60–61; multiple strate-

gies, 74, 108–110; research base
for children's, 70–74; story, 34;
video, 64–65; writing as, 143–144
Project READ: anecdote, 179–181;
defined, 177–178; discovery
learning, 181–184; evaluation,
185, 191–193; and Graystone Elementary School, 179–191; lesson
design, 190; metainstruction, 184
Project Zero, 206
Protoquantitative schemas, 30–32,
56
Purkey, S. C., 192, 202

**Q**

Quellmalz, E. S., 206, 215

**R**

Ransom, K., 127, 130
Reading instruction: and basic
skills vs. critical literacy, 113–
114; decoding-based, 125–126,
189; and disadvantaged students,
7, 126–128; and metacognitive
skills, 114; and natural vs.
taught literacy, 114–115, 132–
133; and reciprocal teaching,
116–126; reductionist vs. holis-
tic/constructionist, 115–116;
strategies, 135–137, 182; tensions
in, 112–116. *See also* Literacy
instruction
Reasoning-based mathematics program: basic features, 54–55; as
cognitive apprenticeship, 51–52;
and mental model construction,
61–62; principles, 34–46; results,
46–50; teachers' perspective, 59–
60; theoretical framework, 29–
34, 55–59
Reciprocal teaching: and active
teaching/learning, 132–133; for
at-risk students, 116–128, 131–
134; benefits, 131–134; defined,
116; evaluation, 124–126; examples, 117–121; and holistic/con-
structionist approach, 115–116;

and instructional chaining, 127;
motivating factors, 127; and
natural vs. taught literacy, 114–
115, 132–133; research, 124, 138;
and scaffolding, 120; strategies,
116–117; student preparation,
123; and teacher roles, 120; and
teacher/student interaction, 133–
134; and teacher training, 121–
123, 136–137; theoretical princi-
ples, 122
Reflection, 223
Regency Competency Exams, 236
Reimann, P., 222, 241
Reisner, E. R., 25
Research. *See* Cognitive research
Research-based instructional tech-
niques, 210–211
Resnick, L. B., 28, 29, 34, 53, 55, 56,
67, 103, 111, 119, 243
Restructuring programs, 177, 179,
205–206. *See also* Schoolwide
projects
Reyes, M. de la Luz, 159, 166
Richards, J., 106, 110, 111
Richards, L., 105, 111
Richert, A., 202
Richmond, P. A., 176, 203
Rieser, J., 61, 67, 230, 241
Riley, M. S., 34, 53
Rogoff, B., 58, 67
Romano, T., 173, 175
Rose, M., 156, 157, 165, 166
Rosenholtz, S. J., 197, 202

**S**

Salomon, G., 184, 190, 202, 262, 276
Samuels, S. J., 182, 201
Scaffolding: and apprenticeship,
218; defined, 15, 223; examples,
15; in reciprocal teaching dialogues, 120; and writing instruction, 158
Scardamalia, M., 143, 144, 145, 147,
150, 151, 152, 153, 155, 158, 159,
160, 165, 223, 243
Schaefer, R. J., 194, 202
Schlager, M., 240, 242

Schoenfeld, A., 58, 67, 221, 243
School Development Program, 205-206
Schools: as communities of inquiry, 177; restructuring, 179
Schoolwide projects: Chapter 1 program assessment, 213; Chapter 1 program requirements, 208-209; characteristics, 205; Comer model, 205-206; defined, 205; and differently normed student tests, 213-214; evaluation, 212-213; examples, 206; and individual differences, 211-212; organizational elements, 207-209; and research-based instructional techniques, 210-211; and staff development, 208. *See also* Inquiring Schools; Project READ
Scott, J. C., 7
Semantic maps, 182-183, 192
Sequencing: and global before local skills, 225; and increasing complexity, 224-225; and increasing diversity, 225
Sessums, S. K., 147, 167
Sharp, D.L.M., 62, 67
Shaughnessy, M. P., 157, 167
Sherwood, R. D., 10, 26, 230, 241
Shields, P. M., 137, 139, 176, 188, 201
Shinn, M. R., 154, 167
Siebert, J., 32, 53
Silva, C. M., 103, 105, 111
Situated learning, 58, 226
Skills: computational, 69-70; global approach to, 10-12, 51; hierarchical approach to, 1, 4, 27-28, 39; mental model, 62-63; metacognitive, 114; teaching models, 1-2, 7-16; transfer, 62-63. *See also* Advanced skills; Basic skills
Slavin, R. E., 132, 134, 139, 206, 215
Smith, E. B., 186, 201
Smith, E. E., 222, 241
Smith, E. L., 57, 66
Smith, M. S., 192, 202
Snyder, B. L., 262, 276
Sociolinguistic research, 157

Sociology of learning: and community of practice, 226; and exploiting cooperation, 227-229; and intrinsic motivation, 226-227; and situated learning, 226
Sophian, C., 33, 53
Spiro, R. J., 57, 67
Staff development: Central Park East Secondary School, 252-254; and instructional models, 263-266; reciprocal teaching, 121-123; for schoolwide projects, 208; and teachers' needs, 18-19
Stallings, J. A., 257, 276
Steffenson, M., 134, 140
Stein, M., 134, 140
Steinbach, R., 152, 166, 223, 243
Stevens, A. L., 223, 242
Strategic knowledge, 220
Strategy: control, 221; focused instruction, 151-152; heuristic, 221; learning, 221-222; problem-solving, 74, 108-110; reading instruction, 135-137, 182; reciprocal teaching, 116-117
Students: knowledge deficits, 188; learning disabled, 154-155; out-of-school experience, 12-13, 34, 36-37, 94-95; and reciprocal teaching, 123; test scores, 2-3; writing ability, 142. *See also* At-risk students; Disadvantaged students
Students at risk for school failure. *See* At-risk students
Success for All program, 206
Swallow, J., 160, 166

**T**

Teacher training. *See* Staff development
Teachers: and children's mathematical knowledge, 74-75, 88-89, 93-94, 99, 108; classroom experimentation with new approaches, 17; composition recommendations, 173-174; curriculum participation, 18-19; expansive vs.

limited view of children's
knowledge, 86-88, 89-91, 103-
105; learning environment role,
52; and left-/right-brain theory,
108; and reasoning-based mathematics program, 59-60; and reciprocal teaching, 120-123, 136-
137
Teaching: advanced skills, 1-2; and
dialogue, 15-16; master/ap-
prentice metaphor, 52; methods,
222-224; multiple approaches,
14-15; new strategies, 13-16; reciprocal, 116-126; and scaffolding, 15; and thinking strategies,
13-14; and whole-school perspective, 23-25. *See also* Compensatory education; Education;
Instructional models; Lan-
guage/communication arts instruction; Literary instruction;
Mathematics instruction; Reading instruction; Reciprocal
teaching; Writing instruction
Teaching methods: articulation,
223; coaching, 222-223; exploration, 224; modeling, 222; reflection, 223-224; scaffolding, 223.
*See also* Instructional models
Testing: and compensatory programs, 2-3; differently normed,
213-214; and hierarchical skills
assumption, 5
Textbooks: culturally relevant,
135-136; going beyond, 97-98;
and linear vs. geometric learning, 104-105; minority-culture,
159; supplementation, 96-97
Thinking-aloud protocols, 143-
144, 145-147, 150, 172
Tuman, M. C., 182, 202
Turnbull, B. J., 3, 25, 26

U

University of Wisconsin, Madison,
235

V

Van Allsburg, C., 188, 202
Van Lehn, K., 224, 243

Verschaffel, L., 34, 52
Video: and mathematics instruc-
tion, 63-65; problem solving,
64-65
Villasenor, A., 77-78, 101
Vye, N. J., 57, 66, 139, 230, 241
Vygotsky, L. S., 158, 167

W

Waxman, H. C., 134, 140
Weaving, 182-184
Webbing, 182-183, 192, 194, 197
Wheelock College, 104
White, B. Y., 224, 243
Whitehead, A. N., 158, 167
Whittaker, A., 193, 195, 202, 203
Whole-language movement, 177
Williams, B. I., 176, 203
Willinsky, J., 141, 167
Willis, H. D., 129
Wilson, P., 138, 140
Wolf, S., 193, 203
Wong, I., 193, 203
Woodruff, E., 160, 166
Writing: composing process, 147-
148; as dialectic, 150; epistemic,
141-142, 157, 171; evaluation of
student, 142; to learn, 141, 147-
150, 154; as new literacy, 141; as
problem solving, 143-144;
thinking-aloud protocols, 143-
144, 145-147, 150, 172
Writing instruction: for at-risk students, 142, 155-163; cognitively
based, 163-164, 169; deficit
model, 155; and direct instruction vs. direct experience, 172-
173; knowledge-telling model,
142, 144-147, 171; knowledge-
transforming model, 142, 144,
147-150, 171; and modeling, 174;
and Monitoring Understanding
and Strategic Execution
(M.U.S.E.) program, 143, 151;
and procedural facilitation, 174;
process paradigm, 173; remediation, 155-156; and scaffolding,
158, 168; writing-to-learn model,

154, 158. *See also* Monitoring
Understanding and Strategic
Execution (M.U.S.E.) program
Writing to learn, 141, 147–150, 154

**Y**

Ysseldyke, J. E., 154, 167

**Z**

Zeichner, K. M., 197, 203
Zemelman, S., 174, 175
Zigmond, N., 195, 199
Zuboff, S., 216, 243
Zucker, A., 69, 101